The Chronicles of Narnia
and Philosophy

Popular Culture and Philosophy™

Popular Culture and Philosophy™

The Chronicles of Narnia and Philosophy

The Lion, the Witch, and the Worldview

Edited by
GREGORY BASSHAM
and
JERRY L. WALLS

OPEN COURT
Chicago and La Salle, Illinois

Volume 15 in the series, Popular Culture and Philosophy™

To order books from Open Court, call toll-free 1-800-815-2280, or visit our website at www.opencourtbooks.com.

Open Court Publishing Company is a division of Carus Publishing Company.

Library of Congress Cataloging-in-Publication Data

The chronicles of Narnia and philosophy / edited by Gregory
    Bassham and Jerry L. Walls.
        p. cm. — (Popular culture and philosophy ; v. 15)
    Includes bibliographical references and index.
    ISBN-13: 978-0-8126-9588-5 (trade paper : alk. paper)
    ISBN-10: 0-8126-9588-7 (trade paper : alk. paper)
    1. Lewis, C. S. (Clive Staples), 1898–1963. Chronicles of Narnia.
    2. Lewis, C. S. (Clive Staples), 1898–1963—Philosophy.
    3. Children's stories, English—History and criticism. 4. Christian
    fiction, English—History and criticism. 5. Fantasy fiction,
    English—History and criticism. 6. Philosophy in literature.
    7. Narnia (Imaginary place) I. Bassham, Gregory, 1959-
    II. Walls, Jerry L. III. Series.
      PR6023.E926C5324 2005
      823'.912—dc22
                                                        2005015101

To Jonny, Bubba, Corman, Headley, Jesse,
Jump, Leffel, and Major

*—the good men of the Monday
night tradition who love Lewis and,
like Lewis, love a good argument,
a good laugh, and a good cup of tea.
May Aslan deal with the Edmund
in all of us!*

Contents

Part III
Further Up and Further In: Exploring the Deeper Nature of Reality

Part IV

The Deepest Magic: Religion and the Transcendent

Acknowledgments

Thanks are due, first and foremost, to the contributing authors for their hard work, timely production, and patience with not one, but two, pestiferous editors (motto: "True freedom means doing what we tell you to do"). The series editor, Bill Irwin, was a constant source of encouragement and good advice. We particularly thank him for his frequent reminders that "the fountains of prosperity irrigate the garden of prudence and virtue." Open Court's Editorial Director David Ramsay Steele, a devilishly well-preserved fellow who swears by Plumptree's Vitaminized Nerve Food, had faith in this project from the beginning and provided valuable feedback as the book neared completion. Jamie McAndrew, the trusty student aide to the Philosophy Department at King's College, read all the essays in draft and offered many helpful suggestions for improvement. Jerry wishes to thank Elizabeth, Angela, and Jonathan for love and encouragement. Greg also wishes to thank Elizabeth, Angela, and Jonathan—for keeping Jerry sane. In addition, Greg thanks his wife, Mia, and his son, Dylan, for their love, patience, and support. Without the help of all these good people, this book would still be lingering in the Wood between the Worlds.

Abbreviations

The following abbreviations are used in referring to the *Narnia* books.
All quotations are from the one-volume HarperCollins edition of 2001,
and all page references are to that edition.

LWW   *The Lion, the Witch, and the Wardrobe*

PC   *Prince Caspian*

VDT   *The Voyage of the "Dawn Treader"*

SC   *The Silver Chair*

HHB   *The Horse and His Boy*

MN   *The Magician's Nephew*

LB   *The Last Battle*

Narnia and the Enchantment of Philosophy

JERRY L. WALLS

The movie *Shadowlands* begins with a scene in one of the Oxford University chapels, followed by one of those fabulous Oxford dinners, with all the Dons wearing their academic gowns and engaged in spirited conversation. As we listen in, we discover that C.S. Lewis, the main character in the movie, is not only one of the participants in the discussion, he is also the subject of one of the conversations. One of his colleagues, in a rather mischievous manner, asks how it is that Lewis can write children's books since he doesn't know any children. Not to be outdone, Lewis replies that his older brother Warnie was a child at one time, and as unlikely as it may seem, so was he![1]

A few scenes later, some of these same characters are sitting around a fire in a charming English pub engaged in a similar conversation. One of the members of the group volunteers that he has a complaint about "the wardrobe." Fans of C.S. Lewis will readily recognize this as a reference to *The Lion, the Witch, and the Wardrobe*, the first of seven children's books he wrote that are known collectively as *The Chronicles of Narnia*. The "complaint" is that the book describes the house of an old professor who is single, yet his house has a wardrobe full of old fur coats, presumably belonging to a woman. It is through these fur coats, at the back of the wardrobe that the children entered the wonderful land of Narnia. The explanation for why the old

---

[1] Actually part of the original inspiration for the *Chronicles* came from children who lived temporarily with Lewis at his home in Oxford. These were children who had been evacuated from their homes during the Second World War. One of them expressed an interest in an old wardrobe, asking if she could go inside, and if there was anything behind it. See George Sayer, *Jack: A Life of C.S. Lewis* (Wheaton: Crossway Books, 1988), p. 311.

professor had this wardrobe is simple, Lewis replies: it belonged
to his mother.

Now the fur becomes the topic of conversation as one of the
characters playfully offers a Freudian interpretation of the fact
that the children have to push their way through the mother's
fur to reach Narnia. But Lewis will have none of this. The fur is
not important, he insists. Then he jumps to his feet to describe
what he imagined it was like for the children in his story as they
pressed through the coats, almost suffocating. Suddenly, there
are white lights, crisp cold air, and trees covered with snow, a
total contrast to their everyday experience. "It's the gateway to
a magical world," he exclaims.

Countless readers have found their own gateway into this
world of magic through the pages of *The Chronicles of Narnia*.
Indeed, the *Chronicles* is one of the most beloved children's
book series of all time and continues to sell several million
copies a year. And if this were not enough to ensure their ongoing popularity, the books are the basis of a series of major
motion pictures co-produced by Walt Disney Pictures and
Walden Media. The first of these films is *The Lion, the Witch,
and the Wardrobe*, directed by Andrew Adamson, who was also
the director of *Shrek* and *Shrek 2*.

Not only children, but adults as well, have been enchanted
by the world Lewis created. The *Chronicles* are great stories,
well told, and with timeless appeal. Parents and grandparents
who loved the books when they were young now read them as
bedtime stories to their own children or grandchildren, often
with undiminished, and even enhanced, interest and enjoyment.

Though written primarily for children, *The Chronicles of
Narnia* are rich in philosophical themes. Among the philosophical questions raised in the *Chronicles* are these: How can
we distinguish truth from illusion? Does might make right, or
do objective moral rules exist that are binding on everyone?
Why should we be moral? Should some things be accepted on
faith? Could more than one religion be true? What is time, and
can it flow at different rates in different worlds? Could someone be turned into a dragon, as Eustace was, and still be the
same person?

Readers who enjoy the magic may raise a dubious eyebrow
at the prospect of philosophers entering Narnia. Rounding up a
group of philosophers to write about the *Chronicles* may seem

akin to letting loose a horde of Calormenes, with free license to pillage and plunder. At the very least, is there not a danger that they may try to turn these charming children's stories into something ponderous and pretentious ("gas," as Lewis would say), producing essays with titles like "An Ontological Analysis of Dufflepuddian Transubstantial Change" or "Hags and Haecceities in Marsh-wigglean Metaphysics"? This would be even worse than the Freudian interpretation of Lewis's friend in *Shadowlands*. Fearing such a prospect, lovers of Narnia may wish Reepicheep to grab his sword and let the fur fly!

Rest assured, the editors and writers of this volume are fans of the *Chronicles* and have no desire to transform them into something they are not. The *Narnia* tales are first and foremost wonderful stories and should be appreciated on their own terms. However, we believe that such an appreciation is consistent with—and in fact can be considerably enriched by—an awareness of the philosophical and moral themes that are artfully woven into them.

Lewis himself, after all, was something of a philosopher. While his field of expertise was English literature, the subject he taught at Oxford, and later Cambridge, he also studied Philosophy during his undergraduate days at Oxford. Indeed, his first job at Oxford in 1924 was teaching Philosophy, a one-year appointment to replace a professor who had gone to America to teach for a term. The next year, he joined the faculty at Magdalen College in Oxford, where he would stay until his move to Cambridge in 1954. Lewis believed he got the job at Magdalen because he was the only candidate who could teach both Philosophy and English, the combination the college wanted for the position.[2] It's also noteworthy that from 1942 to 1954, Lewis was the President of the Socratic Club, an Oxford University undergraduate debating society whose purpose was to discuss issues related to Christianity. The club hosted skeptics as well as believers, and in the spirit of the famous Greek philosopher who was its namesake, members were encouraged to follow the argument wherever it led. A number of speakers were noted philosophers, and in his role as President, Lewis often engaged them in debate.

---

[2] Sayer, *Jack*, pp. 176–83.

Even more to the point, some of Lewis's most famous and influential books were explicitly philosophical in nature. These dealt with such issues as the problem of evil, the nature and ground of morality, the existence of God, the credibility of miracles, the deficiencies of scientific materialism—in short, the same sorts of issues that appear in the *Chronicles*. While these books are mostly popular in nature, they have received considerable attention and critical comment from professional philosophers.

To note Lewis's philosophical interests is not to suggest that his stories are simply vehicles to express his moral or religious views, nor to imply that "the real point" of the stories is primarily philosophical. However, to ignore or to deny the philosophical when it is there is no more of a virtue than to read the stories as sermons in clever disguise.

The chapters that follow have the modest aim of assisting readers who wish to explore some of the fascinating philosophical and moral terrain that undeniably runs through the Narnia stories. The primary audience we have in mind are Narnia fans who are also interested in philosophy rather than professional philosophers with an interest in Narnia. Given this purpose, along with obvious space limitations, the authors attend mainly to major arguments and issues rather than detailed qualifications and objections that it would be necessary to address if these essays were written primarily for professional philosophers. These essays shine light down numerous trails that interested readers may well want to explore further on their own, once they have learned the lay of the land. As Lucy and her siblings learned to their delight, there are worlds to discover in Narnia that we may not have dreamed existed. So, in the words of Jewel the Unicorn, further up and further in!

Part I

Farewell to Shadowlands

Believing, Doubting, and Knowing

1

Aslan's Voice: C.S. Lewis and the Magic of Sound

STEPHEN H. WEBB

Which would you rather be: ugly or invisible? I don't mean homely or plain looking; I mean really ugly—so ugly that people you don't know would stop and stare at you. Most people, I bet, would choose to be invisible. The ugly are looked down upon in our society, but the invisible can see everything without being seen. To be invisible, as Plato and Tolkien remind us, is to have godlike powers. But wouldn't it be tiresome not to be seen? If you were invisible, you wouldn't be a part of human society. People wouldn't be able to identify you or know how to react to you. As a result, you would lose your sense of self-identity. Yet we live in a culture that places such a high value on beauty that many people, I'm sure, would choose to be invisible rather than ugly.

These issues are posed for us by a curious group of creatures that Eustace, Lucy, and their companions come upon during their great voyage on the *Dawn Treader*, namely, the Dufflepuds. These creatures choose invisibility over ugliness, or, to be more accurate, they choose to be invisible when their master, a great Magician, casts a spell that makes them (in their own eyes) unbearably ugly. Their choice isn't very smart. Indeed, as Eustace of all people points out, the Dufflepuds are "certainly not very clever" (VDT, Chapter 9, p. 491). Even though they are invisible, for example, they are afraid of the dark. They also plant boiled potatoes to save time cooking them when they dig them up. They are such cowards that they force Lucy to sneak upstairs and into the Magician's room in order to reverse the spell. Most of all, they babble on without ever saying anything important, all the while sounding like Rush Limbaugh dittoheads in enthusiastically declaring their agreement with everything their leader says ("Ah, there it is, Chief. There's the point. No one's got a clearer head than you. You couldn't have made it plainer. . . . Keep it up, keep it up" (VDT, Chapter 11, p. 502).

We might be tempted to think our heroes' encounter with these strange creatures is just a bit of comic relief during a treacherous journey to the end of the world. In fact, however, the story is much more than this, for it sheds light on the fascinating topic of C.S. Lewis's approach to the senses. *The Chronicles of Narnia* are about a lot of things, but one of the topics Lewis explores in depth is the nature of the human senses. The Dufflepuds are disturbing because they can be heard but not seen. All through the *Chronicles*, Lewis is interested in how seeing and hearing operate and how those two senses are related to each other.

Several philosophical questions are pertinent. What are the qualities of sound and sight? Do we know the world differently through listening or seeing? If there are fundamental differences in the senses, what does that tell us about human nature? Are some senses better than others for giving us access to truth and reality?

Seen, Not Heard

Here is another seemingly dumb question: Would you rather be deaf or blind? Children love to ponder such questions, but they contain the seeds of serious philosophical puzzles. Lewis asks a variation of this question in the Dufflepuds episode when he has Eustace wish that "the Magician would make them inaudible instead of invisible" (VDT, Chapter 11, p. 504). In other words, if you were surrounded by both ugliness and noise, would you rather be deaf or blind? Eustace would rather see the Dufflepuds than hear them. He would rather be deaf than blind. I think most people would agree with his choice. Does that mean that there is something about sound that makes it more powerful than sight?

As anyone who's been to a good concert knows, sound waves seem to penetrate us more intimately than light waves. Perhaps that is because we can always close our eyes, while our ears have no lids. Graphic sights can be disturbing, but loud sounds can be so jarring that military planners have researched ways to use them to deafen and disorient enemy troops. Even quiet sounds, like the soft plop of pigeon poop on our shoulders, can make us cringe. Sounds are especially menacing when we don't know where they're coming from. When Lucy climbs the stairs to the Magician's study, for example, things are so quiet that every little sound stands out. She panics when she hears footsteps in the corridor, but is relieved when she finds Aslan at the door.

We are afraid of the dark partly because we can't see the source of the sounds we hear. Indeed, right after the episode with the Dufflepuds, the *Dawn Treader* reaches the Dark Island, which is so pitch dark that it drives people mad. Such absolute blackness is hard to describe. Lewis compares it to a railway tunnel "either so long or so twisty that you cannot see the light at the far end" (VDT, Chapter 12, p. 506). In this darkness, the sailors hear a cry so terrible that they don't know if it's human. It is. It comes from an old man whose eyes "were so widely opened that he seemed to have no eyelids at all, and stared as if in an agony of pure fear" (VDT, Chapter 12, p. 509). It turns out that in that absolute darkness, all one's worst nightmares come true. As the ship floats through the darkness, the crew on board can't help straining their ears for any recognizable sound. When you can't see what you're listening to, you end up being afraid of what you hear. Sure enough, "soon everyone was hearing things" (VDT, Chapter 12, p. 510). The lesson is clear: When deprived of sight, we strain to hear, but the darkness misleads our ears. Once again, only the familiar voice of Aslan saves them from doom.

Sound Sense

There is a long tradition in Western philosophy of connecting vision with knowledge and darkness with terror. When we understand something, we say, "I see." When we want to know more, we seek clarity and illumination. People who know what they're talking about have a vision that others can follow. These observations are so common that we take the relationship between seeing and knowing for granted, but Lewis doesn't. Remarkably, Lewis gives sound, not sight, the fundamental role to play in the construction of knowledge.

Fans of his stories might overlook the role of the senses in a first reading, but Lewis is very deliberate in how he describes Narnia. By portraying Narnia as the consummation of human hopes and fears, Lewis is able to probe the depths of human nature. Narnia is not only a place that tests the courage and integrity of the children who visit there; it's also a place where these visitors discover the innocence of human perception. They learn to trust what they hear and doubt what they see. In other words, Narnia educates their senses.

The Primacy of Sound

Narnia is both like and unlike planet earth. It's sufficiently similar to our world for the children to be at home as they take on new adventures, but it's sufficiently dissimilar for them to be challenged to re-imagine their lives back home. For Lewis, the modern world has destroyed the innocence of our imaginations. We no longer live in the great stories of myth and legend. The twentieth century made life brutal and cynical. Lewis wanted to teach his readers to stretch their imaginations. He didn't think that logic alone could help us find meaning in life. He wanted a renewed appreciation for the senses in all of their innocence over cold, hard logic.

Lewis wrote the *Chronicles* at a time when logical positivism was all the rage in philosophical circles. The manifesto of the movement, A.J. Ayer's *Language, Truth, and Logic* (1936), was one of the most influential works of philosophy of the twentieth century. Ayer accepted as true statements only logical tautologies (statements that are true by definition) and empirically verifiable observations. Both metaphysics and theology are meaningless, according to Ayer, because they seek reality beyond the boundaries of reason. Statements have meaning only if they are logical or factual.

Lewis rejects Ayer's view by developing a completely different theory of truth. For Lewis, sound no less than logic is crucial to meaning. Where Lewis most strikingly makes this point is, of course, in his vivid depiction of the voice of Aslan, the great Lion. Aslan's voice is more than hot air. Aslan breathes the world into being in *The Magician's Nephew*, and in *The Lion, the Witch, and the Wardrobe* his breath awakens the animals that the Witch had turned to stone (LWW, Chapter 16, p. 188). Even his growls are full of meaning. Aslan represents the essence of sound.

Lewis defends a vocative philosophy of sound. What does that mean? In brief, a vocative philosophy of sound argues that the meaning of words is most fundamentally found in the human voice. Historically, of course, writing is secondary to, and derivative of, vocalization. Cultures were oral long before they were literate and textual. There is a philosophical truth to be drawn from the historical priority of speaking over writing. In our culture today, it is tempting to think that meaning has to do with the silent and abstract properties of sentences. Truth is something we see on the written page. Lewis helps us understand that meaning is sonic before it is visual. Even when we read silently, we can hear words in our heads. Moreover, speaking out loud, even in our visual culture, remains the most important way of saying who we are and calling others to account for themselves.

Voices, however, are fragile. We can literally lose our voices due to stress or sickness. We can also be afraid to speak for a variety of reasons. To be given a voice, then, is to be set free. Likewise, to be denied a voice is to be denied one's humanity. This does not mean that all voices are good. We can try to force our views on others by shouting down other opinions. We can twist words into hateful and deceptive forms. Voices, however, can also be used for great good. Through speech we create the world we live in. This, in brief, is what Lewis argues in the world he creates called Narnia.

A Bedtime Story

Many people first encounter the Narnia stories by hearing them read out loud, which is good because the tales are so vividly written. The *Chronicles* are almost like a script that brings out the actor in every parent! Moreover, many episodes in the tales hinge on the consequences of loud sounds. Remember that the whole adventure begins when Digory tells Polly that he heard a yell as he was going past the foot of the attic-stairs on his way to bed (MN, Chapter 1, p. 12). What is Uncle Andrew up to? When the two children begin to explore the attic, they hear a faint, humming sound—almost, Lewis says, like a vacuum cleaner, if vacuum cleaners had been invented in those days.

The humming has a musical tone. When they meet Uncle Andrew in the attic room, Polly thinks the humming is coming from the rings he shows them. Uncle Andrew laughs at this suggestion (he is always wrong about what he hears), but Polly is right. The rings hum, and it is their humming that transports the children to a new world where they will never hear things the same way again.

The new world, or worlds, the children enter are both like and unlike our own world. These worlds allow Lewis to speculate about what our sense perceptions mean by imagining what they might be like under totally different conditions. One of the senses he pays most attention to is the sense of hearing. The *Chronicles* are, among other things, a complex and daring exploration into the nature of sound. For example, the first world they experience, the Wood between the Worlds, is described most vividly in terms of its quietness. It is quiet in a way that is rich and vibrant. The trees seem alive. Digory says the woods are as rich as a plum cake (MN, Chapter 3, p. 25).

The quiet of the Wood is in stark contrast to the world they find in Chapter 3, "The Bell and the Hammer." The silence of this new place is of a different order altogether. Here they find a ruined city where nothing is alive. A noise, Digory thinks, could bring what is left of the ruins down like an avalanche in the Alps (MN, Chapter 4, p. 33). Soon they stumble into a room where they find a pillar with a little golden bell on top and a golden hammer to the side. Cut into the stone of the pillar is a message that dares them to

> *Strike the bell and bide the danger,*
> *Or wonder, till it drives you mad,*
> *What would have followed if you had.* (MN, Chapter 4, p. 35)

Digory can't resist the temptation and rings the bell. Lewis describes the resulting sound in graphic terms. It begins sweet, but soon becomes so loud that the children can't hear each other. Then the sound turns horrible as it rattles the stone floor. It sounds like the roar of a distant train. This description isn't farfetched, because sound waves can be felt as well as heard. In fact, at about twenty hertz, hearing and touch merge as the lower frequencies of sound become tactile vibrations.

Lewis also describes the bell as sounding "like the crash of a falling tree" (MN, Chapter 4, p. 36). This comparison is significant. It is this horrible sound that awakens the Queen, who is soon revealed as a wicked witch. All the trouble in Narnia thus begins with a sound. Why? Lewis is re-imaging in this passage the biblical story of the Garden of Eden and the fall of Adam and Eve. Evil enters into the Garden, after all, when the serpent speaks to Eve; it is the ear that is the first of the senses to yield to temptation. Furthermore, it is a tree that is the object of the act of disobedience, just as it is another tree, later in the biblical story, that reverses the fall and provides the opportunity for salvation. Sound, Lewis is saying, touches us deeply. Sound is a fascinating sense because it enters into us, traveling into the hollow cavity of the ear, and thus becomes part of us even as it is invisible and out of our control. Sound is powerful; it can create and destroy worlds. Just as the words of the serpent begin the exile from Eden, the sound of the bell unleashes an evil force that will threaten the very existence of Narnia. Likewise, the sound of Susan's magical horn will reverse the effects of Digory's hammer and call Aslan to the rescue.

The Wonderful, Awful Beauty of the Queen

What, or whom, the horrible sound awakens is Jadis, the last Queen of Charn, later to be known as the White Witch. Years later, when he was an old man, Digory thought he had never seen a woman more beautiful. The eye, however, can be terribly misleading. Indeed, the Queen's own eyes can see through anything, even to the point of being able to read other people's minds. She is a creature of sight, not sound. She wants to see everything, but she pays the price of not knowing how to listen to voices that have more authority than her own. Her looks are striking, but her voice makes everyone quiver. This is in contrast to Aslan's voice, which "was deep and rich and somehow took the fidgets out of them" (LWW, Chapter 12, p. 169).

In fact, it was her voice that had destroyed an entire world. With an astounding selfishness, she had killed every living thing in Charn by using the Deplorable Word. She used this terrible word when the last of her soldiers lay defeated by her sister. It only takes one word, Lewis seems to be saying, to bring a world to an end. Words indeed can do much greater damage than sticks and stones. Jadis, in fact, is so full of herself—so taken by her own way with words—that she doesn't listen to others. Words are merely tools in her quest for power. She understands how powerful words are, but she has no true understanding of language. She is furious when she visits the children's world (our world), where she can't destroy her enemies with her speech. Her magic fails her on earth. Nevertheless, she is still able to cause havoc with her voice, as when she whispers into the horse's ear to madden him (MN, Chapter 7, p. 55). When the children use their rings to transport themselves, the Cabby, and the Queen to another world, the Queen loses the power of her speech while the children and the Cabby sing a hymn to cheer themselves up.

What a Talking Lion Sounds Like

It is at this moment that the most remarkable event in the book occurs, an event that sheds further light on Lewis's theory of sound. "A voice had begun to sing" (MN, Chapter 8, p. 61). With that simple sentence, Lewis introduces Aslan the Lion into the narrative. Notice, however, that the Lion is heard before he is seen. It is almost as if his voice is what makes the Lion the creature that he is. The form of the Lion is not as significant as his sound, or, better put, the voice of the Lion is able to create or inhabit any form. This is Lewis's way of crediting voice with the property of creativity. When the children, the Cabby, Uncle Andrew, and the Queen first hear the voice, it sounds as if it were coming from all directions simultaneously. The voice wasn't speaking, or even carrying a tune. It was, however, beautiful beyond comparison. The lower notes of the voice, its deep register, sounded as if it arose from the earth itself, and it called forth other voices higher up the scales that seemed to come from the sky and the stars. The Queen understood the sound of the voice and feared it.

The contrast between the Lion's voice and the Queen's could not be more striking. Whereas hers was destructive, his was creative. As Aslan moved back and forth, coming nearer the group, life sprang into being. The various tones and overtones of his voice gave birth to grass, trees, and flowers. Then came the animals, who also were called forth by the sound of the Lion's song. The Lion brought some of the animals into a circle, and finally he speaks. What he says is a command for Narnia to awaken and for the animals in the circle to speak. Life comes to know itself through the power of sound.

When one of the animals says something silly, Aslan doesn't mind. "For jokes as well as justice," he says, "come in with speech" (MN, Chapter 10, p. 72). This is really a remarkable statement. Indeed, justice and humor seem to be inextricably related. Justice is the harmony of society, but such harmony is impossible without humor. Aslan could have chastised the perky jackdaw who had spoken out of turn, but that would have instituted a hierarchy of law based on fear and mistrust. Only if we can laugh at each other without resorting to violence can we learn to get along as a community. The acceptance of a joke, then, is the beginning of justice, just as justice provides the condition without which it's impossible to laugh freely. We should remember, for example, how humorless Russian communism was. A society that lacks justice is a society of fear. In such societies, jokes are no laughing matter.

Not everyone saw the humor in the situation. Lewis makes the argument, through the differing perspectives of the Witch and Uncle Andrew, that "what you see and hear depends a good deal on where you are standing: it also depends on what sort of person you are" (MN, Chapter 10, p. 75). This doesn't mean that Lewis affirms a kind of cultural relativism. The Lion speaks the truth; indeed, truth is first and foremost a property of his character, not propositions, and it is through sound that his character is communicated. The Witch understood the Lion's sound and rejected it. Uncle Andrew, on the other hand, heard a snarl every time Aslan spoke. This sounds less strange than it is. Think about the variety of human languages. If you are not French and have never heard French spoken, then French will sound like gibberish to you, especially if you have never heard any language spoken other than your own. Languages create community. There is a "soundscape" to our social lives every bit as important as the landscape we associate with home. Thus, when Uncle Andrew hears the animals speak, he can't understand them because he doesn't recognize them as belonging to the same community as his own. Animals, for him, don't count as creatures of moral worth. There is no discourse between animals and him, so he can't understand them, even when they are given the gift of human-like speech.

Likewise, they can't understand him. They can't figure out what kind of creature he is, though they understand instinctively that he is evil (or, as the Elephant says, Neevil). Uncle Andrew has made himself the kind of person who doesn't understand the sound of warranted authority. He is tone deaf to the sound of truth, just as some people are tone deaf to music.

When the children first hear the name "Aslan" in *The Lion, the Witch, and the Wardrobe*, they feel an inexplicable shudder of awe. Likewise, when Polly first hears Aslan, she understands his voice as a call and feels certain that "anyone who heard that call would want to obey it" (MN, Chapter 11, p. 81). Sound, in fact, draws us out of ourselves. The first relationship we have with the world is through our grunts and gurgles. Parents coo to their children in order to reach them. When we are called out of ourselves, we are also called to take responsibility for ourselves. We learn who to trust and who not to, even when somebody speaks to us, as the Witch spoke to Digory "more sweetly than you would have thought anyone with so fierce a face could speak" (MN, Chapter 13, p. 94). Dogs recognize their masters by smell but also by the sound of their voice. Likewise, we learn to intuit the meaning of what others tell us in part by listening to the quality of their tones, seeking out sincerity and resisting deception.

The Mystery of Sound

Sound is naturally mysterious. Voices come deep from within other people and enter deeply into ourselves, all without a physical trace. What we see we can inspect, but when we listen to someone, we have to pause and pay attention. Seeing can happen at a distance, but a conversation draws us close to each other, since, without microphones or telephones, we must be physically near the source of the sound. We can see an object all at once, but sound forces us to be patient, since we have to listen to words sequentially. Light speeds toward the eye, granting immediate information, but "sound travels so slowly" (LB, Chapter 14, p. 749). Most mysteriously of all, sound waves travel on invisible frequencies. We can hear a voice without seeing its source in a body. Sound is thus the perfect medium for the supernatural. No wonder in the Bible God is heard but not seen!

Sound is also the perfect medium for our own sense of self-identity. Parents make all sorts of sounds to their newborn babies, surrounding them with a security blanket of comforting baby talk. We learn who we are by listening to others, imitating their voices, and hearing them name us. Our parents anxiously await our first word. When we speak, we become who we were meant to be.

This is the meaning of Shasta's encounter with the voice on his long ride from Calormen to Narnia. He hears a loud, large, and deep voice, but he sees nothing in the dark. Is it a giant, or a ghost? He knew he was being followed by lions, but now he discovers that it was only one lion, and what a lion at that! "Who are you?" Shasta asks. "Myself," the voice answers (HHB, Chapter 11, p. 281). Sometimes when someone calls us, it is enough to hear his or her voice. Something responds, and we know that we are known. Voices carry meaning along their sound-waves, and they reveal who we are if we but listen to them.

Reading or Hearing?

If all of this talk of the supernatural sounds a bit farfetched, consider the following question. What is the act of reading? We think of reading as a silent affair, but people used to read out loud long before the practice of silent reading became widespread. Many people think of the imagination as a visual affair. Books paint pictures with words. A great novel thus portrays a rich landscape. Novels, however, can also give us soundscapes. When we read a great book, we listen for the author's voice. We need a quiet space to read in order to let the silent marks on a page have their say. Reading is as much a matter of hearing as it is of seeing.

At least reading *The Chronicles of Narnia* is that way. Lewis wants us to push our imaginations by trying to hear the sounds that make us who we are. He speaks about sound so much that many different passages could be selected to make this point, but think about this one: "Have you ever stood at the edge of a great wood on a high ridge when a wild southwester broke over it in full fury on an autumn evening? Imagine that sound" (PC, Chapter 14, p. 406). This passage describes the great battle where the woods come alive and march, on behalf of Peter's army against the Telmarines. Lewis has put marks on a page in order to have us activate them with our auditory imaginations. He wants us to think about the ways in which sound is the very stuff of our existence. His *Chronicles* are a very noisy affair, no matter how quietly we read them to our children at bedtime. Perhaps we love to read them so much because we are searching for voices that comfort us and call us home.

2

Virtue Epistemology: Why Uncle Andrew Couldn't Hear the Animals Speak

KEVIN KINGHORN

One of the most fascinating scenes in *The Chronicles of Narnia* features an incident that is truly puzzling. The scene takes place in *The Magician's Nephew*. Four lucky humans (Digory, Polly, Uncle Andrew, and Frank the Cabby) and one very unhappy Witch (Jadis) watch as Aslan sings the new world of Narnia into existence. When the newly-created Talking Animals begin to speak, the human witnesses are amazed to find that they can understand them. Everyone, that is, except Uncle Andrew. All he can hear is barkings, howlings, and the like (MN, Chapter 10, p. 75). But why? Why wasn't Uncle Andrew able to understand like everyone else?

This is the sort of question asked by virtue epistemologists. And as we shall see, virtue epistemology can shed a great deal of light on the puzzle before us. But before looking at the insights that virtue epistemology can bring us, let's get clear on what virtue epistemology *is*.

Epistemology is the branch of philosophy concerned with the study of knowledge and belief. Epistemologists seek to answer fundamental questions like: "What is knowledge?" "How do people come to know things?" "*Can* we really know anything?" "When is a belief justified?" "Are any beliefs one hundred percent certain?" and "Is the hoky poky really what it's all about?"

One hot topic among epistemologists centers on the distinction between *believing* something to be true and *knowing* that it's true. Clearly, I can't *know* something unless it's true. Anyone who says, "I *know* the Eiffel Tower is in London," is clearly mistaken. At the same time, however, not all true beliefs constitute knowledge. After all, a six-year-old, on hearing that C.S. Lewis lived his adult life in England, may form the true belief that Lewis lived in Oxford. But she may do so because Oxford is the only city in England she's ever heard of, and she naïvely thinks that all people from England live in Oxford. Surely in this case the child doesn't *know* that Lewis lived in Oxford; she just made a lucky guess.

Knowledge, therefore, requires something more than just true belief. The person must be *justified* in holding the belief. And what is justification exactly? Philosophers are divided on this question. Some argue that the person holding the belief must herself understand that her belief is based on solid evidence. Others argue that one's belief need only be formed through a process that reliably produces true beliefs, regardless of whether the person understands this process. Such traditional approaches to the issue of justification share what we might call an *outward-inward* approach. These approaches begin by explaining what counts as a good way of acquiring beliefs. And they conclude that if a particular belief has been acquired in this way, then the person holding the belief holds it justifiably.

Virtue epistemology is a recent theory of knowing that seeks to reverse the traditional assumptions about how we determine whether a person is justified in his or her beliefs. In 1980 the philosopher Ernest Sosa suggested that we should define justification in terms of intellectual virtues.[1] Intellectual virtues are kinds of inward excellences, such as the ability to reason skillfully or to perceive truth. Virtue epistemologists, following Sosa, argue that we should define justification in terms of such virtues. So, suppose we ask whether a person is justified in holding a belief in a particular situation. The virtue epistemologist takes an *inward-outward* approach and answers that, if the belief resulted from an appropriate intellectual virtue, then the person justifiably formed that belief.

The general strategy of virtue epistemology is to analyze a person's beliefs in terms of the intellectual virtues the believer possesses—or lacks. By employing this strategy, we will find

---

[1] Ernest Sosa, "The Raft and the Pyramid: Coherence versus Foundations in the Theory of Knowledge," *Midwest Studies in Philosophy* (1980), pp. 3–25.

that a great deal is revealed about why Uncle Andrew failed to form true beliefs about the Narnia animals.

In asking whether Uncle Andrew possessed the intellectual virtues needed to form justified beliefs, we first need to identify what these virtues are. Lorraine Code, one of the first philosophers to respond to Sosa's virtue epistemology, argues that intellectual virtues should be understood in terms of one's *epistemic responsibilities*.[2] Whether a person meets her epistemic responsibilities will be "a matter of orientation toward the world and toward oneself as a knowledge-seeker in the world."[3] More specifically, Code remarks, "[i]ntellectually virtuous persons value knowing and understanding how things really are. . . . They resist the temptation to live in fantasy or in a world of dream or illusion, considering it better to know, despite the tempting comfort and complacency a life of fantasy or illusion can offer."[4]

From Code's general comments on epistemic responsibility, it's possible to identify at least four central virtues of a responsible seeker of knowledge. Such a person:

(1) will value truth for its own sake;
(2) will not believe things simply because she wants them to be true;
(3) will not allow fears to dictate what she believes;
(4) will recognize her own limitations as a seeker of knowledge.

Let's now examine whether Uncle Andrew possessed or lacked these four intellectual virtues. By the time we're finished, it will be clear why Uncle Andrew couldn't hear the Narnia animals talk.

Did Uncle Andrew Value Truth for Its Own Sake?

Code remarks that one characteristic of intellectually virtuous people is that they embrace knowledge as "good in itself, not

---

[2] Lorraine Code, *Epistemic Responsibility* (Hanover, NH: University Press of New England, 1987). "Epistemic" responsibilities are simply those duties of believing, doubting, and so forth that fall within the subject area of epistemology.

[3] *Ibid.*, p. 58.

[4] *Ibid.*, p. 59.

just instrumentally good."[5] Her point is that virtuous seekers of truth will not seek to understand things merely as a means to accomplish further goals. Rather, they will value an accurate understanding of the world as an end in itself.

Importantly, a search for truth is not the same thing as the attempt to ensure that one never holds any false beliefs. Some philosophers have made this mistake. For example, the nineteenth-century philosopher W.K. Clifford, in a famous essay titled "The Ethics of Belief," declares that "it is wrong always, everywhere and for everyone to believe anything upon insufficient evidence." The misguided attempt to avoid at all costs holding any false beliefs was the downfall of the renegade dwarfs in *The Last Battle*. The dwarfs had been fooled into thinking that a donkey dressed up in a lion suit was actually Aslan. In time, the dwarfs discover the trickery and vow never to be taken in by anyone again. When King Tirian later appeals to them to join Aslan's forces, they reply: "You must think we're blooming soft in the head, that you must. . . . We've been taken in once and now you expect us to be taken in again the next minute. We've no more use for stories about Aslan, see!" Tirian explains that he's talking about the *real* Aslan. But the dwarfs simply respond, "Where's he? Who's he? Show him to us!" (LB, Chapter 7, p. 707).

In demanding absolute proof, the dwarfs are not seeking to ensure that they have the facts about Aslan. Rather, their ultimate goal is to make sure they aren't fooled again. This becomes clear when they eventually *do* come face to face with Aslan, who prepares a great feast for them. But the dwarfs are so closed off to the possibility that Aslan is actually before them that they don't recognize him or the goodness of his gifts. Aslan explains that the dwarfs "have chosen cunning instead of belief" (LB, Chapter 13, p. 748).

As anyone who has channel-surfed through late-night infomercials knows, sometimes people develop false beliefs by being too naïve. Yet, it's equally true that a person can fail to acquire true beliefs by being too cynical. The dwarfs' problem is that they don't value truth for its own sake. Instead, they seek to understand the world around them only so far as this is consistent with their ultimate goal of never holding false beliefs.

---

[5] *Ibid.*

Uncle Andrew also seems to have an overarching commitment to avoid naïve beliefs at any cost. When he first hears the roar of Aslan at the creation of Narnia, he recognizes that the sound is indeed a song. But he tells himself that the source of the noise is "only" a lion, remarking for his own benefit, "Who ever heard of a lion singing?" (MN, Chapter 10, p. 75) Lewis comments that Uncle Andrew "tried to make himself believe that he could hear nothing but roaring, . . . [and] the trouble about trying to make yourself stupider than you really are is that you very often succeed. Uncle Andrew did. He soon did hear nothing but roaring in Aslan's song." When at last Aslan spoke and said, "Narnia, awake!" we find that Uncle Andrew "didn't hear any words: he heard only a snarl" (MN, Chapter 10, p. 75).

One reason why Uncle Andrew was blind to things that were perfectly obvious to his companions is that he was "dreadfully practical" (MN, Chapter 10, p. 75). When Uncle Andrew witnesses Narnia's creation, he has no interest in understanding what he's seeing. Instead, he continually seeks a way to leave the place. The only time his interest is piqued is when he considers the financial profits he might reap if he could exploit the miraculous fecundity of Narnia. His only interest in understanding Narnia is purely instrumental.

Contrast Uncle Andrew's attitude with that of Frank, the humble, good-natured Cabby. The Cabby is in awe of what he sees. As Uncle Andrew chatters away about his financial plans and about his dislike for Narnia, the Cabby finally tells him at one point: "Oh stow it, Guv'nor, do stow it. Watchin' and listenin's the thing at present; not talking" (MN, Chapter 9, p. 65). The Cabby is embracing the beauty and inherent worth of what he is witnessing, and he's seeking a better understanding of Narnia simply because it's worth understanding. Uncle Andrew's only interest in Narnia concerns the money he might make if he could find a way to tap its treasures. Because he doesn't value for its own sake the truth about Narnia, his concern to avoid childish beliefs overwhelms his concern for the truth.

Was Uncle Andrew Guilty of Wishful Thinking?

To quote Lorraine Code again, the intellectually virtuous person will "resist the temptation to live in fantasy or in a world of dream or illusion." Such a person will not believe things simply because she wants them to be true.

It's not difficult to see from everyday examples that people's desires often influence what they believe. Think, for instance, of a rabid sports fan's beliefs about a referee's performance during a hotly contested game, or of an overly protective parent's beliefs about whether her child's teachers are treating her child fairly.

The Chronicles of Narnia contain some interesting examples of how people's desires can affect what they believe. In *The Lion, the Witch, and the Wardrobe*, Lucy tells Edmund what she has learned about the White Witch, who calls herself the Queen of Narnia. Edmund realizes this is the same person who had given him Turkish Delight and had promised to give him more if he returned to Narnia with his siblings. Lewis tells us that Edmund "wanted to taste that Turkish Delight again more than he wanted anything else" (LWW, Chapter 4, p. 128). So Edmund challenges Lucy's version of reality. "Who told you all that stuff about the White Witch?" he asks. Lucy explains that it was Mr. Tumnus, the Faun. Edmund tries to act as though he's somehow knowledgeable on the subject and declares, "You can't always believe what Fauns say." Lucy naturally asks, "Who said so?" Edmund of course has no real evidence for his assertion. He simply wants it to be true. And so he can only offer the absurd response: "Everyone knows it. Ask anybody you like" (LWW, Chapter 4, p. 128).

When Edmund later meets up with the Witch, she reneges on her promise to give him more Turkish Delight and treats him harshly. It becomes obvious to Edmund that his desire for Turkish Delight won't be fulfilled even if the Witch remains in power. With this realization, he no longer has the incentive to try to convince himself and others that she's really not so bad. We read of Edmund, "All the things he had said to make himself believe that she was good and kind and that her side was really the right side sounded to him silly now" (LWW, Chapter 4, p. 162). In short, Edmund's belief in the Queen's right to rule Narnia was sustained by a strong desire that she be proved the rightful ruler. Once the desire faded, so did Edmund's belief.

Did Uncle Andrew share Edmund's tendency to allow his desires to rule his beliefs? Consider Uncle Andrew's own response to the Queen in *The Magician's Nephew*. When the Queen first meets Uncle Andrew, who fancies himself a magician, she grabs him by the hair and says, "I see what you are. You are a little, peddling Magician who works by rules and books. There is no real Magic in your blood and heart" (MN, Chapter 6, p. 46). She then barks orders at Uncle Andrew and warns him that she'll cast an evil spell on him at the first sign of his disobedience.

Uncle Andrew retreats to his room, takes a couple of stiff drinks, and puts on his best outfit to impress the Queen. All this makes him feel better about himself. "Andrew, my boy," he says to himself while looking in the mirror, "you're a devilish well-preserved fellow for your age. A distinguished-looking man, sir." Lewis comments: "You see, the foolish old man was actually beginning to imagine the Witch would fall in love with him. The two drinks probably had something to do with it, and so had his best clothes. But he was, in any case, as vain as a peacock" (MN, Chapter 6, p. 49).

To any reasonable onlooker, the Queen's first meeting with Uncle Andrew provided no evidence whatsoever that she might actually like him. But Uncle Andrew's hope that the Queen would admire him clouds his judgment.

As was the case with Edmund, when Uncle Andrew's desires lose their grip on him, his beliefs about the Queen become more realistic. As the Queen begins to address Uncle Andrew as "slave" and "dog," his desire to be admired by the Queen is replaced by fear of her. When this happens, we read of Uncle Andrew that "all the silly thoughts he had had while looking at himself in the glass [mirror] were oozing out of him" (MN, Chapter 7, p. 5).

Uncle Andrew shows in his dealings with the Queen that he does not possess the second intellectual virtue we are considering. He allows his desires unduly to affect his beliefs. He is the kind of person who does not see reality in a clear light. Rather, he sees what he wants to see.

Returning to the scene of Narnia's creation, Uncle Andrew's overriding desire is simply to leave and return home safely. Because he has no real desire to see any of Narnia's wonders, it's not surprising that can't hear the animals speak. As the Greek orator Demosthenes observed, "what a man wishes, he generally believes to be true."

Uncle Andrew's Fear Factor

Our fears can influence our beliefs just as our desires can. Following the work of Sigmund Freud, it has become popular to talk of the possibility of repressing one's beliefs because they represent situations too frightful to entertain. Fears can also cause a person to believe in something that is feared. For instance, a child's fear of monsters might be so intense that she comes to believe that there really are monsters hiding in her closet. Thus, fear can lead one both *away* from believing what one fears, and *towards* it. Either way, an intellectually virtuous person will not allow fears unduly to influence what she believes.

There are examples in the *Chronicles* where this third intellectual virtue is glaringly absent. In *Prince Caspian*, the young Caspian is told by his tutor, Doctor Cornelius, that the old Kings and Queens of Narnia lived in Cair Paravel. "Ugh!" replies Caspian with a shudder. "Do you mean in the Black Woods? Where all the—the—you know, the ghosts live?" (PC, Chapter 4, p. 340). Doctor Cornelius explains that the stories about the woods are pure myths perpetuated by the Telmarines, who now rule Narnia. "There are no ghosts there," he says, explaining that because the Telmarines "quarreled with the trees, they are afraid of the woods. And because they are afraid of the woods they imagine that they are full of ghosts" (PC, Chapter 4, p. 340).

What about Uncle Andrew? Lewis remarks that Uncle Andrew "had never liked animals at the best of times, being usually rather afraid of them." He then adds, "And of course doing cruel experiments on animals had made him hate and fear them far more" (MN, Chapter 10, p. 76). Because of this fear, Uncle Andrew runs in terror when the newly-created Narnia animals run after him in excitement and curiosity. When they catch up to him, they open their mouths to pant and catch their breath. Uncle Andrew thinks they're opening their mouths to eat him. A Bulldog asks him innocently enough, "Are you animal, vegetable, or mineral?" All Uncle Andrew hears is "Gr-r-r-arrh-ow!" (MN, Chapter 10, p. 76).

Not once do we read of Uncle Andrew pausing to reflect on whether his fears of the animals are well-founded. Not even when he sees the other humans interacting peacefully with the animals does he question his own assumptions. Instead, he says to himself, "The fools! Now those brutes will eat the rings along with the children and I'll never be able to get home again" (MN, Chapter 10, p. 76). A moment of calm reflection would allow Uncle Andrew to see the folly of his own distrustful attitude toward the animals. But his assumptions about the animals are so driven by his fears that they are not open to critical scrutiny.

Does Uncle Andrew Recognize His Own Limitations?

To quote Lorraine Code again, intellectually virtuous character is a matter of proper orientation not only toward the world, but also "toward oneself as a knowledge-seeker in the world." As Socrates notes, the beginning of wisdom lies in realizing how little one knows.

A scene in *The Voyage of the "Dawn Treader"* nicely illustrates how self-knowledge can affect one's beliefs. The passengers on the *Dawn Treader*, led by Prince Caspian and the Pevensie siblings, land the ship on an island. While the ship is being repaired, the spoiled brat Eustace sneaks away to avoid doing any work. He falls asleep and, upon awakening, becomes frantic that the others might leave him behind. Lewis tells us that "if he had understood Caspian and the Pevensies at all he would have known, of course, that there was not the least chance of their doing any such thing. But he had persuaded himself that they were all fiends in human form" (VDT, Chapter 5, p. 460).

There is a proverb that says: "As a man thinketh, so is he." When we observe other people's actions, it is only natural for us to assume that their reasons for acting are the same as ours would be if we were acting as they are. Philosophers refer to this tendency as the "Principle of Charity." Eustace believes that the others might leave him because, frankly, this is the kind of thing he would do.

Eustace has both a change of heart and a change of hide after becoming lost on the island. He changes into a dragon and undergoes a series of trying circumstances that bring him to a state of loneliness and despair. A time of soul-searching helps him realize that he hadn't been "such a nice person as he had always supposed" (VDT, Chapter 6, p. 466). Indeed, we read that "Eustace realized more and more that since the first day he came on board he had been an unmitigated nuisance" (VDT,

Chapter 7, p. 472). With this self-discovery comes a decision to make a fresh start. And with a new commitment to others, he sees others in a different light: "He realized now that Caspian would never have sailed away and left him" (VDT, Chapter 6, p. 467).

Unfortunately, Uncle Andrew never comes to such a point of self-discovery.[6] We noted earlier that he has the clear chance to re-evaluate his fear-laden assumptions about the motivation of the Narnia animals when he sees them making friends with Digory, Polly, and the Cabby. But Uncle Andrew can't see that Digory and the others actually *are* making friends with the animals. All Uncle Andrew can see as he observes them is the selfish attempt to show they don't care about him. He exclaims, "What a selfish little boy that Digory is! And the others are just as bad. If they want to throw away their own lives, that's their business. But what about *me?* They don't seem to think of that. No one thinks of *me*" (MN, Chapter 10, p. 75).

Uncle Andrew is the one, of course, who is selfish to the bone. And so he naturally interprets the actions of others in line with his own self-centered commitments. If Uncle Andrew had at least possessed some awareness of the way his personal character was influencing his perceptions, he might have come to a more accurate understanding of his surroundings. But Uncle Andrew lacked the fourth intellectual virtue of self-knowledge. As a result he remained mired in his skewed perspective of the world.

Was Blind, But Now I See

In describing how the creation of Narnia didn't make the same impression on Uncle Andrew as it did on Digory, Polly, and the Cabby, Lewis makes a comment that anticipates much of our discussion. Lewis states that "what you see and hear depends a good deal on where you are standing: it also depends on what sort of person you are" (MN, Chapter 10, p. 76). Our discussion of virtue epistemology can perhaps be viewed as giving philosophical precision to Lewis's insight.

---

[6] Though as an old man he does seem to undergo some change for the better. See LB, Chapter 15, p. 106.

At the same time, Lewis's own well-known religious commitments leave little doubt that his interests in epistemology did-
n't lie merely with general intellectual duties people can have.
He was also concerned with specifically *spiritual* problems that
prevent people from seeing the truth about God. We can
observe in some of our previous examples that Lewis's ultimate
concern seems to be this matter of spiritual blindness. For example, it's not just that Edmund in *The Lion, the Witch, and the
Wardrobe* is mistaken in thinking that the Queen of Narnia is
the rightful ruler of Narnia. More importantly, he is blinded to
the fact that opposition to Aslan, the creator and sustainer of
Narnia, cannot ultimately prevail. Similarly, it's not just that the
dwarfs in *The Last Battle* can't recognize that the feast Aslan prepares for them actually consists in choice food and wine instead
of rotten turnips and dirty water. It's also that they can't recognize the more profound truth that Aslan is seeking their well
being.

A thought-provoking reference to spiritual blindness occurs
in *Prince Caspian*, where Lewis offers an account of the travels
of the Pevensie siblings and the dwarf Trumpkin as they trek
through Narnia to come to the aid of Caspian. The group is
unsure how to navigate a gorge they need to cross. Lucy suddenly spots Aslan in the distance offering them direction. But
her companions don't believe Lucy's story (with the exception
of Edmund, who reminds himself that nobody believed Lucy's
accurate testimony when, in a previous adventure, she made
claims about a magic wardrobe opening up into a land called
Narnia.) So, after a vote, they decide to follow a route different
from the one Lucy advises. After a time, they become hopelessly
lost (PC, Chapter 10, pp. 375–76).

Lucy again spots Aslan, and this time she is determined to
follow him whether any of the others do or not. The others do
come along, for they have no other real option. Aslan appears
repeatedly in the distance to guide them. Lucy leads the others,
as she is still the only one who can see Aslan. Gradually, the
others in the group one by one also come to see Aslan. The
order in which they come to see him corresponds exactly with
the degree of skepticism they originally expressed about Lucy's
testimony. Edmund had originally voted to follow Lucy. And it
is he who is the first of the others to see Aslan. Next, Peter recognizes the shape of Aslan in the distance. Then Susan, who

was originally the most condescending of the children towards Lucy, comes to see Aslan. Finally, the dwarf Trumpkin, who had refused earlier to consider the possibility that Aslan even existed, is forced to come to grips with the reality of Aslan when the Lion confronts him face to face.

The degree to which the members of the group are initially skeptical of Lucy's testimony seems to determine the extent to which they are later able to recognize the truth that Aslan is present with them. The religious implications here are obvious. As Lewis notes in a number of his writings, much of the evidence we have today for the central Christian claims about Jesus Christ comes in the form of testimony from the New Testament eyewitnesses and near-contemporaries. In this sense, the evidence for Christian truth rests on a kind of faith—specifically, a faith in the credibility of certain human testimony. Yet faith, Lewis believed, also produces its own authenticating evidence. Sin blinds, and faith opens our hearts and minds to God's gracious presence in our world and in our lives.

We've looked at four intellectual virtues central to being a responsible seeker of knowledge: valuing truth for its own sake; refusing to believe something simply because one wants it to be true; not allowing fears to dictate what one believes; and recognizing one's limitations as a seeker of truth. We've seen that Uncle Andrew utterly lacks these virtues. As a result, he, like the renegade dwarfs, lives in untruth and makes a prison of his own mind (LB, Chapter 13, p. 748).

3

Trusting Lucy: Believing the Incredible

THOMAS D. SENOR

Lucy is breathless with excitement as she tells her siblings her remarkable tale—how she had walked through the wardrobe into a wintry world, had tea with a Faun named "Mr. Tumnus," and listened to his stories of dancing Dryads, deep-delving Dwarfs, and a wicked White Witch who had cast a spell that made it "always winter and never Christmas" (LWW, Chapter 2, p. 118).

Lucy's excitement quickly turns to frustration, however, when it becomes clear that her brothers and sister simply don't believe her. And who could blame them? After all, what she told them was unbelievable.

Later, Edmund ducks into the wardrobe during a game of hide-and-seek and soon finds himself in Narnia, gorging on the White Witch's Turkish Delight. He confesses to Lucy that he has been through the wardrobe, although when she happily tells the others that Edmund can corroborate her story, he viciously turns on her and says that he was making the whole thing up. Edmund continues in this lie, making Lucy appear worse and worse for insisting on the truth of her tale.

The older kids, Peter and Susan, decide to seek the advice of the Professor who owns the house in which they are all staying. They tell him about the conflict between Edmund and Lucy, and explain that they are worried about Lucy because they've never known her to do anything like this before. They reason that she's either become a bald-faced liar (and a bad one at that) or else has lost her mind. They don't like the thought of either alternative.

The Professor's response surprises them. He asks who is generally more trustworthy, Lucy or Edmund? Peter says there is little doubt that Lucy is. But, they say, they don't suspect her of lying as much as they fear she's gone mad. This possibility the Professor has little patience with. Madness is, after all, a general condition and Lucy has shown no signs of dementia. There are, the Professor reminds them, just three options: she's lying, she's crazy, or she's telling the truth (LWW, Chapter 5, p. 131). But past experience tells against the first option, and there is ample reason to disbelieve the second. Therefore, the Professor suggests, Lucy is probably telling the truth!

Peter and Susan are not sure what to think as they leave the Professor's study. On the one hand, the idea that what Lucy is saying could be true is utterly fantastic. How could there possibly be another world accessed through the back of a wardrobe? And not just any old world, but a world of Fauns and other mythical creatures who are ruled by a witch who has cast a spell of perpetual winter? Yet, on the other hand, there is no doubt that Lucy believes with all her heart in the reality of her experience. And with the exception of these wild stories about Narnia, Lucy is the rational, sensible person they've always known her to be. What are they to think?

What Would You Think?

What would you think? What *should* you think? This is an important issue because at some time or other we all will find ourselves in Peter and Susan's shoes. We have all heard stories, sometimes from apparently credible sources, of unidentified flying objects, "miracle" cures, apparitions, and mystical visions. What do we think when we hear such tales? Does reason require us to be always skeptical? And what does skepticism come to here? Or does reason sometimes surprise us with the advice of the Professor? Exploring questions such as these will be the purpose of this chapter. We will begin by considering in some detail the factors that Peter and Susan must weigh when figuring out whom to believe. We will then apply the results of our discussion of the credibility of Lucy's reports to the kinds of situations we face on this side of the wardrobe.[1]

---

[1] Those who have studied a little philosophy may be familiar with eighteenth-century philosopher David Hume's famous essay "Of Miracles" (from his book

The Predicament

Although clear enough once pointed out, questions about what we ought to believe are rarely in the forefront of our minds. Indeed, I would guess that when you've read *The Lion, the Witch, and the Wardrobe*, you never stopped to ask yourself what you'd do if you were in the older siblings' shoes. This is natural enough since we readers know that Lucy's story is true. But it doesn't take a lot of thought to see that Peter and Susan are in a bit of a predicament. In fact, they are in what philosophers call an *epistemic* predicament. What makes the problem epistemic is that it is concerned with what one should believe if one wants to believe the truth. And it is only true beliefs that allow us to know what is good for us, and how to change the world for the better. Yet the desire to acquire truth is even deeper than this; one fundamental way humans differ from the rest of the animal kingdom is our intellectual curiosity. Gaining knowledge of how the world does and should work is an intrinsic good.

Weighing the Evidence

We have good reason, therefore, to be concerned with epistemic matters. And among such matters, Peter and Susan's situation is particularly perplexing. For rational reflective belief comes about by carefully considering the evidence for and against a claim, weighing the totality, and then making a judgment in favor of the side the evidence favors. Normally, the factors one considers are of the same general kind on both sides of the issue. For example, if you are trying to figure out which of two driving routes to take to get from one city to another, you'll weigh, in each case, considerations such as total distance, speed limits, traffic density, possible road construction delays, and so

---

An Enquiry Concerning Human Understanding, published in 1748). Hume argues that one is never justified in accepting the report of a miracle. Although there are obvious parallels between purported miracles and Lucy's testimony, I've not included a discussion of Hume in this essay because it is essential to his argument that a miracle is a violation of a law of nature. But Lucy makes no claim to have experienced a literal miracle. For all she is claiming, her adventure in Narnia has an explanation that is perfectly in keeping with natural laws.

forth. You'll also weigh other, more subjective factors, such as a preference for freeway or back-road driving, and the scenic qualities of the respective routes—but in both cases, you'll look at the same kind of evidence for the two routes and compare them.

Part of what makes Peter and Susan's position so difficult is that the kinds of considerations that lead them to accept Lucy's testimony and the kind that lead them to be suspicious of it are of drastically different types. Against Lucy is much of what they think they know about reality. Undoubtedly, these imaginative, well-educated children retain some sense of wonder about the world; they don't expect to it to be devoid of mystery. Yet all of their experience seems to teach that there simply are no worlds of Fauns and witches. Doubtless, if the source of these claims were someone they didn't know, they would have no qualms about dismissing them out of hand. But the counterevidence in this case is precisely the character of the messenger. They know Lucy to be honest, and they have no reason (apart from her bizarre story) to doubt her sanity. So part of what makes Peter and Susan's position so difficult is the fact that the evidence against her testimony, and the evidence for it, are of very different types.

In addition to having to weigh two very different sorts of evidence, Peter and Susan's predicament is made all the worse by the strength of the evidence on either side. Certainly, their evidence that Fauns and witches are creatures of mere fantasy is very strong. Yet they've likely never been in the position of being unable to believe the trustworthy and sincere Lucy. Were anyone else to claim what Lucy is claiming, her testimony would be summarily dismissed. Were Lucy to be saying practically anything else, her word would be unquestioningly accepted. What's a rational person to think?

A Closer Look at the Predicament

The crux of the problem for Peter and Susan is that they are in the following situation. Let "Lucy's Story" stand for the entire story Lucy has told about her trip to Narnia put in purely objective terms. That is, Lucy's Story does not include the fact that it is Lucy who has made these claims; it includes only what she has said and not that it was she who said it. So Lucy's Story includes claims like "By stepping into a wardrobe, Lucy discovered a magical kingdom" and "Lucy had tea with a Faun."

Now just before Lucy tells Peter and Susan of her experience, what should we say is the probability of Lucy's Story's being true given what Peter and Susan believe? For example, suppose that just before Lucy relates her experience, we were to play a little game with Peter and Susan in which we ask them to consider various statements and whether, given the totality of what they believe, these statements are likely to be true. We give them, for instance, statements like "In a hundred years there will be no king or queen of England" and "The Professor knew Winston Churchill when they were both boys." We then ask them to judge, given all they believe about the world, how likely these statements are to be true or false. So, for example, the kids might judge it highly unlikely that the Professor knew Churchill (because they think that they'd know about something so remarkable if it were true), and not particularly likely or unlikely that there will be a monarch of England in a hundred years (because they take themselves to not have much of a basis for making such a judgment).

Now suppose we then have Peter and Susan consider Lucy's Story, and we ask them whether it is likely or not that most of the claims that make up Lucy's Story are true. The answer will be that these claims are unlikely indeed. The probability that there is a magical kingdom accessed through the wardrobe is, they will think, awfully close to zero. On the other hand, they know Lucy to be reliable and trustworthy. And that is an important factor to be weighed.

A First Lesson

There is a lesson here. When confronted with testimony you are tempted to disbelieve, you should ask yourself the following two questions: (1) how does the testimony fit in with my overall system of background beliefs?[2] and (2) how trustworthy is

---

[2] There is a further complication that I will mention only in passing. If a person has been intellectually irresponsible or irrational in forming a great many of her beliefs, then her background system itself will be epistemically tainted. It might be, then, that even if a claim she is now considering coheres well with her background beliefs, we might hesitate to think she should add it to her

the testifier, both in general and with respect to this particular topic? It is important to see that the answer to the first question does not have to be that the probability is high. The truth is actually that if the testifier is generally reliable, then even if what she is saying is somewhat improbable given your background beliefs, you still ought to believe her. For example, suppose I have some friends over for a dinner party. A half an hour after my guests leave, one of them calls to tell me that there has been a bad automobile accident on a certain street not far from my home, but that no one from my party was involved in the accident. Now the probability that there would have been a serious accident at that particular time and place is rather low if only because such accidents are rare. However, judgments based only on general probabilities are easily overridden by testimony to the contrary by a reliable source. After all, even if the probability is low that there would be an accident just there and then, I have no particular reason for thinking that there isn't an accident there now. Indeed, I have good reason to believe that there are accidents happening right now at many different locations and no reason to believe that the location my friend is referring to isn't one of them. So it won't take too much to override my initial evidence to the contrary.

If you lack a specific reason to believe that some particular testimony is false, and if your evidence against it is only that there is a general statistical reason for believing it is unlikely to be true, then you are surely justified in believing the testimony. Yet the accident case is importantly unlike the case of Lucy. For, assuming the person reporting the accident is reasonably trustworthy, we won't have any inclination to disbelieve her. Yet Peter and Susan quite rightly have a strong initial disinclination to believe Lucy.

The difference between the accident case (in which we readily believe the statistically unlikely testimony of our friend) and

---

stock of beliefs. After all, why should coherence with a set of irrationally formed beliefs confer rationality? This is a good question, and one without a clear answer. However, we can leave it aside because the primary issue we are dealing with in this essay is what you should do when you hear potentially incredible testimony. Now even though your past irresponsibility or irrationality may have put you in a poor position to evaluate the truth of a surprising claim, nevertheless, the best you can do now is to make a judgment about its acceptability on the basis of what you believe.

Lucy's case (in which we are naturally more skeptical) is that in the latter Peter and Susan have beliefs that are straightforwardly inconsistent with what Lucy is telling them. Peter and Susan believe that outside of make-believe, there are no worlds of the sort that Lucy is describing. It isn't as though they think there are such worlds but are dubious that they can be accessed via the wardrobe. Rather, they believe that there are no such places. And they believe this very strongly. So they take the probability of Lucy's Story, relative to their background beliefs, to be virtually zero. In contrast, although it would, of course, be very hard to assign any specific probability to the claim that there has been an accident at that particular place and time, the probability of that given our background beliefs is low but still many times higher than the probability of Lucy's Story is for Peter and Susan.

Lucy Disbelieved a Second Time

Let's now compare the epistemic position of Peter and Susan in the case we've been discussing with that of Lucy's three siblings in a pair of scenes from another book in the *Narnia* series. About midway through *Prince Caspian*, the four Pevensie children and the brave dwarf Trumpkin are on a journey and are having trouble finding their way. Suddenly, Lucy sees Aslan and takes him to be trying to lead them in his direction. But when the others look, Aslan is nowhere to be seen. Lucy reports that she is absolutely certain that she has seen Aslan, but Peter and Susan don't believe her. It's not clear whether Edmund believes her either, but he admits that she was right the last time she reported something remarkable, so he supports Lucy. However, Edmund and Lucy are outvoted (PC, Chapter 9, p. 374).

A short time later, Lucy has a conversation with Aslan while the others sleep. Aslan tells Lucy that the others won't be able to see him at first, but that she is to wake them up and tell them that Aslan says they must be on the move at once. Lucy does as she is told and stirs her resting siblings. She tells them that she has seen Aslan—in fact, that she can still see him—and that Aslan has instructed her to do as she is doing. Peter, Susan, and Edmund look where Lucy is pointing but they see nothing. When Edmund asks Lucy straight out how it could be that she sees Aslan but he doesn't, Lucy answers honestly that she doesn't know but that Aslan said he might not.

So once again, Lucy has remarkable experiences that she reports to her siblings. And once again they find her story incredible. Yet this time we might be excused for taking Lucy's side. Her later story is likely to strike us as more worthy of belief than was her original tale. We now can see why Lucy is more believable in these later episodes. Recall that what made the original predicament so sticky was that Lucy's testimony directly contradicted deeply held beliefs about the nature of reality. So even though she is the model of reliability, believing her required rejecting some fundamental beliefs to which, like the rest of us, her siblings were deeply committed. However, the epistemic position of her siblings when she tells them of her sightings of Aslan is rather different. First, and most significantly, all of the parties involved share a relevant body of background beliefs according to which Lucy's seeing Aslan is a live possibility. For they now believe all kinds of wild things they didn't believe before they came to Narnia. They believe, for instance, that animals can speak, that trees can become fully animated, and that at least one lion has been killed and come back to life. Now, given all these current beliefs that previously they would have regarded as absurd, the claim that this powerful, resurrected lion could appear selectively to Lucy seems not only to not contradict any deeply held background beliefs but coheres reasonably well with what they do know. In these circumstances, believing Lucy is a no-brainer. Shame on Peter and Susan!

We've seen that in order to assess whether a person's testimony is believable, you need to consider the reliability of the testifier, and then consider the content of what is being claimed in light of your system of background beliefs. If you have good reason to believe that the source is highly reliable, and if the content of what is being claimed is not deeply at odds with the other things you know or rationally believe, then you should generally believe the testifier. For instance, if it's a gray, overcast day and your sister comes home and says, "It's raining," you will immediately believe her because (a) you know her to be generally reliable, and (b) what she is saying fits in well with your background information.

Most cases of testimony are like this. Most of what we are told comes from sources that are reliable with respect to the messages being relayed, and the messages cohere well with our prior beliefs. However, when what we hear is highly surprising, we are likely either to reconsider the reliability of the messenger (at least with respect to this particular testimony) or to rethink some of what we thought we knew.

With these considerations in mind, let's turn our attention to a type of real world situation that bears a significant resemblance to Lucy's case. Among the hard-to-believe stories we sometimes hear are those in which people apparently have direct experience of God, or encounter aliens, or know of someone who has had a sudden and completely inexplicable recovery from a disease that had put him at death's door. Because we don't have time to consider each of these kinds of reports, and because the epistemic issues are basically similar, we'll limit ourselves to a discussion of just one of these topics: reports of religious experiences.

A Case of Testimony of Religious Experience

Suppose a friend, Julia, comes to you and tells you the following story:

> I had the most remarkable experience last night. I came home from a Bible study and began to pray for a good friend who has been struggling with a debilitating depression. As I was praying, the room seemed to me to become very warm. At first I figured that I had just worked myself up into a sweat, but then I felt as though there was someone in the room with me. My eyes shot open and I looked around frantically. I was sure that someone had come into my apartment. But after looking in every room, I became convinced that there was no other human there but I felt a presence still. Then I heard a voice. Actually, I didn't hear it audibly, but it was not something I was thinking—it was something said to me. It's as though the words were put directly in my head without the need to be spoken. And what was said was that God loved my friend and that no permanent harm would come to her. I'm sure this sounds crazy but that's the way I see it. After I received the message the voice stopped, the presence left, and the room cooled. I sat up all night thinking about it.

What is one to make of a report like this? Given the principles we drew out of the Lucy cases, we should have some idea of how to proceed. To decide whether Julia's story is credible, we must consider two primary factors: (1) the degree to which

Julia is a reliable person, and (2) the fit of what Julia is saying with our background beliefs. Let's consider these issues in order.

Knowing whether Julia is reliable can be a tricky business. And as with most questions of even minimal complexity, some distinctions are in order. First, when we wonder about Julia's reliability, we might have in mind her *general* reliability. What percentage of the statements that Julia makes with apparent sincerity turn out to be true? Obviously, the higher the percentage, the more reliable Julia is. The trouble is, of course, no one other than God is really in a position to know the answer to this with any precision. Nevertheless, if we know a person reasonably well, we can be in a position to make a pretty fair judgment about his or her general reliability. However, general reliability is not infallibility. Even a reliable source will sometimes be misleading.

Recall that after their discussion with the Professor, Peter and Susan came to believe that there were only three options regarding Lucy's testimony: she was either insane, lying, or telling the truth. Given that the first two possibilities were completely inconsistent with what they knew to be true of Lucy, they saw good reason to accept what she was saying. Now these three options do seem to pretty much exhaust the possibilities for Lucy. But it is important to see that in most cases there is one more, very common, way in which a bit of testimony can go wrong: the testifier might be sincerely mistaken. She might be sane and believe she's telling the truth but simply be wrong about the cause of her experience. It's easy to see why this possibility doesn't apply to Lucy: she's claiming to have gone into a wardrobe and thereby entered a world of talking Fauns and wicked witches. While this story might be the result of an insane hallucination or knowingly concocted out of whole cloth, is there really any possibility that she just was *mistaken* about her experience in the wardrobe? That what she took to be a talking Faun was really just an old coat? No, in her case, an honest mistake seems out of the question. But in most real-world cases, an honest mistake is very much a live possibility.

There are two ways these considerations are relevant to the acceptability of testimony. First, if you know that the testifier frequently gets things wrong and yet sincerely and confidently reports these errors as facts, then you have good reason to be suspicious of his reports generally. Second, even when a person isn't frequently unreliable, a healthy recognition of the limits of human knowing can still tell against what she says. When someone reports an experience that doesn't cohere with your background knowledge, then even if you have good reason to believe in the person's general reliability, the possibility of simple error is a real one. So when someone reports an experience that is rightly hard to believe, there are three ways the testimony might be wrong: the person is insane, lying, or simply sincerely mistaken.

Now what are we to make of Julia's report? Should it be believed? Having completed our discussion of Peter and Susan's predicament, we are now in a position to tackle this question. Let's take the above reasons for rejecting her testimony one at a time:

Julia is insane: we can state for the purposes of the case that you know Julia well, and you have no prior reason for questioning her sanity. Furthermore, in talking with Julia after she tells you her story, you get no sense at all that her rational faculties have been compromised.

Julia is lying: we can also pretty much rule this out. You know Julia well and have never had any reason to doubt her. If you have vast experience with a person and have never known her to lie, and if you can't think of any good reason for this situation to be any different, then there is no reason to take the lying possibility seriously.

Julia is sincerely mistaken: this is clearly the most likely skeptical possibility. Unlike Lucy's experience, Julia's could plausibly be thought to be produced by a sane, yet anxious and emotionally upset mind. Although she might be honest in reporting what she believes her experience to be, she might be mistaken about the nature of that experience. She felt the room heat up because she was praying so intensely. Perhaps her feeling of the presence of someone was caused by the strength of her conviction that God draws nearer to us in prayer and in times of distress. And the explanation for the inaudible voice could possibly be the workings of a subconscious wish-fulfillment process. This explanation is consistent with Julia's sincerely reporting her experiences. But if her experience is the result of purely natural processes, and there is good reason to think that God was not atypically present to her, then her report is false.

We should tread carefully here and notice that there are two ways of taking what Julia is saying. First, you might read her as merely reporting what her experience was like and the way things *seemed to her*. On this interpretation, believing Julia means only believing that she had a peculiar experience of some sort or another. This interpretation is consistent with both Julia's experience being caused by God and is also consistent with its being the result of purely natural psychological processes.

The second, more robust understanding of Julia's testimony is that she is asserting that the presence in her room was that of God, and that God did indeed speak comforting words to her about her friend's prospects. If you take Julia to be saying this, you are committed to the claim that her experience is genuinely caused by God; furthermore, you must deny the naturalistic psychological explanation of her unusual experience. Clearly, this is a more substantial commitment. Should you make it?

So What Should We Say about Julia?

We've said that you reasonably judge Julia's general reliability to be high, and that you can pretty much eliminate the insanity and lying possibilities. So your remaining choices are that she is honestly mistaken or that she's right. Now the reason you have for thinking she's right is that she usually is. This is a significant point in favor of accepting her testimony. Indeed, you *should* believe her unless what she says is quite unlikely given your background beliefs. So is what she says quite unlikely given your background beliefs? I can't answer this question for you.

"Why not?" I hear you silently objecting, "You've not been bashful about telling me what to think until now!" Fair enough, and what is stopping me now is not a sudden rush of shyness. Rather, I can't tell you if this belief is unlikely given your background beliefs because I don't know what your background beliefs are. As we've seen, one of the two key issues to consider when someone relates an experience is how well what is said fits with your background beliefs. And while most of us share a great many such beliefs, there is also a lot of variation from person to person. One possible belief that is clearly relevant to your consideration of Julia's testimony is belief in the existence of God. If you are a theist, and if you also believe that God does sometimes draw close to those in prayer, then although Julia's story might be somewhat surprising, it will not conflict with anything that you hold deeply. Indeed, it seems to confirm some of your convictions. On the other hand, if you have a firm belief that God doesn't exist, then you will quite reasonably disbelieve Julia—at least if her testimony is understood in the stronger way. Instead, you'll likely weigh what you know about Julia's trustworthiness against your conviction that she can't have an experience of something that doesn't exist, and come to the conclusion that although she is mistaken about the ultimate cause and significance of her belief, she surely did have an unusual experience that she sincerely believes to be an experience of God.

Throughout this essay, I have been writing as though when you hear a surprising report you must respond either by believing or else by disbelieving what has been said. However, there is a third option that will, in many circumstances, be the most reasonable. To see this, again consider Julia. Now suppose that you aren't sure what to think about the existence of God. You think you see some reason for belief, but those reasons don't seem overwhelming and, in your eyes, are at least counterbalanced by the evil and suffering that seems too prevalent for a world designed and ruled by an all-powerful, benevolent creator. In short, you're an agnostic. Julia, your good friend who has always struck you as sensible and reliable, reports a truly unusual experience. There is no question that you believe that something out of the ordinary happened on that night. And while you think it might be that she experienced God, you also think there is about an equal chance that some purely naturalistic cause produced her experience. In this case, the rational response for you is to *withhold* belief. To withhold from believing something is to neither believe nor disbelieve it; it is to not have a settled opinion on the matter.

Notice that withholding belief is not only rational for the agnostic; the theist and atheist might also reasonably withhold belief about Julia's testimony. A believer might withhold belief if she thinks that even though God exists and sometimes becomes directly present to people, the great majority of such reports are false. She might think that people are far too quick to think that their every high or low experience has a supernatural cause. On the other hand, someone might believe that God doesn't exist, but have such confidence in Julia's discriminating intelligence that her report of the presence of God causes the atheist to have less confidence in her atheism. Such a person might then simply withhold belief (and thereby withhold disbelief) in Julia's testimony.

In addition to the possibility of withholding belief, there is one more complication that needs to be mentioned. Although it is common to think of belief as an all-or-nothing phenomenon, the truth is that it is not. Beliefs come with a wide variety of conviction. Some beliefs are clung to so firmly that it would take a great deal to dislodge them; others we hold by a thread. This means that there are lots of possible ways to respond to Julia. While the primary categories are *believe*, *disbelieve*, and *withhold*, there are many different degrees of strength with which one can do the first two.

A Modest Conclusion

So what should we conclude about Julia's experience? In general, what should one do when confronted with an unusual or surprising testimony? Should you ever believe reports of UFOs or disappearing cancers? As this essay shows, these are neither particularly easy questions to answer nor questions for which there is a single reply. What we can say is that whether it is rational for you to believe such reports will depend on what you know about the reliability of the testifier together with your background knowledge relevant to the subject of the testimony. Generally, if you have good reason to think the person is usually reliable, and you've got no reason to think that she's lying or in some other way mistaken about this particular report, and what is being said does not contradict well-considered, firmly held beliefs, then you should believe her. But applying these considerations to specific cases often yields no straightforward answer.

Is this disappointing? Perhaps a bit. But that doesn't mean that our reflections have not been of value. For we began by recognizing Peter and Lucy's epistemic predicament, but without any clear sense of the nature of the predicament or how to think about what should be done in such cases. We now have a clear understanding of their situation and what rationality requires of us when we are presented with surprising (if not strictly incredible) reports. Philosophy is often a great help in getting us to see how to think about problems, even if it offers answers only sparingly.

4

Breaking the Spell of Skepticism: Puddleglum versus the Green Witch

STEVEN LOVELL

As readers of the stories, we can all agree that Narnia isn't real, that "there is no Narnia." But we don't expect those in the stories themselves to agree with us. And yet, at a crucial moment in *The Silver Chair* several of the main characters are found with these philosophically puzzling words on their lips. We begin by reminding ourselves of how this odd-sounding situation came about.

How the Enchantment Begins

Jill Pole and Eustace Scrubb have been summoned from our world into Narnia to find Prince Rilian, lost son of the now aged King Caspian. The children and their pessimistic guide, Puddleglum the Marsh-wiggle, eventually come to an underground world where the wicked Queen of Underland, the Green Witch, has Rilian under her spell. Following the signs that Aslan has given, the three release Rilian from the bewitching silver chair while the Queen is away. But she returns just as the four are about to make their escape, and immediately attempts to bring them all under an enchantment.

Since Jill, Eustace, Puddleglum and Rilian aim to escape to Narnia, the Witch's strategy is to bring them to believe that no such world exists. The green powder the Witch throws on the fire fills the room with a sweet and soporific smell that makes it hard to think, and her monotonous thrumming on a mandolin has a similarly hypnotic effect. In this situation, the Queen begins to reason with our company of four. The arguments and counter-arguments that follow provide the focus of this chapter.

The Enchantment Deepens

The powder and the mandolin soon begin to take effect, and before long Puddleglum is the only one still resisting the spell.

> "You can play that fiddle till your fingers drop off, and still you won't make me forget Narnia. . . . I know I was there once. I've seen the sky full of stars. I've seen the sun coming up out of the sea of a morning and sinking behind the mountains at night. And I've seen him up in the midday sky when I couldn't look at him for brightness."
>
> Puddleglum's words had a very rousing effect. The other three all breathed again and looked at one another like people newly awaked. (SC, Chapter 12, pp. 630–31)

The victory is short-lived, however. When asked to explain what the sun is like, Rilian compares it to the lamp illuminating the room. The sun is like the lamp, only "far greater and brighter." Both are round and yellow, and whereas the lamp gives light to the whole room and hangs from the roof, the sun gives light to the whole Overworld and "hangeth in the sky."

> "Hangeth from what, my lord?" asked the Witch; and then, while they were still thinking how to answer her, she added, with another of her soft, silver laughs: "You see? When you try to think out clearly what this *sun* must be, you cannot tell me. You can only tell me it is like the lamp. Your *sun* is a dream; and there is nothing in that dream that was not copied from the lamp. The lamp is the real thing; the *sun* is but a tale, a children's story."
>
> "Yes, I see now," said Jill in a heavy, hopeless tone. "It must be so." And while she said this, it seemed to her to be very good sense. (SC, Chapter 12, p. 631)

The other three soon give in, at least until Jill remembers about Aslan. But the Witch is now in full flow, and Aslan suffers the same fate as the sun. When Eustace explains that a lion is like a huge cat, the Queen replies.

> "I see," she said, "that we should do no better with your *lion*, as you call it, than we did with your *sun*. You have seen lamps, and

so you imagined a bigger and better lamp and called it the *sun*. You've seen cats, and now you want a bigger and better cat, and it's to be called a *lion*. Well, 'tis a pretty make-believe, though, to say truth, it would suit you all better if you were younger." (SC, Chapter 12, p. 632)

The Lady of the Freudian Slip

The Witch's arguments have several parallels in philosophy. We shall be looking at just one: the Freudian critique of religious belief. According to that critique, religious beliefs are illusions. Sigmund Freud argues that belief in God results from the wish for a father figure to protect us, as in childhood, against forces beyond our control. Freud writes:

> The derivation of religious needs from the infant's helplessness and the longing for the father aroused by it seems to me incontrovertible. . . . I cannot think of any need in childhood as strong as the need for a father's protection. . . . The origin of the religious attitude can be traced back in clear outlines as far as the feeling of infantile helplessness.[1]

In short, Freud argues that "at bottom God is nothing other than an exalted father."[2] So similar is this critique of religious belief to the Witch's case against the Overworld that it's tempting to think this is what the whole passage is "really about." Indeed, if we replace "sun" or "lion" with "God," the Witch's arguments virtually *become* the Freudian critique: "When you try to think out clearly what this *God* must be, you cannot tell me. You can only tell me *He* is like a father. Your *God* is a dream; and there is nothing in that dream that was not copied from an earthly father. Earthly fathers are the real thing; *God* is but a tale, a children's story." "You've seen fathers, and now you want a bigger and better father, and it's to be called *God*. Well, 'tis a pretty make-believe, though, to say truth, it would suit you all better if you were younger."

---

[1] Sigmund Freud, *Civilization and its Discontents* (1930), in *Civilization, Society and Religion; Penguin Freud Library*, Volume 12 (London: Penguin, 1990), p. 260.

[2] Sigmund Freud, *Totem and Taboo* (1913), in *The Origins of Religion: Penguin Freud Library*, Volume 13 (London: Penguin, 1990), p. 209.

A Puzzle about Aslan: How Do You Tell a Copy from the Original?

In *The Last Battle*, the poor gullible donkey, Puzzle, is duped into dressing up as Aslan by the scheming ape, Shift. Many Narnians are fooled into accepting this charade as the real thing and, as a result, are led to all kinds of evil deeds. Their problem was that they couldn't tell the copy from the original.

An important part of the Queen's case against Overworld is the claim that the Sun is nothing but a copy of the lamp. Similarly, Freud's argument assumes that God is nothing but a copy of an earthly father. While Freud's assertion may seem plausible, readers of *The Silver Chair* know that the Witch's argument is unsound. If we are going to speak of copies and originals here, it would seem more appropriate to say that the lamp is a copy and the Sun is the original. But what about Freud's claim? How do we tell a copy from the original?

At first sight it might seem that if we cannot answer this question then we cannot reply to Freud. But since it is *Freud's* argument that depends on God being a copy, it is Freud, rather than his opponents, who needs a way of answering the question. Unfortunately for Freud, it's not at all clear how the question should be answered. But one thing seems obvious: from the mere fact that two things are similar, it is impossible to tell which, if either, is the copy. But similarity is all that Freud has to go on.[3]

Indeed, if God does exist, it seems reasonable to believe that earthly fathers are in some way a copy of our heavenly one.[4] The similarity between God and our earthly fathers is not an embarrassing fact that those who believe in God must explain away. Rather, it is just the sort of thing one might expect if God does exist.

Whose Illusion Is It, Anyway?

Part of Freud's argument against God that isn't so neatly paralleled in the Witch's arguments is the claim that belief in God is

---

[3] Compare Richard L. Purtill, *C.S. Lewis's Case for the Christian Faith*, second edition (San Francisco: Ignatius Press, 2004), p. 22.

[4] For a little more on this theme, see C.S. Lewis, *The Pilgrim's Regress* (London:

the result of wish-fulfilment. The closest the Queen comes to saying anything like this is the constant patronising of the companions' beliefs as childish, though this does include saying that the beliefs are a "pretty make-believe."

Freud claims that we believe in God because that belief provides comfort in a cold and dangerous world. But is the God of Christianity really the sort of thing one would wish for? After all, as one leading Christian philosopher has pointed out:

> [M]any people thoroughly dislike the idea of an omnipotent, omniscient being monitoring their every activity, privy to their every thought, and passing judgement on all they do or think. Others dislike the lack of autonomy consequent upon there being a Someone by comparison with whom we are as dust and ashes, and to whom we owe worship and obedience.[5]

Edmund's early feelings about Aslan in *The Lion, the Witch, and the Wardrobe* are surely similar to the feelings many of us have about God: "the mention of Aslan gave him a mysterious and horrible feeling just as it gave the others a mysterious and lovely feeling" (LWW, Chapter 9, p. 151). As Edmund makes his way to the White Witch's house he sees what he eventually realizes is a stone lion. To him it seemed a "lovely idea" that this might once have been the Aslan that everyone was talking about. As harsh as it may sound, far from wishing for him, Edmund wanted Aslan dead. Indeed, if one were to wish for a God at all, it probably wouldn't be the God of Christianity, just as Lucy and Susan wished that Aslan might have been something rather more tame than a lion.

> "Ooh!" said Susan, "I'd thought he was a man. Is he—quite safe? I shall feel rather nervous about meeting a lion."
> "That you will, dearie, and no mistake," said Mrs Beaver; "if there's anyone who can appear before Aslan without their knees knocking, they're either braver than most or else just silly."
> "Then he isn't safe?" said Lucy.
> "Safe?" said Mr Beaver; "don't you hear what Mrs Beaver tells

Fount, 1977; first published 1933), pp. 81–89. Freud is represented in this work by the character of "Sigismund."

[5] Alvin Plantinga, *Warranted Christian Belief* (New York: Oxford University Press, 2000), p. 195.

you? Who said anything about safe? 'Course he isn't safe. But he's good. He's the King, I tell you." (LWW, Chapter 8, p. 146)

Is it really plausible to say that belief in God results from wish-fulfillment? Contrary to Freud, it is far from clear that anyone would wish for the existence of a being such as God, and it may in fact be atheism that results from wish-fulfillment.[6]

The God-Shaped Hole

As readers of the story, we are in no danger of being taken in by the Witch's arguments. We know that Jill, Eustace, Puddleglum, and Rilian are being deceived: Narnia is real, just as Aslan and the Sun are real. And since we know this, we also know that the Witch's argument can't be right.

Since the Witch's conclusion is wrong (as she knows), there must be a mistake somewhere in her reasoning. But if the Witch's reasoning is wrong, and Freud's reasoning is essentially the same, then there must be a mistake somewhere in his reasoning too! The mistake in question is often called "the genetic fallacy," and involves illegitimately rejecting a belief simply because of where it comes from.[7] A belief might be true whatever its origins, whether this be wish-fulfillment, tea-leaf reading, or anything else. Indeed, this is quite obvious in our case; wishes do sometimes come true, although admittedly not as often as most of us would like.

In fact, Freud admitted that his argument didn't prove that religion is false, but he still thought his arguments showed that religious belief is irrational. If religion is to be rational, it surely ought to be based on good evidence, not on our "infantile wishes."

Suppose we grant that religion is based on a desire for God. Does it follow that religious belief is irrational? That depends on

---

[6] For more on this theme, see Lewis, *The Pilgrim's Regress*, pp. 81–96. See also P.C. Vitz, *Faith of the Fatherless: The Psychology of Atheism* (Dallas: Spence, 1999), pp. 9–16.

[7] In other words the genetic fallacy relates to the origin or *genesis* of the belief—hence the name of the fallacy. For an entertaining critique of the fallacy, see Lewis's essay "Bulverism," in C.S. Lewis, *God in the Dock: Essays on Theology and Ethics* (Grand Rapids: Eerdmans, 1970), pp. 271–77.

the desire itself. If the desire is a mere "wish," and the resulting belief a "wish-fulfillment," then we must agree with Freud. But what if the desire is better described as an *inherent need* for God? What if, as the early medieval philosopher St. Augustine (354–430 A.D.) said, "You have made us for Yourself and our hearts are restless until they find their rest in You"? To paraphrase Blaise Pascal (1623–1662), it may be that humans have been created with a God-shaped hole, a need that only God can fill.

The idea of a deep desire for something beyond the physical world is a theme that comes up again and again in Lewis's writings. In *The Voyage of the "Dawn Treader,"* King Caspian sets out in search of seven Lords, friends of his father who had been sent to explore the Eastern Seas by the usurper Miraz. Among others, Caspian is accompanied by the incomparably gallant mouse, Reepicheep. Although Reepicheep would have sailed with Caspian out of valor and loyalty alone, his main reason for joining the crew was something quite different.

> "But Reepicheep here has an even higher hope." Everyone's eyes turned to the Mouse.
>
> "As high as my spirit," he said. "Though perhaps as small as my stature. Why should we not come to the very eastern end of the world? And what might we find there? I expect to find Aslan's own country. It is always from the east, across the sea, that the great Lion comes to us." . . .
>
> "But do you think," said Lucy, "Aslan's country would be that sort of country—I mean, the sort you could ever *sail* to?"
>
> "I do not know, Madam," said Reepicheep. "But there is this. When I was in my cradle, a wood woman, a Dryad, spoke this verse over me:
>
> > Where sky and water meet,
> > Where the waves grow sweet,
> > Doubt not, Reepicheep,
> > To find all you seek,
> > There is the utter east.
>
> I do not know what it means. But the spell of it has been on me all my life." (VDT, Chapter 2, p. 433)

In *Mere Christianity*, Lewis puts it like this:

> Creatures are not born with desires unless satisfaction for those desires exists. A baby feels hunger: well, there is such a thing as

food. A duckling wants to swim: well, there is such a thing as
water. Men feel sexual desire: well, there is such a thing as sex. If
I find in myself a desire which no experience in this world can satisfy, the most probable explanation is that I was made for another
world.[8]

So, far from counting against religious belief, a deep desire for
God may provide evidence for His existence.

In sum, Freud's critique, like the Witch's, fails. It fails for four
reasons. First, the similarity between the concept of God and the
concept of an earthly father does not tell us which (if either) is
the copy and which is the original. Second, atheism seems just
as likely as religious belief to be the result of wish-fulfillment.
Third, one cannot show that God doesn't exist from the
(alleged) fact that we wish Him to exist. Fourth, if God does
exist and created us with a need to be in relationship with Him,
believing in Him on the basis of that need would not constitute
wishful thinking.

The Spell Is Broken: The Meditations
of a Marsh-wiggle

Puddleglum and company didn't respond to the Witch in the
way that I have responded to Freud. Puddleglum's first response
is purely practical. He stamps out the fire with his bare feet,
clearing the air of the fumes that have been clouding their thinking and replacing them with the rather less enchanting smell of
burnt Marsh-wiggle. The pain in his feet also brings a certain
clarity of thought:

> "One word. All you've been saying is quite right, I shouldn't won-
> der. . . . But there's one thing more to be said, even so. Suppose
> we *have* only dreamed, or made up, all those things—trees and
> grass and sun and moon and stars and Aslan himself. . . . Then all
> I can say is that, in that case, the made-up things seem a good deal
> more important than the real ones. . . . That's why I'm going to
> stand by the play-world. I'm on Aslan's side even if there isn't any
> Aslan to lead it. I'm going to live as like a Narnian as I can even if

---

[8] C.S. Lewis, *Mere Christianity* (London: Fount, 1977; first published 1952), p.
118.

there isn't any Narnia. So . . . we're leaving your court at once and setting out in the dark to spend our lives looking for Overland. Not that our lives will be very long, I should think; but that's a small loss if the world's as dull a place as you say." (SC, Chapter 12, p. 633)

One of the surprising things about Puddleglum's speech is the way it starts: by admitting that the Witch is probably right. Unlike the previous attempts, this defense of the reality of Narnia and Aslan is not based on any claim to have experienced these things, nor on any other straightforward argument for their existence. Puddleglum seems to be arguing that the belief is legitimate even though he doesn't have any evidence for it.

In attempting to defend belief in Narnia and Aslan without evidence, Puddleglum's argument echoes famous defenses of religious belief by the philosophers William James (1842–1910) and Blaise Pascal. Both argue that belief in God can be perfectly rational, even in the absence of rationally compelling evidence. While Freud argues that religious belief is irrational because it is based on wish-fulfillment and not evidence, James and Pascal deny that proof is necessary.

Puddleglum's Wager

Puddleglum's argument seems, at least in part, to be that if the Witch is right then nothing real is of value: the made-up things are the most important ones. But perhaps, just perhaps, Narnia and Aslan are real. Either way, Jill, Eustace, Puddleglum, and Rilian have little to lose by staking their lives on the small chance that the valuable things are real after all. If there is no Narnia, nothing will be lost in seeking it, since life in the Witch's world has nothing to offer. But if Narnia does exist, then giving in to the Witch would be the worst mistake possible.

Pascal's argument for belief in God is remarkably similar. Whether God exists or not, we have nothing to lose by committing ourselves to Him. If there is no God, then the decision of whether or not to believe is ultimately inconsequential: nothing will be lost if we believe or if we do not. But if God does exist, not believing in him will prove a terrible mistake. If we believe in God and are wrong, we lose little, but if we are wrong in our disbelief we miss out on eternity with Him (and may have a much worse fate to endure). The risks of believing in God are infinitely lower, and the possible gains infinitely higher, than those of not believing.

Puddleglum's speech is also reminiscent of a famous argument by William James. In his essay "The Will to Believe" (1896), James points out that in our intellectual life we have two important aims: to believe truths and to avoid errors.[9] Those who think we need to have evidence for everything we believe seem to place more weight on the second of these aims than on the first—"better risk loss of truth than chance of error" is their motto.[10] But, as James points out, there are many important existential questions that cannot be decided by evidence. And since these decisions cannot be based on evidence, it is perfectly legitimate to let some questions be decided not by evidence but by our "passions"—that is, by our hopes, desires, and interests. Perhaps the existence of God is one of these vital and undecidable existential questions.

James didn't think every question could or should be decided without evidence, but only questions of a particular sort. To qualify, a question must meet four conditions. It must be one that the person cannot decide on intellectual grounds alone; it must be genuinely open in a person's mind; there must be no way of evading the question; and the question must be an important one.

For a question to be open, the possible choices must "appeal as a real possibility." For example, to most of us, the proposition *Zeus is god above all other gods* is not a live hypothesis: "The notion makes no electric connection with your nature—it refuses to scintillate with any credibility at all."[11] In short, all hypotheses are either "live" or literally beyond belief. James admits that what is a live hypothesis for one person may be beyond belief for another. If a question cannot be settled on intellectual grounds and is, in James's terms, *living*, *forced* and *momentous*, then we not only may, but must, decide the issue on "passional grounds."

The decision facing Jill, Eustace, Puddleglum, and Rilian is very much of this sort. It certainly seems possible to them that Narnia does not exist, but while the enchantment is not com-

[9] William James, "The Will to Believe," reprinted in *Pragmatism: The Classic Writings*, edited by H.S. Thayer (Indianapolis: Hackett, 1982), pp. 186–208.

plete, the reality of Narnia remains a live hypothesis. The decision cannot be evaded: either they believe in Narnia or they do not. Any attempt to suspend judgment on the issue will leave them under the Witch's spell. The decision is also momentous. The only possibility worth living for is Narnia, and if they don't take their chance now, Narnia will never again be in their reach.

In this situation it is surely unreasonable to suppose that our companions shouldn't believe without better evidence. As James said, "a rule of thinking which would . . . prevent me from acknowledging certain kinds of truth if those truths were really there would be an irrational rule."[12] While the four remain in the Underworld, the rule "better risk loss of truth than chance of error" is just such a rule, and must be rejected as irrational.

James applies the same reasoning to religious belief. The existence of God is a live hypothesis for most of us. In addition, the question of his existence cannot really be evaded: if you remain an agnostic long enough, death will turn your "perhaps" into a "no." This is similar to Jill's decision early in *The Silver Chair* to approach Aslan so she can drink from the stream. Had she never made her decision she would have died of thirst just as surely as if she decided against drinking from the stream. The decision for or against God is clearly a momentous one: we have only one life in which to make it, and the associated risks and possible benefits could not be bigger, as Pascal's Wager makes clear. So the case of belief in God meets James's criteria, and it is therefore legitimate to decide the issue without conclusive evidence.

Look Out! It's a Live Hypothesis[13]

A common objection to the arguments of both Pascal and James is that they ignore the possibility of different religious options. For instance, against Pascal it is often claimed that it is possible that there is a malicious god who, after our deaths, would torture those who had believed in God and give everlasting pleasures to those who had not. If we were to take this idea into

---

[10] *Ibid.*, p. 205.
[11] *Ibid.*, p. 187.
[12] *Ibid.*, p. 206.
[13] C.S. Lewis, *Miracles*, second edition (London: Fontana, 1960), p. 98.

account, it would seem that Pascal's argument no longer works, for believing in God would be just as risky as failing to believe.

James and Puddleglum can help us here. Puddleglum wasn't faced with a choice between all logically possible theories of the universe; he was faced with a choice between believing in Narnia and believing only in the Witch's dark, gloomy caverns. It would be absurd to fault him for not considering the possibility of the existence of Tolkien's Middle-earth.[14] Middle-earth was not a live hypothesis for Puddleglum. Similarly, the possibility of an evil god who tortures believers is not one that many of us can take seriously. Pascal's argument is not designed to rule out such options. His argument is directed to those who are choosing between classical theism and atheism, and for such persons the argument has force.

Puddleglum's Speech: Attack or Defence?

It may be that some readers will now complain that no traditional form of religious commitment is a live option for them. But this doesn't mean that James's and Pascal's arguments are without value. Indeed, the value of Puddleglum's argument would not have depended on its ability to convince the Witch's still enchanted Earthmen servants. Fending off the attacks of one's opponents is quite a different thing from launching attacks of one's own. If the arguments are supposed to convince outright skeptics they will probably fail. On the other hand, if the arguments are addressed to those for whom God is a live hypothesis or to believers who need rational reassurance, they may succeed.

If, as my reader, you find that religious belief is not a live option, then James's and Pascal's arguments are not addressed to you. However, you should be warned that if belief in God no longer appeals to you, that may be because your enchantment is complete.

---

[14] Middle-earth was the setting of Tolkien's *The Lord of the Rings*. Incidentally, Tolkien and Lewis were, after a rocky start, good friends. There are many passages in *The Chronicles of Narnia* that were clearly influenced by *The Lord of the Rings*. To cite just one example: the hypnotic voice of the Green Witch is strongly reminiscent of the scene in *The Lord of the Rings* (*The Two Towers*, Chapter 10) in which Saruman's seductive voice nearly convinces the conquering armies of Rohan to release him.

5

At Any Rate There's No Humbug Here: Truth and Perspective

BRUCE R. REICHENBACH

We haven't let anyone take us in.
—THE RENEGADE DWARFS

The great fear of philosophers over the past four centuries has been that they might be taken in, deceived, duped, caught without any clothes of sufficient evidence. Their motto was to avoid the uncertain and the subjective. Better to lose a world of truth than once to be mistaken. But a rising counter-chorus is being heard. The American philosopher and psychologist William James notes, "For my own part, I have also a horror of being duped; but I can believe that worse things than being duped may happen to a man in this world."[1] C.S. Lewis had a similar perspective, as suggested by this telling description of the Dwarfs in the final volume of the *Chronicles*: "Their prison is only in their own minds, yet they are in that prison; and so afraid of being taken in that they cannot be taken out" (LB, Chapter 13, p. 748).

The Holy Grail of Certainty

From the early seventeenth century to the middle of the twentieth century, the pursuit of certitude dominated Western thought.

---

[1] William James, "The Will to Believe" (1896), reprinted in *Philosophy of Religion: Selected Readings*, second edition, edited by Michael Peterson *et. al.* (New York: Oxford University Press, 2001), p. 88. Compare Alfred North

Philosophers looked back at past philosophy, science, and religion and wondered why so little progress had been made. The father of modern philosophy, René Descartes (1596–1650), looked at his past education, the achievements of science, and the state of philosophy and morals, and was profoundly disappointed. "There is nothing about which there is not some dispute—and thus nothing that is not doubtful."[2] Relying on reason to produce the clarity and distinctness characteristic of certainty, Descartes began his quest for certainty by turning to the one thing we know directly: our own thoughts. The problem for Descartes was that while some things like my own and God's existence seem certain, knowledge of the world around us, provided by sense experience, is often uncertain.

At the end of the seventeenth century the Englishman John Locke assumed the task of trying to put our sensory beliefs on a firmer footing. The senses reveal qualities such as color, shape, taste, hardness, and sound. But how can we be sure these qualities are real? Locke's response is that our understanding is mostly passive. Objects stimulate our senses, which in turn convey to us simple ideas of various qualities. We cannot refuse to receive or alter these simple ideas, though we can combine simple ideas to form more complex ideas. Objectivity is guaranteed, because we add nothing to this incoming simple data. Whenever we have clear and distinct perceptions of simple ideas, we can claim objective knowledge.

But alas, things are not that simple, because as Locke recognized, simple ideas do not simply mirror perceived things. While some of our perceptions represent the real properties of objects, others do not. We can be certain that the objects around us are solid, are extended in space, have shape and are in motion when we sense them. But we cannot have the same certainty about colors, tastes, sounds, and odors, for various persons often have different perceptions when experiencing the same thing. Even in our sensory experience objectivity remains elusive.

At the end of the eighteenth century Immanuel Kant sought to prove the objectivity of sense experience by grounding all

---

Whitehead, *Modes of Thought* (New York: Macmillan, 1938), p. 22: "Panic of error is the death of progress."
[2] René Descartes, *Discourse on Method*, Part I.

knowledge in structures of the human mind. Like a computer, the mind receives data. But the preservation of that data requires that they be saved in files that, for Kant, are preset (*a priori*). By great fortune all humans have the same model of mental computer and preset files, which guarantees that knowledge can be objective and certain. The price of this turn to subjectivity to guarantee certainty is great, however, for Kant restricts our knowledge to the way things appear to us; about the world as it really exists we can at best speculate.

When we come to the twentieth century we find that the elusive animal of objectivity is still being stalked, this time by the Positivists. Taking their cue from Francis Bacon (1561–1626), the Positivists found objectivity in the empirical sciences. If sense experience can't verify an empirical claim, the claim is not merely false but meaningless. Objectivity, they claimed, is found in public confirmation and repeatability. But again, Positivism paid a heavy price. Because many ordinary beliefs such as those found in history or in our memories are unverifiable, they are meaningless according to Positivism.

C.S. Lewis was no stranger to Positivism; indeed, his noted tutor, "The Great Knock" (William Kirkpatrick), had Positivist leanings. Lewis writes, "If ever a man came near to being a purely logical entity, that man was Kirk. Born a little later, he would have been a Logical Positivist."[3] Yet Lewis's grounding in Plato, Northernness (the Germanic and Scandinavian myths), and the Classics made him immune to long-term Positivist influence, so that even before the likes of Thomas Kuhn and Jacques Derrida made such ideas fashionable, we find in Lewis a clear rejection of this search for certitude and objectivity. Three themes supporting this claim run through his Narnian stories. First, knowledge is perspectival; second, knowledge is value-laden; and finally, knowledge is personal. We will consider each in turn.

"The inside is bigger than the outside":
Perspectival Knowing

The first assumption of objective knowing is that everyone can have the same perspective if only they put themselves into the

---

[3] C.S. Lewis, *Surprised by Joy: The Shape of My Early Life* (New York: Harcourt, Brace, 1955), p. 125.

proper experiential position. Lewis saw through the enchantment of this assumption:

> Tirian looked and saw the queerest and most ridiculous thing you
> can imagine. Only a few yards away, clear to be seen in the sun-
> light, there stood up a rough wooden door and, round it, the
> framework of the doorway: nothing else, no walls, no roof. . . . He
> walked round to the other side of the door. But it looked just the
> same from the other side: he was still in the open air, on a summer
> morning. The door was simply standing up by itself as if it had
> grown there like a tree. . . .
>
> "It is the door you came through with that Calormene five min-
> utes ago," said Peter smiling.
>
> "But did I not come in out of the wood into the Stable? Whereas
> this seems to be a door leading from nowhere to nowhere."
>
> "It looks like that if you walk *round* it," said Peter. "But put
> your eye to that piece where there is a crack between two of the
> planks and look *through.*"
>
> Tirian put his eye to the hole. At first he could see nothing but
> blackness. Then, as his eyes grew used to it, he saw the dull red
> glow of a bonfire that was nearly going out. . . . So he knew that
> he was looking out through the Stable door into the darkness of
> Lantern Waste. . . .
>
> "It seems, then," said Tirian, smiling himself, "that the Stable
> seen from within and the Stable seen from without are two differ-
> ent places."
>
> "Yes," said the Lord Digory. "Its inside is bigger than its out-
> side." (LB, Chapter 13, pp. 743–44)

Lewis suggests that our tools of knowing are like Tirian's
door: perspectival. Things might look one way from one perspective and quite different from another. Most of us are wired
in pretty much the same way, though there are enough exceptions to keep neurologists interested and busy. But ask any two
persons how they see something in the world and suddenly we
are thrust into a world of diversity. Colors are shaded, sounds
have timbre, tastes run rampant. A connoisseur of coffee I am
not. Gourmet flavors are completely lost on me because I have
never developed the taste for coffee. It is not that my taste buds
are not working or working properly. It is not that I am not
"receiving" the simple ideas of the flavors. Rather, it is that I
bring to the drinking experience a different context and set of
experiences than the coffee aficionado brings. My coffee expe-

rience is not merely a matter of appreciation; it is a matter of the taste itself. The coffee really tastes differently to each of us because of what we bring to the experience.

The Lockean view that we receive the world in atomistic bits has been replaced with a Gestalt view of experience. This means the world comes organized and structured with complex richness. For example, we don't see the star

composed of isolated points. Neither do we construct the star out of the discrete points. We actually see a star. As philosopher of science Thomas Kuhn has shown, we possess no pure observation-language that yields complete objectivity and certainty about our experience. In moving from one conceptual framework, or "paradigm," to another, we actually see the world as different.[4] This is precisely Lewis's point. The Stable seen from the outside and the one seen from the inside are really in different places; it is not a matter merely of interpretation. The world depends upon the perspective, just as the perspective depends upon the world. Each accommodates and corrects the other.

This view of knowledge does not wallow in fuzzy subjectivity. Tirian *knows* that the Door stands in the field surrounded by no walls, just as he once knew that the Door was attached to and opened into the Stable. It is a matter of seeing, however surprising that may be in different contexts. For Lewis, the point about seeing extends beyond perception to a concern about the world itself. The theistic paradigm, affirming the existence of a creator God who intervenes in the world, competes with the atheistic paradigm. For Lewis, the atheistic paradigm only sees the Stable as a small, ramshackle building housing animals. For the theist, the Stable can hold more. As Lucy notes, "In our world too, a Stable once had something inside it that

---

[4] Thomas Kuhn, *The Structure of Scientific Revolutions* (Chicago: University of Chicago Press, 1962), p. 127.

was bigger than our whole world" (LB, Chapter 13, p. 744). Lewis holds that some cannot see or hear God or, in the Narnian stories, Aslan, however hard they try; "what you see and hear depends a good deal on where you are standing: it also depends on what sort of person you are" (MN, Chapter 10, p. 75).[5] Lewis argues that theism provides a superior paradigm, and from this paradigm the world is richer because it once housed God himself. In any case, the question of the nature of the world depends on one's perspective.

"The smelly little hole of a stable":
Value-Laden Knowing

The second thesis of objective knowing is that knowledge must be value-free. The model of knowing assumed by Enlightenment thinkers and their heirs was science. Scientists allegedly rejected any intrusion of values into the knowing process. A good experiment can be repeated by anyone in similar circumstances following the same procedures. Repeatability guarantees that what one person discovers to be the case will be discovered by all others, whatever the values of the investigators.

In his influential book *The Structure of Scientific Revolutions*, Thomas Kuhn rejects the widely-held thesis that scientific knowledge grows through the steady, linear accumulation of new data. Rather, science develops through the struggle of competing general theories, or paradigms. Often paradigms accepted by the scientific community encounter anomalies, data that will not fit into the current explanatory structure. The geological theory of fixed landmasses could not explain the way continents like South America and Africa fit into each other or the identical geological formations on the respective coasts. The normal approach is to alter some features of the paradigm to account for the anomalies, and usually this successfully resolves the anomaly. But at times

---

[5] Similar insights are often found in Eastern philosophical and religious traditions. Consider this story told by Buddhist monk Thich Nhat Hanh: "One man who wanted to see the Buddha was in such a hurry that he neglected a woman in dire need whom he met along the way. When he arrived at the Buddha's monastery, he was incapable of seeing him. Whether you can see the Buddha or not depends on you, on the state of your being." Thich Nhat Hanh, *Living Buddha, Living Christ* (New York: Riverhead, 1995), p. 52.

mere adjustment of the current paradigm is insufficient to deal with the anomaly, and new paradigms—like continental drift— are suggested. For awhile the paradigms compete until one emerges the winner. The struggle is not painless; old paradigms are not easily abandoned, nor are new ones readily accepted. No obvious method for deciding between them is available. Facts themselves cannot determine a clear winner, and criteria for making a decision are already embedded in paradigms. Since each paradigm faces its own anomalies, one has to decide which has the fewest important anomalies. The decision between paradigms, then, requires not only factual but value judgments. The acceptance of a paradigm is not an objective research project but a value-laden intellectual activity.

Lewis, in his treatment of competing worldviews, agrees. Jill and Eustace chose their fundamental paradigm not by logic but out of their very personal encounter with Aslan. Their adoption of their worldview was grounded on the virtue of faith, not evidence or argument. For Eustace, it was the faith that Aslan could strip him of his dragonish skin and ways (VDT, Chapter 7, pp. 474–75). For Jill, it was faith to accept Aslan's invitation to drink from the stream despite her fear of being eaten (SC, Chapter 2, p. 558). Faith, in the Narnian stories, is responding without assurance, often in the midst of despair, to the invitation of God. Accepting this invitation brings the beginning of a new paradigm. "It would be nice, and fairly nearly true, to say that 'from that time forth Eustace was a different boy'. To be strictly accurate, he began to be a different boy. He had relapses. . . . But most of those I shall not notice. The cure had begun" (VDT, Chapter 7, p. 476).

Not only do the acceptance and rejection of paradigms invoke values, the very paradigms themselves introduce values into knowledge claims about the world. Lewis explores the values found in competing paradigms in Lucy's encounter with the Dwarfs in *The Last Battle*.

[The Dwarfs] had a very odd look. They weren't strolling about or enjoying themselves nor were they lying down and having a rest. They were sitting very close together in a little circle facing one another. . . .

"Look out!" said one of them in a surly voice. "Mind where you're going. . . ."

"All right!" said Eustace indignantly. "We're not blind. We've got eyes in our heads."

"They must be darn good ones if you can see in here," said the same Dwarf whose name was Diggle.

"In where?" asked Edmund.

"Why you bone-head, in *here* of course," said Diggle. "In this pitch-black, poky, smelly little hole of a stable."

"Are you blind?" said Tirian.

"Ain't we all blind in the dark?" said Diggle.

"But it isn't dark, you stupid Dwarfs," said Lucy. "Can't you see? Look up! Look round! Can't you see the sky and the trees and the flowers? Can't you see *me*?"

"How in the name of all Humbug can I see what ain't there?" (LB, Chapter 13, p. 746)

The Dwarfs adopt the view that they are in a dark, smelly stable. Their dismal paradigm determines the way they see the world. When Lucy holds aromatic wild violets under their noses they take them to be filthy stable-litter. Aslan's roar is the machine noise created by the gang at the other end of the Stable. The glorious feast of pies and tongues, trifles and ices, that Aslan prepares for them tastes like hay, old turnips, and dirty water from a donkey's trough. The paradigm they have chosen will not allow them to see or to value differently. What for Lucy and the others is filled with joyous beauty, for the Dwarfs is only the occasion for a blind brawl. As Aslan remarks, "Their prison is only in their own minds, yet they are in that prison; and so afraid of being taken in that they cannot be taken out" (LB, Chapter 13, p. 748).

As the twentieth-century philosopher John Dewey notes, action calls for decision, and decision calls for knowledge without certainty. Lewis too sees values as part of the underlying paradigm used in decision-making directed toward action. In *The Silver Chair*, Eustace, Jill, and Puddleglum have to make a quick but momentous decision about whether or not to release Prince Rilian from his chair. Which of his utterances derive from the enchantment and which reflect the sane Prince? To cut his restraining ropes might mean their death. Yet the finding of Rilian and his release was the very mission Aslan gave them.

"Quick! I am sane now. Every night I am sane. If only I could get out of this enchanted chair, it would last. I should be a man again.

But every night they bind me, and so every night my chance is gone. But you are not enemies. Quick! Cut these cords."

"Stand fast! Steady," said Puddleglum to the two children. . . .

"Oh, if only we knew!" said Jill.

"I think we do know," said Puddleglum. . . . "You see, Aslan didn't tell Pole what would happen. He only told her what to do. That fellow will be the death of us once he's up, I shouldn't wonder. But that doesn't let us off following the sign." (SC, Ch. 11, pp. 625–26)

Although Puddleglum was uncertain, he had the knowledge needed for action. He knew what he needed to do, and this included obedience to the commands of an Aslan he had never met.

Knowing is a relationship between the knower and the known, such that each contributes to the task. Post-moderns like Jacques Derrida contend that neither sense data nor texts have intrinsic meaning; they achieve significance from the meanings we attach to them. The meaning we bring into the context comes from ourselves, and there is no self devoid of values or normative structures. In his denial of intrinsic meaning, Derrida goes too far, but the point stands that knowing is a balancing act between the contributions of the knower and the known. The dichotomy between value-free objectivity and value-laden subjectivity is false.

"I know nothing about Aslan": Personal Knowing

The third thesis of the Enlightenment model of knowing is that knowing is impersonal. Since knowing is objective, knowledge claims are interchangeable. What one perceives, so should another.

Rejecting the ideal of scientific detachment, philosopher of science Michael Polanyi contends that knowing involves the passionate, personal participation of the knower. Knowing is an act of commitment in which we bring ourselves to the experience in a variety of ways. We bring theories to the knowing experience, because we cannot understand the data apart from theories. We bring our bodies to the knowing experience, because our very thought processes originate from and are shaped by our body. Even the process of discovery is personal, for from beginning to end it is guided by our "personal vision and sustained by a personal conviction."[6]

But doesn't this make knowing a subjective rather than an objective process? Polanyi argues that it doesn't, for there is an objective world that is given to us in our experience, whereas in complete subjectivity all meaning and understanding is contributed by the knower. Theories, for example, are not merely personal but are expressed for the use and evaluation of the community, guarding us against being misled by our own desires or perceptions. The objective component to knowledge is maintained through our contact with reality. Personal knowledge, then, is the fusion of the personal and the objective.

In *Prince Caspian,* the four Pevensie children and the dwarf Trumpkin have become lost searching for a way to meet up with Prince Caspian. "Look!" Lucy suddenly cries out.

> "Where? What?" asked everyone.
> "The Lion," said Lucy. "Aslan himself. Didn't you see?" Her face had changed completely and her eyes shone. . . .
> "Where do you think you saw him?" asked Susan.
> "Don't talk like a grown-up," said Lucy, stamping her foot. "I didn't *think* I saw him."
> "Where, Lu?" asked Peter.
> "Right up there between those mountain ashes. . . . And he wanted us to go where he was—up there."
> "How do you know that was what he wanted?" asked Edmund.
> "He—I—I just know," said Lucy, "by his face." . . .
> "The only question is whether Aslan was really there," [said Peter].
> "But I know he was," said Lucy, her eyes filling with tears.
> "Yes, Lu, but we don't, you see," said Peter.
> "There's nothing for it but a vote," said Edmund. . . .
> "Down," said the Dwarf. "I know nothing about Aslan." (PC, Chapter 9, pp. 373–74)

Lewis's treatment of Lucy's sighting suggests that he, like Polanyi, sees knowing as personal. Lucy did not merely think or believe she had seen Aslan; she knew that she had. But how to

---

[6] Michael Polanyi, *Personal Knowledge: Towards a Post-Critical Philosophy* (Chicago: University of Chicago Press, 1958), p. 301.

convince the others? It is not clear that she could, for she had no proof, only her own word. But still she knew.

Lucy exemplifies what Polanyi calls tacit knowledge; she could tell by Aslan's face what he wanted. But what was it about Aslan's face that conveyed this knowledge? As Polanyi writes, "We can know more than we can tell." For example, we can recognize someone, distinguishing them from many others. But we usually cannot tell *how* it is that we recognize that person. Or again, "we recognize the moods of the human face, without being able to tell except quite vaguely, by what signs we know it."[7]

Saying that knowledge is personal doesn't imply that knowledge is merely subjective. Not every knowledge claim has equal merit. There are what Alvin Plantinga calls *defeaters*—reasons for abandoning one's belief. Some experiences might suggest that our senses are unreliable. A hallucinogenic weed might have got into Lucy's rations, causing her to think she had seen a lion. Or perhaps Lucy saw a wild lion, as Trumpkin suggests. The possessor of personal knowledge has no right to ignore countervailing evidence. But neither are believers like Lucy compelled to abandon their personal knowledge simply because others have not had similar experiences. What might be a defeater for one person might not be so for another. Thus, although all knowing is grounded in the knower, it can still be objective because the paradigms in which one works are often public possessions of communities, subject to the challenge of potential defeaters.

Spells

Perhaps in one way or another we are all, like Prince Rilian, bound by the Queen of Underworld, under some sort of spell or other. The spell-makers are the paradigms that govern our ways of knowing. The Enlightenment thinkers were under the spell of objectivity and certainty, lest they be fooled or taken in. The history of philosophy testifies to the problems this view of knowing faced and was unable to solve. Lewis helps us in his

---

[7] Michael Polanyi, *The Tacit Dimension* (New York: Doubleday, 1966), pp. 4–5.

Chronicles of Narnia to see a different paradigm, one in which we are all in one way or another "taken in" in the pursuit of truth. Truth and action based on knowledge are no less important for Lewis than for the Enlightenment philosophers. But he realizes that knowledge involves both the world to be experienced and the knowers themselves, rich with context, concepts, values, and indeed, their very being. Either we stay in our dark castle, protecting our paltry and diminishing certitude, or with Rilian we advance, realizing that action requires risk and uncertainty. "He walked resolutely to the door and flung it wide open" (SC, Chapter 11, p. 627).

Part II

The Tao in Narnia

Morality and the
Good Life

6
Worth Dying For: Narnian Lessons on Heroism and Altruism

LAURA GARCIA

Narnia swarms with heroes and villains, and usually it's easy to tell which is which. But sometimes heroes appear in villainous form, and villains disguise themselves as good guys (or gals). The truth comes out in the end, of course, and in time we can detect a clear portrait of the Narnian hero(ine): a person who would die rather than betray a friend, a promise, or a moral principle. The ancient Greeks and Romans are famous for their celebrations of heroic deeds, and the stories of America's birth are filled with such deeds as well. But heroism seemed to have fallen out of vogue in this culture until the events of September 11th, 2001, when we witnessed the utter selflessness of police and firefighters who risked their lives, and sometimes lost them, in order to save others. The day was a stark reminder that there are things worth dying for. Saving the lives of others is one of those things. Freedom is another. What seems less plausible to us today is that it might be worth dying to avoid betraying a person or a serious moral principle. "Death before dishonor" no longer sounds as compelling as it once did. Still, it is the motto of Narnia and Narnia's heroes, so let's consider the case they make for it.

Heroism in Narnia

Jill and Scrubb

Jill (Pole), Eustace (Scrubb), and Puddleglum the Marsh-wiggle are sent by Aslan, the Lord of Narnia, to seek a lost prince. After many trials and brushes with death, they meet a young knight in a deep underground labyrinth whom they quickly come to dislike. When he is later bound to an enchanted silver chair, deeply agitated almost to the point of madness and struggling against his bonds, he tries to persuade them to set him free. They have no reason to do so out of trust or friendship, and the knight had warned them beforehand not to listen to any of his pleas once he was under the spell, as great harm would come to them if they did. When he invokes the name of Aslan, however, they remember that this was a sign Aslan had given them for recognizing the true Prince, and that obeying Aslan's instructions means setting the knight free. Given the evidence they have, it is quite likely that setting him free will mean their own deaths. There is little time, and our heroes worry that Aslan's instructions might have been intercepted somehow, or that they may not even apply in this life-threatening situation. Jill laments,

> "Oh, if only we knew!" "I think we do know," said Puddleglum. "Do you mean you think everything will come right if we do untie him?" said Scrubb. "I don't know about that," said Puddleglum. "You see, Aslan didn't tell Pole [Jill] what would happen. He only told her what to do. That fellow will be the death of us once he's up, I shouldn't wonder. But that doesn't let us off following the sign." They all stood looking at each other with bright eyes. It was a sickening moment. "All right!" said Jill suddenly. "Let's get it over. Good-bye everyone." They all shook hands. (SC, Chapter 11, p. 626)

Like the passengers who fought the hijackers on Flight 93 on September 11th, Jill and her companions faced a moment of decision and rose above fear and despair to perform an act of true bravery.

Eustace

In *The Voyage of the "Dawn Treader,"* Eustace is on board a ship commanded by King Caspian, and has previously declared himself a pacifist in order to avoid a duel with Reepicheep the Mouse. But when a Sea Serpent attacks the ship, "Eustace . . . now did the first brave thing he had ever done. He was wearing a sword that Caspian had lent him. As soon as the Sea Serpent's body was near enough on the starboard side he jumped on to the bulwark and began hacking at it with all his might. It's true that he accomplished nothing beyond breaking Caspian's second-best sword into bits, but it was fine thing for a beginner to have done" (VDT, Chapter 8, pp. 478–79). We are surprised to see Eustace in the hero's role, since up to this point he has been the picture of a spoiled, immature "poltroon," as Reepicheep calls him. While most of Narnia's heroes develop their courage over time, Eustace shows that real heroism is possible even for those who have never been called upon to exercise it.

Shasta

In *A Horse and His Boy*, two runaways on horseback, Shasta and Aravis, race toward the gate of a walled garden with the Calormene army close behind them. Just short of the gate, Shasta hears a new sound, the snarling roar of a lion, and he sees it closing in on Aravis and her mount. Failing to get his horse to turn back, Shasta leaps from the saddle and runs on foot back toward Aravis and the lion.

> Before they reached him, the lion rose on its hind legs, larger than you would have believed a lion could be, and jabbed at Aravis with its right paw. Shasta could see all the terrible claws extended. Aravis screamed and reeled in the saddle. The lion was tearing her shoulders. Shasta, half mad with horror, managed to lurch toward the brute. He had no weapon, not even a stick or a stone. He shouted out, idiotically, at the lion as one would at a dog. "Go home! Go home!" For a fraction of a second he was staring right into its wide-opened, raging mouth. Then, to his utter astonishment, the lion, still on its hind legs, checked itself suddenly, turned head over heels, picked itself up, and rushed away." (HHB, Chapter 10, pp. 271–72)

As with Eustace's brave assault on the Sea Serpent, we read that Shasta "had never done anything like this in his life before and hardly knew why he was doing it now" (HHB, Chapter 10, p. 271). Nearly every one of the Narnia tales reports incidents like this one, which become a defining moment for the characters involved. There is a sense that these moments of decision have a significance beyond themselves, determining not just what one will do here and now but what kind of person one is. While there may be other opportunities, it also seems possible that this choice is the truly crucial one, setting a course from that time on. The philosopher St. Augustine (354–430 A.D.) says that even one who believes in God can walk with one's back toward him. The same is true of the moral good, and Lewis may be suggesting that the further one goes in this direction the harder it is to turn and face both the good and oneself.

Digory

Lewis clearly expects his characters to willingly risk their lives, even knowingly to sacrifice their lives, if others are in mortal danger or if loyalty demands it. But what if the stakes are even higher? What if the life one risks is not one's own but another's, and the loyalty demanded seems almost trivial by comparison? This is the situation Digory finds himself in, near the end of a long quest in search of a cure for his mother who is terminally ill. He has accepted a mission from Aslan, promising to bring back a magic apple that will protect Narnia (for a time) from the evil Digory had brought into it. "Evil will come of that evil," says Aslan, "but it is still a long way off, and I will see to it that the worst falls upon myself. In the meantime, let us take such order that for many hundred years yet this shall be a merry land in a merry world. And as Adam's race has done the harm, Adam's race shall help to heal it" (MN, Chapter 11, p. 80).

Following Aslan's directions, Digory and Polly have undertaken a long and difficult journey, until at last Digory enters a very private garden and takes one silver apple from the magical tree within it. He resists a strong urge to taste the apple, recalling the inscription on the gates of the garden:

> *Come in by the gold gates or not at all,*
> *Take of my fruit for others or forbear,*
> *For those who steal or those who climb my wall*
> *Shall find their heart's desire and find despair.* (MN, Chapter
>   13, p. 92)

As Digory turns to go, the evil Witch Jadis calls out to him and chases him down. She has obviously climbed over the wall and has just finished eating an apple from the tree. She tells Digory that the apples give eternal youth and health to whoever eats them; she herself is feeling younger and more powerful every minute. Digory has little interest in the Witch's proposition that

he and she should rule as King and Queen of Narnia after everyone else has grown old and died.

Finally in desperation Jadis tries another ploy:

> "But what about this Mother of yours whom you pretend to love
> so? . . . Do you not see, Fool, that one bite of that apple would heal
> her? . . . What has the Lion ever done for you that you should be
> his slave? . . . What can he do to you once you are back in your
> own world? And what would your Mother think if she knew that
> you *could* have taken her pain away and given her back her life
> and saved your Father's heart from being broken, and that you
> *wouldn't*—that you'd rather run messages for a wild animal in a
> strange world that is no business of yours?" (MN, Chapter 13, pp.
> 93–94).

Digory *has* promised, to be sure, but as the Witch points out,
he didn't know what was at stake when he made the promise.
If it is simply a matter of keeping one's promises, surely these
circumstances justify an exception. To make things worse,
Digory already asked Aslan whether something could be done
for his mother without receiving any firm reply. Yet when at last
he looks into Aslan's face, he sees that the Lion's eyes are filled
with tears, so that "for a moment he felt as if the Lion must really
be sorrier about his Mother than he was himself." But Aslan says
only, "My son, my son. I know. Grief is great. Only you and I
in this land know that yet. Let us be good to one another" (MN,
Chapter 12, p. 83). Still, in his moment of greatest temptation,
Digory finally recognizes that the Witch's motives are cruel and
selfish, and he and Polly choose to return to give the apple to
Aslan.

Is True Unselfishness Possible?

Examples of this kind of heroism abound in the world of Narnia,
and I think most readers will agree that the heroic actions
recounted here are truly praiseworthy. More than that, we
deeply admire the courage and resolve behind these deeds and
even hope that we ourselves might rise to such heroism in time
of need. For philosophers since Thomas Hobbes (1588–1679),
however, this presents a bit of a paradox. Hobbes famously
argued that given human nature (individualistic and combative)
and the natural human environment (a war of all against all),

selfishness is simply sanity and any apparent tendency toward self-sacrifice or altruism is likely nothing more than disguised self-seeking. Only fear of others could motivate us to accept relative tranquility under the terms of a social contract. John Aubrey's account of Hobbes in *Brief Lives* tells of a conversation between Hobbes and a clergyman after Hobbes had just given some coins to a beggar. The clergyman asked Hobbes whether he would give alms if Jesus had not commanded it. Hobbes replied that in giving alms he merely helped alleviate his own distress over seeing another's suffering.[1] If Hobbes is right that human nature is inherently competitive and self-seeking, can there be any rational justification for altruism or self-sacrifice? To put it another way, if virtues are qualities that enable us to fulfill our nature, how can unselfishness be a virtue, since it seems to serve others, sometimes at the cost of our own fulfillment?

Narrowly Self-interested Considerations

Modern philosophers who want to find a place for altruism in a Hobbesian world propose various strategies for bringing it into line with what is assumed to be a primary and more fundamental commitment to *egoism*—the view that all human actions are, or ought to be, motivated by self-interest. Hobbes suggests one such strategy above. If seeing the suffering of others naturally distresses us (for unknown reasons), helping them is one way to get something we desire for ourselves—greater emotional peace. (Another would be to remain as ignorant as possible of others' distress, but this is not often within our control.) Hobbes's explanation for altruism doesn't seem to take seriously enough the admiration we feel for the heroes and heroines of Narnia, however. Perhaps giving alms can be motivated by a dislike of encountering poverty, but the actions of Eustace and Shasta could hardly be explained in the same way. It makes little sense to risk one's life simply in order to avoid the prospect of witnessing someone else's death or suffering.

A second strategy for defending altruism is to introduce greater complexity into human nature by recognizing natural

---

[1] John Aubrey, *Brief Lives*, edited by Oliver Lawson Dick (Ann Arbor: University of Michigan Press, 1957), p. 157.

tendencies toward benevolence alongside self-seeking tendencies. Bishop Joseph Butler (1692–1752) claims that virtue and happiness ultimately coincide for human beings.[2] Confronted with counterexamples to this cheerful view, Butler appeals to divine providence. God will see to it in the next life that goodness and self-interest always coincide, pointing us toward the same actions in each instance. This does little to explain why we should act unselfishly in this life, of course. Perhaps the idea is to start training for eternity here and now in hopes of being "in shape" for the afterlife where duty and happiness dovetail.

Third, anyone who believes in an afterlife could argue that altruism coincides with one's ultimate, long-run self-interest, since unselfish actions are more likely to lead to eternal happiness with God. The reward is built in now, as it were, but the payoff won't come until the next life. William Paley (1743–1805) and Abraham Tucker (1705–1774) defend views along these lines, making God the bridge between morality (altruism) and happiness. Tucker proposes that all human happiness gets deposited in a kind of "bank of the universe" [3] which God will ultimately divide into equal shares for distribution to the stockholders (ourselves). By increasing the happiness of others one adds to the bank, and so to one's own share of happiness in the eternal long run. Not surprisingly, Tucker's complex and theologically suspect theory met with a lukewarm reception. Perhaps a theological utilitarianism of some kind could justify run-of-the-mill generosities—putting spare change into the box at McDonald's, yielding to another driver, buying a raffle ticket. But here again, it's hard to see how these considerations would make it wise to put one's life on the line for the sake of others, as Eustace and Shasta do, especially when there's little hope of success. Finally, there is something off-putting about a divine arrangement that rewards those who act for the sake of others only because they expect a reward for themselves.

This is not to reject the view, central to Christianity, that God will reward the righteous and punish the wicked, or better

---

[2] Joseph Butler, *Fifteen Sermons Preached in Rolls Chapel: A Dissertation on the Nature of Virtue* (Indianapolis: Hackett, 1985 [1726]), Sermons 11 and 12.
[3] Abraham Tucker, *The Light of Nature Pursued* (1768–1778), quoted in Alasdair MacIntyre, *A Short History of Ethics* (New York: Collier, 1966), p. 168.

perhaps, that God will reward the repentant and punish the unrepentant. This belief can certainly motivate a person to live an upright life and to seek a constant inner conversion of heart, but the heroic actions described above take us into another arena. For one thing, it's hard to imagine in any of these cases that failing to make the heroic choice would be morally wrong or sinful. These sorts of deeds are what ethicists call *supererogatory acts*—meritorious acts that are "above and beyond the call of duty." For another thing, believing that God rewards good deeds is no guarantee that God will reward this particular act, since one's eternal destiny is not decided by it. Even if there were a surefire connection between the act and the (ultimate) reward, I think we will still find it implausible (even mildly offensive) if it turns out that this connection is what motivated our heroes in making choices that *seemed* to be genuinely selfless.

When David Hume (1711–1776) enters the fray on this question, he adds to the human motivational mixture a kind of natural sympathy that we feel for others, especially family, friends, and neighbors.[4] This emotional spring of action coexists with our natural self-interested desires and sometimes leads us to act for the good of others independently of how this impacts our own good. Hume makes no attempt to integrate the various springs of action into a rational or coherent system; various motives impact our actions in an apparently causal way and the strongest motive wins out. On the other hand, Hume's theory had the advantage of not subordinating benevolent motives to selfish ones, and so has no need to show that actions motivated by sympathy will also lead to one's own self-interest, whether in the short or the long run. At the end of day, however, it's hard to imagine that a feeling as weak as sympathy or fellow-feeling would win out over more basic and instinctive desires for self-preservation. Some forms of benevolence can be accounted for by Hume, but our cases of heroic actions remain puzzling on this view.

---

[4] David Hume, *Enquiries concerning the Human Understanding and concerning the Principles of Morals*, second edition, edited by L.A. Selby-Bigge (Oxford: Clarendon, 1902), Section V, Part II.

Broadly Self-interested Considerations

In the article on "Egoism and Altruism" in the *Encyclopedia of Philosophy*,[5] Alasdair MacIntyre notes that many ego-centered explanations of altruism simply assume that humans care mainly about pleasure and the absence of pain. Bringing in considerations of sympathy just adds emotional pleasures and pains to the list. MacIntyre points out that "what is to my interest depends upon who I am and what I want."[6] Motives for action might be much more complex than the simple me-or-them analysis suggested by Hobbes. "If I want to lead a certain kind of life, with relationships of trust, friendship, and cooperation with others, then my wanting their good and my wanting my good are not two independent, discriminable desires."[7] MacIntyre's remarks evoke an earlier conception of human happiness found in Plato and Aristotle, where happiness or flourishing as a human being, achieving our deepest goal or end, requires wisdom, virtue, and friendship. Clashes between one's own interests and those of others might be relatively rare on this view, so that motives for acting seldom fall out along a clear self/others line. Aristotle justifies acts of heroism in battle, for instance, partly on the grounds that one's goal is to live a certain kind of life or, if one dies in the attempt, at least to *have lived* a certain kind of life.

Some contemporary philosophers who disagree with Aristotle on the good for human beings nonetheless hold that we define ourselves to a great extent by our actions and that we often act in order to maintain our sense of identity. Perhaps one wants to be the kind of person who would die rather than abandon a friend or compromise a moral principle. Let's leave aside for now questions about whether this is a desire everyone has, or should have. Would such a desire explain the actions of Eustace, Shasta, Jill, and Digory? I think the answer is a tentative yes. It also seems plausible that motives along these lines, if not exactly natural to everyone, can be instilled through various forms of training. These are the principles of the military, for example: death before dishonor, no man left behind, *semper fi*.

---

[5] Edited by Paul Edwards (New York: Macmillan, 1967), Volume 2, pp. 462–66.
[6] *Ibid.*, p. 465.
[7] *Ibid.*, p. 466.

Consistently affirming and acting on motives like these could make a person willing to take enormous risks for the sake of the mission or of his or her comrades.

Here again though, Narnia presents a puzzle. Our heroes are very young; they have no military training and no battlefield experiences. They are still developing a moral identity and so have no obvious stake in preserving a pre-existing self-definition. Nor have they acquired deep-seated virtues of fortitude over a lifetime of making courageous decisions. They arrive at a moment of truth, when they are called upon for perhaps the first time to choose between selfish desires and the good of others (Eustace and Shasta) or between self-interest and obedience (Jill and Digory). Each of them has weaknesses as well as strengths, moral failures along with successes. We almost hold our own breath at these moments, which shows that we don't know what the characters will choose or how it will turn out for them. Even if they want to live a certain kind of life, as MacIntyre suggests, the connection between the present choice and that kind of life could hardly be paramount in their thinking in the moment of crisis. This is why even a broadly self-interested theory cannot really explain these heroic actions. Nor can it explain why we admire the actions as we do, or why we hope that the characters make the right decision, regardless of personal consequences. Further still, most readers (I think) hope that they would make the right decision here as well; maybe some of us even hope that we would be given the chance to make such a decision. Why is this?

Other-centered Considerations

I believe the answer to this question means taking a different view of human nature. If humans are simply driven by various appetites and desires, then genuinely selfless actions are inexplicable. Evolutionary psychologists can account for these only by postulating a human psyche that acts "selflessly" only in order to further the survival or reproductive success of the self.[8]

---

[8] See, for example, Herbert Simon's article, "A Mechanism for Social Selection and Successful Altruism," *Science* 250 (December 21st, 1990), pp. 1665–68, in which he explains Mother Teresa's selfless and celibate life as resulting from "docility" and "bounded rationality."

On the other hand, if humans have spiritual capacities for thought and choice that transcend the physical realm, their actions can be explained in part by what they believe about themselves and others. Someone who believes in the tooth fairy will put a lost tooth under the pillow at night—an action that would otherwise make no sense. Actions also influence beliefs. A child who refuses to try it may never come to believe that she can float on water.

The young heroes in Narnia act as they do, I submit, because of what they believe, and they believe as they do in part because of what they are willing to see. Eustace and Shasta, who begin their adventures as self-absorbed and even self-pitying, come to recognize the value of others and the demands of true friendship. Genuine love for others pulls them out of themselves and makes them want to do whatever they can to help, even when the most likely result is that no one will come out of the situation alive. Our heroes have come *to love others for their own sakes*, not just to satisfy their own desires or urges. Suppose we leave aside for now the problem of what *grounds* the moral requirement to love persons for their own sake. My contention is that only a commitment to this kind of love can explain the actions of Shasta and Eustace. Beyond this, I believe only our commitment to this moral requirement can explain why we admire Narnia's heroes as we do. We are proud of them, as it were, and would be proud to have acted as they did. I believe we would feel the same way even if they had lost their lives in the attempt.

The decisions of Jill in Underworld and of Digory in the enchanted garden present a different challenge. Both have been sent on a mission by Aslan, and find themselves torn between obedience to his orders and their own judgment as to the best course of action. The stakes are high: Jill and her companions could lose their lives, and Digory stands to lose the only clear chance he has to save his mother from dying. The situations are so dire in fact, that it's hard to imagine that these characters are *morally required* to carry out the missions entrusted to them. There are grounds for doubt in both cases. Jill's friends wonder whether Aslan's orders apply in this situation, and whether they might have been intercepted and turned to the purpose of the enemy. Digory hadn't known that the apples held the power of eternal youth, and the Witch makes it seem that he is putting the

wishes (or "whims") of a relative stranger (Aslan) above the wel-
fare of his own mother. The decision both characters face is not
so much a choice between duty and self-interest as it is a question of whom they will trust. Aslan has shown himself worthy of
trust, but there is reason to doubt the wisdom of his orders.
While Jill has only her own judgment of the circumstances,
Digory has the influence of the Witch as well. Still, in both cases
it seems the real conflict is between trust in one's own judgment
and trust in Aslan.

Since trust is warranted only when we believe in a person's
wisdom and goodness, the decision here is about whether to
continue to believe in Aslan's wisdom and goodness when it's
not obvious—that is, whether to have faith. Given that lives are
at stake, it's easy to imagine that our heroes might have chosen
differently. Instead they choose faith and their faith is rewarded.
But their faith is not blind. Like the men who followed Ernest
Shackleton to the South Pole, they know something of their
commander's quality. Still, it might be that a truly unconditional
faith should not be given to any human being. In that case, Jill
and Digory are admirable only if the one they trust is more than
human. Those who know Aslan will have to decide that question for themselves.

7

Work, Vocation, and the Good Life in Narnia

DEVIN BROWN

Everyone knows what *work* means. Like the gnomes of Underland, we've all had days when we've felt like saying, "I'm blessed if I know why I'm carrying this load, and I'm not going to carry it any further" (SC, Chapter 14, p. 642).

Vocation is a less common term. "Vocation"—if you're interested in this kind of thing—comes from the Latin word *vocare*, which means *to call*, the same root from which we get *vocal*, *voice*, and even *vociferous*. When people refer to their vocation, they mean the task or occupation they have been called to—as opposed to just doing what their father or mother did, picking it out of a hat, or using a dart and a dartboard, for example. Sometimes people may talk about having a divine calling, but people can also talk about vocation without referring to the supernatural. They might talk about being called by some *thing* rather than some *one*.

Finally, the "good life" is a term that philosophers have been talking about for, well, for as long as there have been philosophers. Like a response in *Jeopardy*, this term typically appears in the form of a question: What is the good life? By this philosophers don't mean, "How many plasma TVs and vacation homes do you own?" but rather, "What is the best and most fulfilling way to live?"

First Things First

Before we start talking about the philosophy of work, vocation, and the good life in *The Chronicles of Narnia*, we should ask about our presuppositions. What are the general things we are supposing or accepting as true before we even begin?

Here's one presupposition: When we—more importantly, when the philosophical giants—ask the question, "What is the good life?" of course we realize that people in different places, times, and situations will answer it in somewhat different ways. However, just by asking, "What is *the* good life?" we are assuming there is an answer which in some ways will be true for everybody.

Here's a second presupposition: Looking for a general answer to questions about work, vocation, and the good life—something that will hold true for everyone—presupposes that there is something common to all of us, some universal nature we all share. If this were not true, if each of us was essentially a separate species, we would each have our own separate answer. It would be like asking, "What's the good life for a cat? For an elephant? How about for a goldfish?"

Here's a final presupposition. In creating the fantasy world of Narnia, Lewis certainly intended to transcend the bounds of known reality—life for most of us does not include wardrobes that open onto a world filled with fauns, centaurs, and unicorns. But at the same time, not *despite* his use of fantasy but specifically *through* his use of fantasy, Lewis set out to communicate important truths about the world of human beings.

As Thomas Arp and Greg Johnson have pointed out, "Some of the world's greatest works of literature have been partly or wholly fantasy: *The Odyssey, The Divine Comedy, The Tempest, Pilgrim's Progress, Gulliver's Travels,* and *Alice in Wonderland* all offer profound and significant insights into the human condition."[1] Lewis himself referred to "beings other than human" found in fairy tales that can serve as "admirable hieroglyphic[s]" of some aspect of human life and behavior.[2]

---

[1] *Perrine's Literature: Structure, Sound, and Sense*, eighth edition, edited by Thomas R. Arp and Greg Johnson (New York: Harcourt, 1999), p. 301.
[2] C.S. Lewis, "On Three Ways of Writing for Children," reprinted in *Of Other Worlds: Essays and Stories* (New York: Harcourt, Brace, 1966), p. 27.

Epicurus and the Tom Sawyer
Philosophy of Work

In Shakespeare's *Hamlet* we are told that, often through indirection, direction can be found, meaning that we can frequently learn a great deal by coming at something in a roundabout way. With this in mind, let's begin looking at the philosophy of work, vocation, and the good life in *The Chronicles of Narnia* by first briefly noting what Lewis is *not* saying.

Epicurus, a Greek philosopher who lived from 342 to 270 B.C., taught that the goal of life is to maximize pleasure and minimize pain, a philosophy that is called hedonism. You may have heard of the modern-day resort named Hedonism that claims to be "a lush garden of pure pleasure," and in fact the Greek word *hedones* means pleasures. As Epicurus explained to a young disciple, "We recognize pleasure as the first and natural good; starting from pleasure we accept or reject; and we return to this as we judge every good thing, trusting this feeling of pleasure as our guide."[3]

Like Kleenex, Epicurus has the distinction of having had his name made into a general noun, although one not as well-known. If you look up *epicure* in the dictionary, you'll find that it refers to a person who takes great pleasure in eating, drinking, or other bodily pleasures.

There is more complexity to Epicureanism than you might think, however. For example, what if what you think of as the height of pleasure—staying in bed all day, eating Turkish Delight, and watching MTV—ends up being, well, not all that pleasurable? As a point of fact, Epicurus didn't advocate a life of wild sex and parties, as many people wrongly assume. But the goal of pleasure is certainly central to his thought, and in this sense we can see Epicurus as the great-grandfather of what we might call the Tom Sawyer philosophy of work.

In the second chapter of Mark Twain's *The Adventures of Tom Sawyer*, Tom appears on the sidewalk with a bucket of

---

[3] Epicurus, "Letter to Menoeceus" translated by Russel M. Greer, reprinted in *Philosophical Classics*, third edition, Volume 1, edited by Forrest E. Baird and Walter Kaufmann (Upper Saddle River: Prentice Hall, 2000), p. 467.

whitewash in one hand, a long-handled brush in the other, and a "deep melancholy" in his heart. Aunt Polly has ordered him to paint the fence. In the end, he convinces every boy who passes by that painting a fence is actually a privilege, not a chore. But Tom doesn't fool us for a minute.

We know Tom hates work, any kind of work. At the merest thought of work, we are told, "all gladness left him," life "seemed hollow," and "existence a burden." Tom, normally a very upbeat guy, doesn't see whitewashing the fence as a privilege. He sees it, and work in general (including going to school), as an obstacle to the fun things he would rather be doing.[4]

In *The Chronicles of Narnia* we find a character that, while not as lovable as Tom, definitely adheres to Tom's philosophy of work. Through him we can see what Lewis's view of work, vocation, and the good life is *not*. In *The Voyage of the "Dawn Treader,"* Eustace Scrubb is clearly one who practices his own brand of hedonism and sees his highest good as his own comfort and pleasure. Eustace, like Tom, looks on any kind of work, even what is rightfully his own share, with dread and foreboding because it interferes with his selfish pursuit of pleasure and avoidance of pain. (Note that these comments apply only to the early Eustace because, as you know if you have read the book, he later becomes quite a different character, which of course is Lewis's point.)

One of the best examples of Eustace's hedonism occurs when the *Dawn Treader* puts ashore on Dragon Island. At this point, the ship is a bit of a wreck. Casks have to be brought ashore, fixed, and refilled. A tree has to be cut down and made into a new mast. Sails must be repaired, a hunting party organized, and clothes washed and mended. In short, "there was everything to be done" (VDT, Chapter 5, p. 459).

Everyone immediately jumps in and begins working—everyone, that is, except Eustace. Here's what Lewis says about him:

> As Eustace lay under a tree and heard all these plans being discussed his heart sank. Was there going to be no rest? It looked as if their first day on the longed-for land was going to be quite as

---

[4] Apparently Twain agreed. Consider his famous quip, "I never let school interfere with my education."

hard work as a day at sea. Then a delightful idea occurred to him. Nobody was looking—they were all chattering about their ship as if they actually liked the beastly thing. Why shouldn't he simply slip away? He would take a stroll inland, find a cool, airy place up in the mountains, have a good long sleep, and not rejoin the others till the day's work was over. (VDT, Chapter 5, p. 459)

The other crew members—who begin working not only without complaining but even with a sense of a happiness—have a vastly different philosophy of work, vocation, and the good life than Eustace does.

By having Eustace grow and develop, from someone who at first cares only about his own pleasure, Lewis suggests that this pleasure-seeking state is an immature one. It's a position that might be understandable in a child but not in someone who has grown up. After his transformation, Eustace remarks, "I'm afraid I've been pretty beastly" (VDT, Chapter 7, p. 475). In associating the word *beastly* with Eustace's first condition, Lewis further suggests that if the love of pleasure is something we share with the animals, being human requires that we acquire a purpose in life that is greater than just our own hedonistic desires.

John Stuart Mill and the Sherlock Holmes Philosophy of Work

In the eighteenth century, the British thinker Jeremy Bentham (1748–1832) founded the philosophy of Utilitarianism, which claims that the aim of action should be the largest possible amount of pleasure or happiness for the greatest number of people.[5] Building on the foundations laid by Epicurus, he writes, "Nature has placed mankind under the governance of two sovereign masters, *pain* and *pleasure*."[6] Bentham goes on to distinguish several sources from which pleasure and pain flow, with the physical realm as only one source.

---

[5] At his request, Bentham's embalmed body is kept on display at the University of London, which he helped found. Apparently, he believed that more people would take pleasure at the sight of his corpse than the reverse. Maybe not, but students get a kick out of it when they hear this story.

[6] Jeremy Bentham, *Introduction to the Principles of Morals and Legislation* (1789), Chapter 1, Section I.

His philosophical successor John Stuart Mill (1806–1873) took the next step by ranking these sources. Mill writes, "some kinds of pleasure are more desirable and more valuable than others," and asserts that we "assign to the pleasures of the intellect, of the feelings and imagination, and of the moral sentiments, a much higher value as pleasures than to those of mere sensation."[7]

No matter how content your dog, cat, or gerbil might seem to be, Mill argues, nobody would "consent to be changed into any of the lower animals, for a promise of the fullest allowance of a beast's pleasures."[8] Why? Because these lower pleasures of mere sensation are not truly fulfilling for a human being, as Eustace discovers for himself.

Shortly after sneaking off to avoid working on the ship, Eustace falls asleep on a dragon's hoard "with greedy, dragonish thoughts in his heart" (VDT, Chapter 6, p. 466). He wakes to find he has changed into a dragon. "There was nothing to be afraid of any more," Eustace quickly recognizes. "He was a terror himself and nothing in the world but a knight (and not all of those) would dare to attack him" (VDT, Chapter 6, p. 466). As a powerful dragon, Eustace can have anything he wants to eat and as much of it as he wants. He can sleep all day and certainly will never have to work again.

But as Eustace almost immediately realizes, a life of ease and pleasure isn't what will make him happy. What he wants are the distinctively human pleasures that are higher than "those of mere sensation." What he wants, as Lewis says, is "to be friends" and to "get back among humans and talk and laugh and share things" (VDT, Chapter 6, p. 466). And he wants this even though it means giving up a life of comfort and ease for one that will include hardship and toil.

Early in *The Lion, the Witch, and the Wardrobe*, the children are not the brave kings and queens they will later become, but still just regular children. Narnia is not very pleasurable at this point—it's cold, they are in danger, and everyone is hungry. And for a moment Susan wants to turn around and not help the Faun, Mr. Tumnus, who has been arrested by the White Witch.

---

[7] John Stuart Mill, *Utilitarianism* (1863), Chapter 2.
[8] *Ibid.*

"What about just going home?" Susan suggests.
"Oh, but we can't," Lucy replies. "We can't." (LWW, Chapter 6, p. 137)

In Lucy's response we find Lewis's position also. The children can't just go home, although this would clearly be the more comfortable choice—not if they are to live as they should. We see Lewis making a similar point in *The Silver Chair* when Jill forgets Aslan's signs at Harfang because all she can think of are "baths and beds and hot drinks" (SC, Chapter 7, p. 596). The view Lewis presents in these passages is what might be called the Sherlock Holmes philosophy of work.

Sir Arthur Conan Doyle, the author of the Sherlock Holmes stories, begins *The Sign of Four* like this: "Sherlock Holmes took his bottle from the corner of the mantelpiece, and his hypodermic syringe from its neat morocco case."[9] When Dr. Watson protests his friend's use of cocaine, Holmes replies, "Give me problems, give me work. And I can dispense then with artificial stimulants." Holmes claims that the only time he is in his "proper atmosphere" is when he is using his talents to work on a case.

Lewis agrees with Holmes that life should be—in fact must be—something more than comfortable idleness. Part of this something more involves work—some task, some goal beyond simply "having fun" or making life more pleasurable for oneself.

Near the end of *The Lion, the Witch, and the Wardrobe,* Susan again wants to turn back, this time from hunting the White Stag. Peter replies, "Never since we four were Kings and Queens in Narnia have we set our hands to any high matter, as battles, quests, feats of arms, acts of justice and the like, and then given over" (LWW, Chapter 17, p. 196). In *The Voyage of the "Dawn Treader"* we find a similar illustration of Lewis's philosophy. When asked what use their quest is, Reepicheep replies: "Use, Captain? If by use you mean filling our bellies or our purses, I confess it will be no use at all" (VDT, Chapter 12, p. 507).

Peter and Reepicheep have radically different philosophies of work, vocation, and the good life than Eustace does. They

---

[9] Sir Arthur Conan Doyle, *The Sign of Four,* reprinted in *The Complete Sherlock Holmes,* Volume 1 (Garden City: Doubleday, 1930), p. 89.

embody Lewis's own position, one that is also seen in *The Last Battle*. In talking to Eustace before a skirmish where the odds look grim, Jill says: "I almost wish. No I don't though. I *was* going to say I wished we'd never come. But I don't, I don't. Even if we *are* killed. I'd rather be killed fighting for Narnia than grow old and stupid at home and perhaps go about in a bath-chair and then die in the end just the same" (LB, Chapter 9, p. 720).

The Life of Thought versus the Life of Action

According to Lewis, the good life must be more than idle comfort and pleasure; it must involve some kind of action or work. Aristotle (384–322 B.C.) took a similar view. In his *Nicomachean Ethics*, Aristotle argues that happiness is an *activity*, not a feeling or a state of mind.[10]

What kind of work makes for the good life? Aristotle believes that complete happiness consists in contemplation of the highest, noblest, and most enduring objects of human thought. For him, the contemplative life is far more valuable than a life of mere physical activity. As Adriano Tilgher points out, Aristotle (and Plato as well) holds that the solution to the question of the good life is "to have the hard, troublesome work of transforming raw material for the satisfaction of our needs done by a part—the majority—of men, in order that the minority, the elite, might engage in pure exercise of the mind—art, philosophy, politics."[11]

Though Lewis strongly disagreed with Aristotle's social and economic elitism, he also saw great value in the contemplative life, and this sentiment is echoed many times throughout *The Chronicles of Narnia*. For a start, we have the Professor, whose house has a whole series of rooms "lined with books" (LWW, Chapter 2, p. 112). Later we find him coaching Peter, another scholar, for his college entrance exams (VDT, Chapter 1, p. 425). The children's father, Mr. Pevensie, is also a college professor, and we learn in *The Voyage of the "Dawn Treader"* that he has been invited to lecture in the United States (VDT, Chapter 1, p.

---

[10] Book X, 1176b.
[11] Adriano Tilgher, *Work: What It Has Meant to Men Through the Ages* (New York: Arno, 1977), p. 5.

425). Mr. Tumnus, while not quite as scholarly as the Professor or Mr. Pevensie, has a bookshelf "full of books" on one wall of his little cave (LWW, Chapter 2, p. 116).

Readers are told that Caspian has a deep love for history and for his tutor Doctor Cornelius (PC, Chapter 4, p. 336). Caspian values learning so much that despite the danger he continues his lessons in secret after his uncle has forbidden them. In *The Voyage of the "Dawn Treader"* we meet Coriakin the Magician, who has a large room "lined floor to ceiling with books, more books than Lucy had ever seen before, tiny little books, fat and dumpy books, and books bigger than any church Bible you have ever seen, all bound in leather and smelling old and learned and magical" (VDT, Chapter 10, p. 494).

As a child, Lewis grew up in a house with rooms like Coriakin's, and throughout his sixty-five years he led a mostly contemplative life—from his years of private tutoring with William Kirkpatrick (the "Great Knock," who served as the model for the Professor in *The Lion, the Witch, and the Wardrobe*), to his rare "triple-first" as an Oxford undergraduate, to his long tenure as a fellow at Oxford, and finally to his position late in life as Professor of Medieval and Renaissance English at the University of Cambridge. Lewis claimed he was the product of the "endless books" he had been surrounded by as a youth: "books in the study, books in the drawing room, books in the cloakroom, books (two deep) in the great bookcase on the landing, books in a bedroom, books piled as high as my shoulder in the cistern attics, books of all kinds."[12]

Clearly, Lewis agrees with Aristotle about the worth of the contemplative life, but he doesn't stop there. Unlike Aristotle, Lewis sees equal value in the life of action, as is evident from the fact that the *Chronicles* are mostly about adventures, battles, and quests.

We see this emphasis on action from the very outset of *The Lion, the Witch, and the Wardrobe* when it's raining and the children are looking for something to do. When Susan suggests that there are "lots of books" they might read, Peter replies, "Not for me. I'm going to explore in the house" (LWW, Chapter 1, p.

---

[12] C.S. Lewis, *Surprised by Joy: The Shape of My Early Life* (New York: Harcourt, Brace, 1955), p. 10.

112). Everyone agrees to Peter's suggestion, and we are told "this was how the adventures began."

Each of the Narnia books opens with some kind of crisis. Each character is then called upon to help in whatever way is appropriate to him or her. Again, the point is that what is needed in these situations is a willingness to act.

Karl Marx in Narnia

In his *Critique of the Gotha Program* (1875), Karl Marx, the father of communism, penned the famous dictum "From each according to his ability, to each according to his needs." Marx did not exactly originate this idea, as it had earlier expressions such as in the Saint-Simonian movement in France in the 1820s and even in the New Testament (Acts 4:34–35), so perhaps we should not be so surprised to see Lewis embracing a similar idea in *The Chronicles of Narnia*.[13]

In *The Lion, the Witch, and the Wardrobe*, Aslan plays a major part—you could say *the* major part—in rescuing Narnia from the White Witch. However, in spite of the fact that it is Aslan who in a somewhat gruesome battle scene kills the Witch in the end, the children and the Talking Animals are expected to assume active roles, each in accordance with their abilities. Immediately after Aslan overcomes the Witch, we are told that "all war-like creatures whom Aslan had led from the Witch's house rushed madly on the enemy lines," including "dwarfs with their battleaxes, dogs with teeth, the Giant with his club," . . . "unicorns with their horns, and centaurs with swords and hoofs" (LWW, Chapter 10, p. 191).

Earlier, there is a scene in which the children receive gifts from Father Christmas, gifts that are appropriate to their natural capacities and temperaments, and are to be used for the good of Narnia. Peter gets a sword and shield, Susan receives a bow, arrows, and an ivory horn, and Lucy is given a healing cordial and a small dagger (LWW, Chapter 10, p. 160). Father Christmas

---

[13] Though not in the socialist sense intended by Marx. Like his friend J.R.R. Tolkien, Lewis wasn't a fan of big government or officious "busybodies and interferers" (LWW, Chapter 17, p. 194). In fact, this is the very thing Lewis is criticizing in *The Last Battle* when the Ape says, "It's all been arranged. And all for your good" (LB, Chapter 3, p. 685).

tells the girls that, unlike Peter, they are to use their weapons "only in greatest need."

Is Lewis here saying that girls can't be fighters and guys can't be healers? Not at all. What Lewis is illustrating, in this scene and elsewhere, is what I like to call the Acorn Philosophy of Vocation.

What is an acorn supposed to do in life? Based on its natural tendencies, we would have to say it's supposed to grow up to become an oak tree. The late Joseph Campbell took this same approach to questions about vocation. He told his students, "Follow your bliss."

So what are the characters in Narnia —including Peter, Susan, and Lucy—to do? To put their natural abilities and inclinations to use—and not just in their own service, but when necessary in the service of Narnia. As Shasta explains in *The Horse and His Boy*, when Narnia is in need, "everyone must do what he can do best" (HHB, Chapter 14, pp, 302–03).

After Aslan frees the animals that the White Witch had turned to stone, he calls for those who are fast to help carry those who are slow, those who are good with their noses to help smell out where the battle is, and for the Giant Rumblebuffin, who is good with his club, to break down the castle gates (LWW, Chapter 16, p. 190).

With this Acorn Philosophy of Vocation, Lewis was taking the same tack seen in Tolkien's *Lord of the Rings*. There we find a Fellowship made up of nine quite different individuals, each contributing according to his own ability. In one scene early in the quest, the members of the Fellowship find themselves stuck in the snow. Aragorn and Boromir, the two strongest members, are trying to tunnel a way through the drifts, but they need to know how far the snow extends. As Legolas springs lightly upon the surface of the snow to go find out, he utters these words which epitomize Lewis and Tolkien's philosophy of vocation: "The strongest must seek a way, say you? but I say: let a ploughman plough, but choose an otter for swimming, and for running light over grass and leaf, or over snow—an Elf."[14]

Perhaps one of Lewis's clearest illustrations of the Acorn Philosophy of Vocation occurs in *The Last Battle*. On their way

---

[14] J.R.R. Tolkien, *The Fellowship of the Ring* (New York: Ballantine, 2001 [1954], p. 328.

to rescue Jewel, King Tirian, Eustace, and Jill must force their way through dense thickets where it's hard to get a bearing. Lewis tells us, "It was Jill who set them right," and as soon as Tirian notices that she is "the best pathfinder of the three of them," he puts her in front to lead (LB, Chapter 6, p. 700).

During the Middle Ages, the term *vocation* came to used exclusively for the religious vocations of priests, monks and nuns, as though other professions were not something you could be called to. Martin Luther challenged this concept. In a treatise written in 1520 he wrote that "a cobbler, a smith, and a peasant" each has a vocation in the work they do, just as much as a priest or bishop does. To Luther's list, Lewis would add a centaur, a dwarf, a unicorn—in short, all rational beings.

Wrong Livelihood

Thomas Aquinas (1225–1274) was the leading European philosopher of his time. His philosophy is called "Aristotelian" because Aquinas took Aristotle's premises and developed his own conclusions. Like Aristotle, Aquinas had much to say about work and its relationship to the good life. In his *Summa Theologica* he wrote, "To live well is to work well" (I-11, q. 57, a. 5). For Aquinas, good living and good working went together. Likewise, one of Buddha's basic teachings was that one's livelihood must be ethical and not inconsistent with one's deepest values and ideals.

It's not enough to just say that life must consist of more than idle pleasure. If one can work well or correctly, then it follows that one can also work wrongly, and Lewis provides a number of examples of wrong work in Narnia.

One example of wrong livelihood is working against one's deepest wishes. In *The Last Battle*, when a wicked ape takes over Narnia as its tyrant, he orders all the animals to work against their will, telling them, "You think freedom means doing what you like. Well, you're wrong. That isn't true freedom. True freedom means doing what I tell you" (LB, Ch. 3, p. 685). Even if the task is itself good, coercion makes it wrong.

Of course, this isn't to deny that sometimes we have a duty to do something, even when we're strongly inclined not to. Here perhaps we must distinguish between our selfish inclinations and our deepest inclinations. While duty may call us to act against our selfish inclinations, it will fulfill our deepest ones. Near the end of *The Voyage of the "Dawn Treader,"* Caspian wants to abandon his ship and go with Reepicheep to the end of the world. Reepicheep appeals to his sense of duty to persuade him he shouldn't: "You are the King of Narnia. You break faith with all your subjects, and especially Trumpkin, if you do not return. You shall not please yourself with adventures as if you were a private person" (VDT, Chapter 16, p. 537).

Another of Lewis's illustrations of wrong livelihood has to do with the ends justifying the means. His point is that they don't. In *The Voyage of the "Dawn Treader,"* Governor Gumpas has achieved his goal of economic prosperity through profits from the slave trade, by allowing the ends to justify the means. When Caspian orders him to end the wicked practice, Gumpas replies, "But that would be putting the clock back. Have you no idea of progress?" (VDT, Chapter 4, p. 450) It turns out that Caspian not only has an idea of progress, he also has an idea of what is right and wrong, and Gumpas is immediately relieved of his duties. So for Lewis, not only is *what* you do important, but also *how* you do it, the means as well as the ends.

Leisure and Play

No discussion of Lewis's philosophy of work, vocation, and the good life in the *Chronicles* would be complete without a brief look at his philosophy of leisure.

In *The Last Battle* Jewel explains to Jill that because the children were brought out of their world "only at times when Narnia was stirred and upset," she must not think it was always like that. In between these times came whole centuries when dances, feasts, and tournaments "were the only things that could be remembered, and every day and week had been better than the last." Jill wishes they could "get back to those good, ordinary times" as soon as possible (LB, Chapter 8, p. 715).

We find examples of feasting, romping, celebration, and enjoyment of the "good, ordinary" pleasures of life throughout the *Chronicles*, and by including these scenes Lewis balances his philosophy of work with an equally important emphasis on leisure and enjoyment. Mr. Tumnus and Lucy enjoy tea with "a nice brown egg, lightly boiled . . . and then sardines on toast, and then buttered toast, and then toast with honey, and then a sugar-topped cake" (LWW, Chapter 2, p. 116). Later, everyone relaxes at the Beavers' with a wonderful supper that includes "a jug of creamy milk," a "great big lump of deep yellow butter," a "great and gloriously sticky marmalade roll, steaming hot," and "a huge jug of beer" for Mr. Beaver (LWW, Chapter 7, pp. 143–44). Lewis's philosophy requires not only a proper philosophy of work but also a proper stance towards these good, ordinary pleasures—namely, one of enjoyment but not enslavement. On a recent CD, ultra-hip Canadian folksinger Bruce Cockburn has a song titled "Don't Forget about Delight," a point Lewis makes over and over in *The Chronicles of Narnia.*

Lewis explores the same point about pleasure in his book *The Screwtape Letters.* There the devil Screwtape tells his nephew:

> Never forget that when we are dealing with any pleasure in its healthy and normal and satisfying form, we are, in a sense, on the enemy's ground. I know we have won many a soul through pleasure. All the same, it is His invention, not ours. . . . All we can do is to encourage the humans to take the pleasures which our Enemy has produced, at times or in ways, or in degrees, which He has forbidden.[15]

And so we have come full circle. We began by saying that for Lewis life must be about more than just self-centered pleasures, but we finish with just two of the scenes of pleasure that occur over and over in the *Chronicles.* And here we might return once more to Aristotle and his famous claim in the *Nicomachean Ethics* that "virtue . . . is a state of character concerned with choice, lying in a mean."[16] Aristotle goes on to develop his famous principle of the *golden mean,* which is often restated in a somewhat simplified form as "moderation in all things."

If Aristotle found virtue in the golden means, we could say that in a sense Lewis's philosophy of work, vocation, and the good life in *The Chronicles of Narnia* advocates the *golden extremes.* If you are going to romp and celebrate, then really romp and celebrate. If it is your task to save Narnia from the White Witch, then don't be moderate, give it your all. Keep first

---

[15] C.S. Lewis, *The Screwtape Letters* (New York: HarperCollins, 2001 [1942]), p. 44.
[16] *Nicomachean Ethics,* 1107a.

things first by always thinking of the greater good ahead of the lesser good, and never forget that Aslan, who created Narnia with his Voice, is "at the back of all the stories" (HHB, Chapter 4, p. 302) and indeed all true callings.

8
The *Tao* of Narnia

TIM MOSTELLER

There is a *Tao* of Narnia. It's not an Eastern *Tao*. It's not a Western *Tao*. The *Tao* of Narnia isn't Northern or Southern. The ancient Chinese called it the greatest thing, but every rational being in every world can know it. For the *Tao* of Narnia is what C.S. Lewis in *The Abolition of Man* calls

> the Way in which the universe goes on . . . the Way which every man should tread in imitation of that cosmic and supercosmic progression, conforming all activities to that great exemplar. . . . This conception in all its forms, Platonic, Aristotelian, Stoic, Christian, and Oriental alike, I shall henceforth refer to for brevity simply as 'the *Tao*'. . . . It is the doctrine of objective value, the belief that certain attitudes are really true, and others really false, to the kind of thing the universe is and the kind of things we are.[1]

The *Tao* of Narnia is what philosophers and theologians call Natural Law. It is the notion that there are moral truths present in the natural world that can be known by all intelligent beings, whether human, dwarf, faun, centaur, or god. It doesn't matter if you live in London, Cairo, Archenland, Tashbaan, or Cair Paravel. The Natural Law, the *Tao*, is always present to you.

The greatest expositor of Natural Law in the history of western philosophy is St. Thomas Aquinas (1225–1274). Aquinas states that Natural Law allows our minds to "discern what is

---

[1] New York: Macmillan, 1955 [1947], pp. 28–29.

good and what is evil,"[2] that is, to perceive objective moral properties that are present in the world. The most fundamental principle of morality and the first precept of Natural Law knowable by us is that "good is to be done and promoted, and evil is to be avoided."[3] Aquinas also holds that Natural Law is the same in all people, primarily at the level of "common principles," but that it can vary in application to specific situations. The truth of Natural Law is the same for all, but it isn't necessarily known equally by all, because our rational abilities can be "perverted by passion, or evil habit, or an evil disposition of nature."[4] Lewis follows this classic understanding of Natural Law throughout the *Chronicles.*

Is it fair to call Natural Law in the sense elaborated by Aquinas, the *Tao?* What's a nice Asian idea got to do with a medieval Catholic concept like Aquinas's? The *Tao* of Narnia is not of course *Taoism.* Lewis wasn't a Taoist, and neither is anyone in the *Chronicles.* Taoism (pronounced *Dow-ism*) is a Chinese philosophy or religion that sees Ultimate Reality ("the Tao") as an infinite, inexpressible principle that underlies and flows through all things, and can only be felt or intuited rather than grasped through rational concepts. The *Tao,* as Lewis conceives it, is present in Taoism, but is not exclusive to it or to any other particular religion. The *Tao* is something to which even religious practices and creeds must conform. The term isn't used simply for shorthand; it is used because of its *inclusiveness.* Natural Law is written on our hearts and is present at all times and places.

In the Appendix to *The Abolition of Man,* Lewis provides a mini-catalog of illustrations of the *Tao* to show the similarity of moral creeds in many different cultures and religions. For example, Lewis provides examples from Hindu, Babylonian, Indian, Chinese, Viking, and Native American traditions praising the good of kindness. Of course, these kinds of examples don't prove that there are objective values, but they do show that the concept of objective value is present across culture, time, religion and race. I'll be using some specific examples of Lewis's

---

[2] St. Thomas Aquinas, *Summa Theologica,* I–II, Question 91, Art. 2.
[3] *Ibid.,* I–II, Question 94, Art. 2.
[4] *Ibid.,* I–II, Question 94, Art. 4.

illustrations of the *Tao* to show how the concept of objective
value is a central idea throughout the *Chronicles*.

Totally *Tao*

Lewis doesn't argue for the *Tao* in the *Chronicles*. He illustrates
it. If his illustrations are sound, and there really are natural moral
laws that apply to us readers and fans of the *Chronicles*, then
there are only three possible responses we can have to the *Tao*:
we can accept it as a whole, accept part of it and reject part of
it, or reject it entirely. Lewis discusses these three responses in
detail in *The Abolition of Man*, but the responses are also illustrated by various characters in the *Chronicles*.

The first option is to accept the *Tao* as a whole and to strive
to live by it. The great Narnian heroes did just this: Peter, Lucy,
Tirian, Emeth, Puddleglum, and Reepicheep to name a few. To
accept the *Tao* involves three things: (1) a commitment to an
objective moral order that is independent of what I or anyone else
thinks, (2) an openness to moral development only within the
Tao, and (3) a willingness to follow the *Tao* in all situations, not
just those that are easy or convenient. Take Peter, for instance.
From the beginning, with only a few minor lapses, the High King
of Narnia did what was right because he saw it was right. Peter
obeyed Aslan's commands and was willing to learn how to be a
good and righteous leader and person in every area of his life. As
we learn at the conclusion of *The Last Battle*, this acceptance of
the *Tao* leads to the possibility of a good life and allows one to
be a good person for all eternity. The participation of the soul in
the *Tao* makes that soul more suitable for life in the Real Narnia.

Tao and Again

Instead of following the *Tao* completely one might choose to
accept some parts of the *Tao* and reject others. Shift and Miraz
are good examples of this approach. In *The Abolition of Man*,
Lewis calls these types of people "Innovators." These are people who try to live as if there were objective values in only some
areas of life, but not in others. The consequences of trying to do
this are usually disastrous, as Shift and Miraz discover.

Shift, the ugly ape, knew that it was a good thing to have a
ruler, especially if the ruler was him. But he rejected the basic

principle of Natural Law that a ruler should have the interests of the people in mind when he or she rules. (Take a look at Plato's *Republic*, Book 1, for a classic argument for this principle.) Shift demanded that people respect those in authority, and this seems to be a valid principle of traditional morality. But another concept that is present through the Natural Law is the concept of ruling fairly and justly. Shift thought he could pick the former principle as something that was true and valuable, but at the same time deny the latter. The problem with this moral selectivity is that it leads to a kind of arbitrariness that undermines the very possibility of there being any real objective value for any ethical judgments. One cannot consistently claim that honoring authority is a real value without at the same time maintaining that caring for one's people is a real value. Shift had to learn the hard way with his rather objective encounter with Tash that we can't pick and choose our morality.

In a similar way, Miraz denied that loyalty to Caspian, the rightful King, was a legitimate moral demand, yet insisted that his own men be loyal to him, which as he painfully discovered, they declined to do. In both cases, these characters denied the validity of a part of the *Tao*, while attempting to retain others. This tension couldn't be held consistently, as each of them learned. One cannot pick which parts of the *Tao* to accept and which parts to reject, because all parts of the Law rest on the same self-evident moral axioms and any moral values the picker-and-chooser may appeal to have no authority outside the Tao as a whole.[5]

According to Lewis, Friedrich Nietzsche (1844–1900) is a prime example of a moral "Innovator." For Nietzsche, the *Tao* is something to be made up by those who have power, the masters like Miraz, Shift, and Jadis.

Nietzsche describes his paragon of morality, the noble or strong man. The strong man "conceives the root idea 'good' spontaneously and straight away, that is to say, out of himself, and from that material then creates for himself a concept of 'bad!'"[6] For Nietzsche, morality is fundamentally about power, not truth; values are invented, not discovered.

---

[5] Lewis, *The Abolition of Man*, pp. 52–59.
[6] Friedrich Nietzsche, *The Genealogy of Morals*, Essay 1, Section 11, in *The Philosophy of Nietzsche* (New York: Random House, 1954), p. 650.

In Lewis's essay "The Poison of Subjectivism," which is a kind of summary of *The Abolition of Man*, Lewis points out the problem with Nietzsche's ethics. He writes, "The Nietzschean ethic can be accepted only if we are ready to scrap traditional morality as a mere error and then to put ourselves in a position where we can find no ground for any value judgments at all."[7] The real problem with accepting a subjectivist morality, according to Lewis, is that one can't non-subjectively ground one's own morality. If, as Nietzsche claims, there are no moral truths, only personal preferences rooted in a universal "will to power," then there are "no *arche*, no premises"[8] to ground one's moral judgments at all. All that remains is the clash of subjective preferences, with force the only arbiter.

The *Tao*? Curse You and Your Stupid Lion Too

The third option that characters in the *Chronicles* had with respect to the *Tao* was to reject it entirely and to create their own moral code from whole cloth. Uncle Andrew and Ginger the Cat illustrate this type of response. These people are what Lewis calls "Conditioners."[9] They want to get rid of the *Tao* entirely and create an artificial one based on their own subjective "values." But since, on this view, there are no real values, the values on which their artificial *Tao* are based can be nothing but what these people prefer. It is their whim that drives them, and their whim means nothing other than their bodily desires. Thus, when one denies the objectivity of the *Tao* one has reduced morality to nothing more than bodily desires. In other words, being a person, a rational, intelligent being, has been entirely abolished.

Consider Ginger the Cat. Ginger denies all of the truth or reality behind Aslan and what he stands for. Ginger wants nothing but his own power and seeks it in league with Shift and the Calormene invaders. But notice what happens when Ginger takes seriously the denial of all natural moral laws. He comes

---

[7] C.S. Lewis, "The Poison of Subjectivism" (1943), reprinted in *Christian Reflections*, edited by Walter Hooper (Grand Rapids: Eerdmans, 1967), p. 77.
[8] *Ibid.*
[9] Lewis, *Abolition of Man*, p. 74.

face to face with his own abolition. He is undone as a Talking Beast, and is changed back into a dumb irrational animal:

> "Aii—Aii—Aaow—Awah," screamed the Cat. . . . Tirian felt quite certain (and so did the others) that the Cat was trying to say something: but nothing came out of its mouth except the ordinary, ugly cat-noises you might hear from any angry or frightened old Tom in a backyard in England. And the longer he caterwauled the less like a Talking Beast he looked." (LB, Chapter 10, p. 727)

Poor Uncle Andrew encountered the same problem. He wanted to make up his own *Tao* and was willing to get it no matter what he had to do to guinea pigs or innocent children. After his failed attempt to invade and exploit Narnia, Uncle Andrew tries to talk to the Narnian Talking Animals, but the "beasts could not understand him any more than he could understand them. They didn't hear any words: only a vague sizzling noise" (MN, Chapter 11, p. 77). Even the rational power of communication was lost to the old Magician, and it might have been lost for good if it he could have pursued his schemes indefinitely. For rationality itself, of which speech is a part, isn't the kind of thing that can be whatever we want it to be. To make reason into our own tool to be used however we wish, is to abandon the very essence of reason and to surrender to the irrational in us. Like Ginger, Uncle Andrew was ultimately undone and functionally reduced to a non-Talking Animal. Fortunately, his end wasn't as bad as Ginger's. Though to the end of his days he continued to think of wicked Queen Jadis as a "dem fine woman," he eventually "learned his lesson, and in his old age he became a nicer and less selfish old man than he had ever been before" (MN, Chapter 15, p. 106).

This is the inescapable logic of the *Tao* of Narnia. You can live within it and enjoy the good life and the possibility of eternal life, able to move ever "further up and further in" (MN, Chapter 15, p. 755) into God's eternal kingdom. You can be a picker and a chooser and end up in a deadly, self-destructive contradiction. Or you can abolish Man and Beast, Naiad and Dryad, Centaur and Satyr, and every other Talking Person, by replacing objective values with personal preferences grounded in bodily desires. Lewis's hope is that we will emulate Lucy, Peter, Tirian, and the other Narnian heroes who choose to embrace the *Tao* in its entirety.

The *Tao* of General Beneficence

Who meditates oppression, his dwelling is overturned.
—BABYLONIAN. *Hymn to Samas*[10]

The *Tao* shows up quite early in the *Chronicles*. Mr. Tumnus, the first Narnian we meet, sees that there is a law of general beneficence. He meets Lucy, a stranger, who is cold and alone. He brings her to his home, a place of safety and warmth. Mr. Tumnus has orders to turn this young Daughter of Eve over to the White Witch, and at first he intends to do so. But something happens to Mr. Tumnus. He sees that something is not quite right with what he is about to do. He sees that oppressing the innocent is morally wrong. He says, "I've pretended to be your friend and asked you to tea, and all the time I've been meaning to wait till you were asleep and then go and tell *Her* [the White Witch]" (LWW, Chapter 2, p. 118).

When Lucy asks Mr. Tumnus to let her go home, Mr. Tumnus says that he's *got to* let her go. He now *sees* that he can't hand her over to the White Witch. He *knows* that what he was about to do was wrong, objectively bad. He *knows* that letting Lucy go free is right, objectively good. How did he come to know this? Did Lucy give him an argument for it, demonstrating through rigorous logic that kidnapping little girls and handing them over to White Witches is morally bad? No! Mr. Tumnus looked at Lucy. He saw what it is to be an innocent stranger in need. He understood that treachery and deceit are wicked. He saw and decided to live by one of the truths of the *Tao*.

But there were still consequences for Mr. Tumnus. He was complicit in oppression. He had already joined with the White Witch, and as a result his house in Narnia was overturned. "The door had been wrenched off its hinges and broken to bits. . . . The crockery lay smashed on the floor and the picture of the Faun's father had been slashed into shreds with a knife" (LWW, Chapter 6, p. 136). There are consequences, sometimes disastrous ones, for living in opposition to objective moral reality.

---

[10] *Ibid.*, p. 98. This is one of many illustrations of the *Tao* that Lewis presents in the Appendix to *The Abolition of Man*. This one and the ones listed below are taken from a variety of cultural and religious contexts in order to show the universality of Natural Law.

And sometimes we pay a heavy price when we turn away from moral compromise in favor of the *Tao*. However, Mr. Tumnus's decision to obey the *Tao* was ultimately rewarded in the New Narnia (LB, Chapter 15, p. 765).

The *Tao* of Special Beneficence

This first I rede thee: be blameless to thy kindred.
Take no vengeance even though they do thee wrong.

—OLD NORSE. *Sigrdrifumál*[11]

The Calormenes, "a wise, wealthy, courteous, cruel and ancient people" (VDT, Chapter 4, p. 452), seem to have a different morality in the *Chronicles*. They dress differently, preferring robes to trousers, and scimitars to straight-edged swords. Their customs, poetry, and food are different. Even their gods are different. But the *Tao* applies to Tarkheenas as well as to English schoolchildren.

Aravis found this out first hand, or rather first back. It was on her back that Aslan applied his long claws. Why? Aravis tells us herself. When she first meets Shasta in *The Horse and His Boy*, Aravis tells the story of her escape to Narnia and the North. To get away from her forced marriage to an ugly and oppressive old man, she drugged a servant girl who was working for her evil stepmother. Shasta asks what happened to the servant girl who was drugged, and Aravis replies, "Doubtless she was beaten for sleeping late. . . . But she was a tool and spy of my stepmother's. I am very glad they should beat her" (HHB, Chapter 3, p. 224).

Is it good to be glad that a member of one's household has been beaten? Even if the punishment is deserved, should we be happy about it? Lewis doesn't seem to think so. He thinks that repaying evil for evil is wrong. But how do we know this? How did Aravis come to know it?

In this case, Aslan had to point it out to her. He says, "The scratches on your back, tear for tear, throb for throb, blood for blood, were equal to the stripes laid on the back of your stepmother's slave because of the drugged sleep you cast upon her.

---

[11] *Ibid.*, p. 88.

You needed to know what it felt like" (HHB, Chapter 14, p. 299.) Now Aravis knows. She sees that her cruel treatment of her servant was wrong. She understands the pain of an unjust beating. She felt it. Aslan didn't argue with her. He didn't take her through a whole semester of Ethics 101. He simply showed her. This showing is something different from proving. Proof is accomplished through reasons and arguments. But Aslan offers no reasons or arguments to show Aravis that what she did was wrong. He simply shows her that it is wrong.

There are some things that must be known without proof. This doesn't make them irrational. In fact, unless some things can be known without proof, nothing can be proved at all. Unless one can see that it is wrong to take pleasure in the sufferings one has caused, one can make no progress in moral growth at all. This is one of the lessons of the *Tao* of Narnia.

The *Tao* of Good Faith and Veracity

> The Master said, Be of unwavering good faith.
>
> —Ancient Chinese. Confucius, *Analects*[12]

What's with the dwarfs? They seem generally like a good bunch. Good food. Good artwork. Good smokes. But some of them just never seem to get it with respect to certain crucial parts of the *Tao*. In *Prince Caspian*, Nikabrik, a black dwarf, provides a good illustration of bad faith when he treacherously betrays both Aslan and his rightful leader, Prince Caspian.

Nikabrik doubts the old stories about Aslan. He doubts the old traditions of the proper rule of the Kings and Queens in Narnia. He questions whether there should be any constraints on what should be done for the sake of expediency. Nikabrik is a pragmatist, a believer in *Realpolitik*. Moral truth is what works. Aslan and the great kings haven't worked. Miraz has nearly defeated the Narnian rebels, and now Nikabrik proposes a plan that will work. The White Witch is to be conjured up from the dead. Fidelity to tradition is to be swept aside. Faithfulness to the laws and offices that have always been a part of the moral

---

[12] *Ibid.*, p. 112.

fabric of Narnia are to be sacrificed for the sake of winning the war. Nikabrik winds up dead, slain by the rightful leaders of Narnia (PC, Chapter 12, p. 395). His plan to jettison tradition and proper rule in favor of an expedient morality is defeated. Nikabrik fails to see that the *Tao* is not just one morality among many. It is the only morality—Aslan's Owner's Manual for true success and fulfillment, for Humans and Talking Beasts alike.

The *Tao* of Magnanimity

Nature and Reason command that nothing uncomely . . . be done or thought.

—ROMAN. CICERO, *The Offices*[13]

Even Queen Lucy the Valiant, the principal heroine of the *Chronicles*, with her simple, childlike faith in Aslan, had to learn to live within the *Tao*. In *The Voyage of the "Dawn Treader,"* when she is examining the Magician's book, seeking a spell to cure the invisibility of the Dufflepuds, Lucy is greatly tempted. First, she is tempted to utter the spell that will make her beautiful, even more beautiful than her big sister Susan. (Think of the *Brady Bunch*. Lucy feels about Susan much as Jan did about Marsha). Lucy doesn't give in, of course, but Lewis makes it clear that she was severely tempted.

This doesn't mean Lucy is perfect. She, like the rest of us, might have been able to avoid something huge, like choosing to become the most beautiful person in the world for vain or selfish reasons. But it's often the little things that are the hardest to be good at. Just about anyone can say, "Yeah, I'm a good person . . . I ain't never killed nobody."

Lucy did give in on one of the little things. When she utters the spell in the Magician's Book "which would let you know what your friends thought about you" (VDT, Chapter 10, p. 496), she hears her friend Marjorie saying that she really didn't like Lucy after all. This upsets her, and she vindictively calls her friend a "two-faced little beast" (VDT, Chapter 10, p. 496).

Lucy, like so many others in the *Chronicles*, has to be confronted with what she did wrong. When Aslan is made visible to her, he reminds her that eavesdropping is wrong. It's wrong

---

[13] *Ibid.*, p. 119.

if you do it on the telephone; it's wrong if you do it outside someone's office; it's wrong if you do it with a magic spell. It's disrespectful of people's privacy and has long-term effects on human relationships. Aslan says as much to Lucy. She won't be able to forget what she overheard her friend say (VDT, Chapter 10, p. 498).

Lewis, through Aslan, doesn't offer an argument for the immorality of eavesdropping. He simply shows Lucy that it is wrong. The "showing" that Aslan does throughout the *Chronicles* is not the kind of showing that one sees with one's eyes. It is the kind of seeing that is done with one's mind. Seeing that eavesdropping or kidnapping or treachery is wrong is a rational insight that one has or one doesn't have. Of course, one can sometimes be blind to what is right or wrong. I can be tone-deaf or color blind, but this doesn't mean that there is no such thing as a C-note or the color green.

How do you prove what it's like to see red? You can't prove it. You can't argue someone into being aware of redness. You might give them advice on how they can come to see red. For example, you might point out that seeing red is highly likely if one looks directly at a box of strawberries or a stop sign. But seeing red can't be argued for. It has to be experienced. It's the same with the *Tao*.

The *Tao* of Humility

> Pride goeth before destruction, and an haughty sprit before a fall.
> —Ancient Hebrew. Proverbs 16:18

Like Lucy, Jill Pole had a lesson to learn. In *The Silver Chair*, when she and Eustace are drawn into Narnia, they nearly fall off a massive cliff. When Eustace tries to pull Jill back, and is terrified, Jill scorns Eustace's fear. As Jill edges closer to the edge, not heeding Eustace's warning, Eustace tries to pull her back again, but he falls over the edge instead and has to be rescued by Aslan.

When Jill is confronted by Aslan about Eustace's fall, she admits that she was showing off. Aslan responds, "That is a very good answer, Human Child. Do so no more" (SC, Chapter 2, p. 558). Pride and haughtiness (thinkin' you're hot stuff when you ain't) are inconsistent with the *Tao* and wrong. In this case it's obvious: Pride goeth before a fall!

How Now Thou *Tao*?

I think that Lewis wrote the *Chronicles* with a heavy dose of the *Tao* in response to all the moral nonsense he saw being taught to kids in school. In *The Abolition of Man*, he wrote that contemporary educators teach our kids that there are no objective moral truths. In our society a similar situation prevails, as illustrated by the fact that you can't post the Ten Commandments in any public classroom today. As in Lewis's day, it is often taken for granted that morality is subjective or a matter of personal preference, not a matter of real knowledge. We rip the moral eyes right out of our kids' heads and then expect them to see moral truths. Lewis puts this point even more vividly and memorably: "We remove the organ and demand the function. We make men without chests and expect of them virtue and enterprise. We laugh at honour and are shocked to find traitors in our midst. We castrate and bid the geldings be fruitful."[14]

The various characters we've looked at in the *Chronicles* show us the way to stop the horror of moral castration in contemporary intellectual life. Can we see the point they make for us? It depends. It depends on whether we are willing to look. It depends on whether we will open our eyes and our minds to see the kind of thing the universe is, and the kinds of beings we are. Philosophy is one of the tools that can be used for just such a task. It is a task that is much needed in our post-Columbine and post-9/11 world. Perhaps we should begin where the *Chronicles* end, with Lord Digory's still pertinent question, "[B]less me, what *do* they teach them at these schools?" (LB, Chapter 15, p. 759)

---

[14] *Ibid.*, p. 35.

9
Extreme Makeover: Moral Education and the Encounter with Aslan

BILL DAVIS

The children who enter Narnia are not saintly or heroic characters. All of them are morally immature, and some, like Eustace,
are worthless blighters. Over the course of their adventures they
grow. Most become genuinely brave, kind, and truthful; all
become less selfish. The moral development of the children in
the stories depends largely on the structure of Narnia itself. In
Narnia they discover a rich, and enriching, moral order. They
are forced to undertake difficult tasks and bear heavy burdens.
It is natural to think that the victories in which they take part
would give them affection for their comrades that would blunt
their self-centeredness. But Lewis intends to recommend more
than camaraderie and hard work. The moral wealth of Narnia
goes beyond giving the children difficult missions to accomplish. Narnia is the remedy for their moral shortcomings. And
Lewis, drawing on a classical moral framework rooted in both
ancient Greek philosophy and Christian principles, wants us to
see that our own moral development needs what they found in
Narnia.

The Moral Poverty of Our World

With a few notable exceptions, it's hard to find good moral characters outside of Narnia in Lewis's *Chronicles*. Eustace Scrubb is
a "record stinker" (VDT, Chapter 1, p. 426). He is consumed by
his own problems, thinks himself too good for others, and is
insufferably arrogant. Jill Pole, Eustace's schoolmate at

Experiment House, is painfully timid and indulges in pointless self-pity. The unnamed Head of Experiment House sides with the bullies in the Gang and thinks them interesting psychological cases. Edmund is treacherous, dishonest, and power-hungry. Uncle Andrew has all these faults, and worse, in spades.

The moral immaturity of the children in Lewis's *Chronicles* isn't hard to explain. All of them are products of a modern educational system that Lewis strongly condemns. Modern education, Lewis believed, tends to choke off sympathy and moral vision by emphasizing facts over imagination, sports over logic, and secular science over wisdom and virtue.[1] Moreover, by allowing bullies to oppress and mistreat younger and weaker students, many schools in Lewis's day created an atmosphere in which cruelty was seen as cool, and power was regarded as the ultimate good.[2] Greedy and cruel Uncle Andrew is the perfect embodiment of this system.

The morally atrophied world of Experiment House wasn't a wild fantasy Lewis made up to give his characters something to overcome. It was his attempt to depict the results of years of misguided efforts not only to take science "seriously," but also to accept it uncritically as the ultimate account of reality. By the early 1900s, western civilization had enjoyed the fruits of scientific progress for more than two centuries. Science had revealed many of the secrets of nature and had raised standards of living throughout the industrialized world. To many, it seemed likely that *everything* would eventually be explained by science. The supernatural could be dismissed as the stuff of childish fantasies. Talk about fuzzy, unobservable things like "values" could be seen as nothing more than talk about our feelings.[3] Like the dwarfs in the Stable in *The Last Battle* who "refused to be taken in" (LB, Chapter 13, p. 742), serious-minded people in Lewis's day refused to believe in anything good or beautiful that couldn't be fit into their own fixed categories.

Before science was exalted to a position of ultimate authority, one of the main goals of education was moral development:

---

[1] C.S. Lewis, *The Abolition of Man* (New York: Macmillan, 1955). See, in particular, p. 41n.

[2] C.S. Lewis, *Surprised by Joy: The Shape of My Early Life* (New York: Harcourt Brace, 1955), pp. 83ff.

[3] Lewis, *Abolition of Man*, pp. 13–35.

helping students to become morally good. Moral goodness was not simply about how things seemed; it was about how things are (or are not, in the case of wickedness). Becoming good meant acquiring *virtues* such as courage, truthfulness, and charity. Whatever other benefits it might provide, an education that didn't form virtuous characters was seen as a bad education.

Lewis believed that an uncritical acceptance of the authority of science had changed the way people thought about education. "Objective" subjects such as math and physics had become more important, while "subjective" matters such as art, literature, and ethics were shortchanged. Professor Kirke in *The Lion, the Witch, and the Wardrobe* asks whether they are teaching logic any more (LWW, Chapter 5, p. 131). More than once Eustace is said not to have read "the right books" (VDT, Chapter 6, pp. 463–64) and is condemned for his narrow practical-mindedness. What Lewis is lamenting in these passages is the rise of modern "scientific" education. Teachers still aimed to improve students, but not by encouraging moral goodness. Instead of working to make students courageous, reverent, and wise, schools sought to make them reasonable, informed, and sensible.

The most common way to encourage reasonableness of this scientific kind was to combine instruction about social rules with seriousness about life. The thinking went something like this: "It is an objective fact that we have to get along with each other. Playing by the rules (such as 'Don't lie' or 'Don't steal') is best for everyone. People serious about life will learn the rules and live by them. Good schools teach children the rules and make them into serious people. Thus, schools that worry about virtue or beauty are encouraging frivolousness and childishness." Lewis believed that this way of thinking was badly mistaken. Not only was it wrong about the reality of goodness and beauty, it produced people who were either genuinely vicious (like Uncle Andrew) or morally stunted (like Eustace when he first entered Narnia). What children like Eustace needed, Lewis believed, was not more talk about rules or a more serious outlook. What they needed was a world where objective goodness and beauty are obvious. They needed moral examples worth imitating. In short, they needed a trip to Narnia.

The Moral Wealth of Narnia

Narnia is clearly enchanted. It is charged with an energy that is both comforting and thrilling. But while it is a world of Deep and Deeper Magic, Narnia enchants us because it is fundamentally a *good* place. It is a world of characters whose goodness is worth imitating and where goodness is rewarded. Lewis takes children to a place very different from Experiment House and Uncles Andrew's London. The children are able to see what it means to be good and not simply "correct," "reasonable," or "socially well-adjusted." And they come to see that self-sacrifice, courage, and honor lead to the defeat of evil, even though these virtues can result in pain and sacrifice along the way. Narnia is both comforting and thrilling to us because it is what we hope for from our own world. Lewis takes his human children (and his readers) to Narnia because he believes that at a deep level what is true of Narnia is also true of our world. Like the children, we need a trip to Narnia so that we can see the moral enchantment of our own world.

Just as Lewis's Experiment House captures a depressingly real place, Narnia revives an understanding of the world that was common before the success of science convinced many people that science describes everything there is. Let's call this earlier, morally rich understanding of the world the "classical picture of the world." Lewis believed in this classical picture. So did most of the great philosophers of the ancient and medieval worlds, including Plato, Aristotle, Augustine, and Aquinas.[4] Narnia is comforting and inspiring because it is a "classical" world in this sense. People (and in Narnia, Talking Animals) have virtues and vices. Virtue is rewarded and vice is punished. The entire world is ruled by a Lion who is supremely good, and who is opposed by witches and other creatures that are thoroughly wicked. Good and evil are obvious, making Narnia a world of vivid moral colors and clear choices. And, most important for understanding the stories, people who are not yet virtuous can develop morally in just the way the classical picture claims.

According to Aristotle, Aquinas, and other defenders of the classical picture, moral growth requires three things. First, we

---

[4] Plato, *Republic*, especially books 5–7; Aristotle, *Nicomachean Ethics*, Books 1, 2, and 6; Augustine, *Confessions*, Books 1 and 3; Thomas Aquinas, *Summa Theologica*, the whole of the Second Part.

need to be taught how the moral world works; we need *instruction*. Second, we need virtuous role models to show us how to be morally good; we need exemplars worthy of *imitation*.[5] Finally, we need to do what is right repeatedly even when it is difficult; we need *habituation*. In Narnia the children are provided with all three of these ingredients. Sometimes Aslan himself instructs the children, as when he explains the Deeper Magic the White Witch didn't know. But more often the children are instructed by Narnians like Reepicheep (a mouse), Trumpkin (a dwarf), Ramandu (a star), or Puddleglum (a Marsh-wiggle).

Just as the classical picture would lead us to expect, however, the times of instruction are not nearly as memorable as the moral examples that the children meet in Narnia. The classical world recognized four "cardinal" virtues: wisdom, courage, temperance, and justice. It would take pages to define these virtues, but they can be grasped even more clearly by saying that Doctor Cornelius is wise (and thus has the virtue of wisdom). Reepicheep is courageous. Puddleglum is temperate (as well as brave). And Aslan is just (as well as wise, courageous, and temperate). In the classical picture, justice is the fulfillment of all the virtues.[6]

A few days with Reepicheep teaches the children more about courage than years of reading or classroom lectures ever could. The most effective way to grow morally is to imitate someone who is already virtuous. For example, Jill Pole is selfish and timid when she arrives in Narnia. Time in the company of the selfless and brave Puddleglum leads her to be less self-centered and fearful. The presence of virtuous examples is essential, but it takes time to acquire the virtues. In keeping with the classical picture, the children grow morally through habitually doing what their virtuous mentors are doing. Like becoming a good tennis player, the children acquire virtues by practice or habituation. In Narnia they find themselves with tasks that require them to be fair, brave, and truthful in one situation after another. And because Narnia is a classical world, practice in *doing* good helps them to *become* good.

While the four cardinal virtues were praised by nearly everyone before the rise of modern science, Lewis also emphasizes

---

[5] See Aristotle, *Nicomachean Ethics*, especially Book 2. Aquinas endorses a similar view of moral education.
[6] Plato, *Republic*, Book 4; Aristotle *Nicomachean Ethics*, Book 5.

two virtues that came to be fully appreciated only in the Middle Ages: chivalry and selflessness. These virtues are at the heart of the Narnian moral order. While wicked characters are deceitful and treacherous, good characters are truthful and loyal even when it means discomfort and danger. Similarly, even though vicious characters are proud and selfish, good characters are humble and sacrifice themselves for the sake of others. Puddleglum burns his webbed feet to save Eustace, Jill, and Rilian. Caspian refuses to leave Dragon Island without Eustace. Shasta jumps off his horse to save Aravis from a lion. And, most spectacularly, Aslan submits to the White Witch's cruel execution to save Edmund's life.

A heart for others may go unnoticed in our world, and selfishness is too often found in the "successful." But in Narnia wickedness of all kinds results in eventual ruin. The cruel White Witch and the Queen of Underland are destroyed. Grasping and deceitful Miraz is slain. The wicked Ape, Shift, is carried off by the demonic Tash. The proud and ruthless son of the Tisroc is made ridiculous, and the wickedly foolish Uncle Andrew is planted in the ground like a tree.

The influence of Narnia's classical moral order on the children is a central theme in the *Chronicles*. Before they enter Narnia in *The Lion, the Witch, and the Wardrobe*, the Pevensie children are far from moral paragons. Peter is an indecisive boy who is slow to defend his sister Lucy. Edmund betrays his siblings repeatedly, first by lying about his own adventure in Narnia, and then by slipping away and betraying his brother and sisters to the White Witch. As further proof of his moral weakness, Edmund is carried off by his lust for Turkish Delight. Lucy whines and is envious of Susan's beauty. She responds to the disbelief of Peter and Susan with tears and sulking. Narnia proves to be the cure for all these moral failings.

For the Pevensie children, one trip to Narnia isn't enough. Their first trip introduces them to the attractiveness of real goodness and moral order. It gives them a taste for chivalry and self-sacrifice and a desire for more. In *Prince Caspian* Peter's lack of resolve and indecisiveness is set aside when he must risk single combat in order to save his friends. His life in England was safe and predictable, but what he needed was a cause worth dying for, a goal both noble and good. Narnia provides a moral setting in which everyone takes for granted the necessity of fighting for what is right. Peter grows into a resolute and wise person through these dangers. Even in wartime conditions, this would not have happened in comparatively safe and colorless England.

Edmund and Lucy have very different experiences on their first trip to Narnia. Edmund's moral growth starts with his cruel reception by the White Witch. He comes to see that gluttony and a lust for power lead to nothing but frustration and pain. In England these vices might not have had such obvious consequences, but in Narnia vice is invariably punished. Not only is Edmund made miserable, but his treason also tears the very fabric of the Narnian world: someone must die. Edmund's life is spared only because Aslan is willing to bear Edmund's punishment for him. The depth of the moral order that governs Narnia proves to be fathomless when Aslan returns to life and puts an end to the Witch's oppressive reign.

Lucy is the first to see the risen Aslan. She frolics with him in the first moments of his return and serves his army as a healer in the battle that ends in the White Witch's defeat. Delight in Aslan's triumph and service to a noble cause start to make Lucy selfless and brave in a way that life in England would not have. For Lucy, as well as Edmund, further adventures would be needed. It isn't until *The Voyage of the "Dawn Treader"* that Edmund becomes a truly loyal friend or Lucy overcomes her envy of Susan's beauty. But even this is what the classical picture would expect. True goodness is not the result of a single trial; and backsliding, as Eustace discovered (VDT, Chapter 7, p. 476), is always possible. Virtues are good habits, acquired by repeatedly doing what is right.

Peter, Susan, Edmund, and Lucy are average English children whose moral education had been neglected. Eustace Scrubb and Jill Pole, on the other hand, enter Narnia as children whose characters had been corrupted by the vicious environment of Experiment House. Eustace is a self-centered, cowardly snob, the sort of boy that Lewis himself says he became in boarding school.[7] By the end of *The Silver Chair* Eustace is a very different boy. He takes risks in order to help his friends, he serves others rather than indulging himself, and he is no longer contemptuous of people who don't know what he knows.

---

[7] Lewis, *Surprised by Joy*, pp. 104ff.

The Silver Chair opens with a description of Jill's unhappy life at Experiment House, where bullies and cliques make life miserable for weaker or more decent students like Jill and Eustace. While Eustace had become a stuck-up know-it-all, Jill had become timid, fearful, and nearly invisible. Even though those who ran Experiment House had not intended to crush her spirit and take away her personality, the school was to blame for these results. In Narnia her moral character blossoms. It doesn't happen all at once, but over time she becomes more confident and courageous. By the end of the story she is the one who faces danger alone by climbing out of Underworld without knowing if it is safe. Courageous Prince Rilian and the unselfish Puddleglum showed her what it meant to be good, and the challenges she encountered gave her the practice she needed to grow into a brave girl.

Close Encounters of the Leonine Kind

One of the more curious things about Narnia is that an adventure there doesn't always work in a lasting way. Susan makes two trips there, but when she returns to our world Narnia's influence wears off, and she eventually becomes "no longer a friend of Narnia" (LB, Chapter 12, p. 741). Also puzzling is Lucy's continuing jealousy of Susan's beauty. It isn't until Lucy's third trip to Narnia that she is forced to deal with that vice directly. It might seem that the moral influence of Narnia is limited to Narnia itself, and that moral development is somehow suspended when visitors return to our world.

But this doesn't happen to Digory or Polly. And most of the children don't start over from the beginning of their moral education when they return for later adventures. These visitors to Narnia are changed so deeply that they can resist the corrupting influences of our world. They aren't just virtuous when they are in the morally rich air of Narnia; they have become virtuous at their core. What all these characters share is a life-transforming encounter with Aslan. For most readers these encounters are the most moving and memorable events in all the adventures. Three in particular are worth close attention: Eustace's being ripped out of his dragonish skin, Jill's getting a drink on Aslan's mountain, and Digory's asking for the magic fruit that will heal his mother.

Eustace deserved to be turned into a dragon and left that way. His selfish and arrogant behavior on board the *Dawn Treader* had made him worse than useless, and he stumbled into the dragon's lair because he was defiantly trying to avoid work. He discovered that it is unpleasant being a dragon. The bracelet on his arm was uncomfortable, but not as painful as being unable to talk with the other people on the island. When Aslan came to him, Eustace was afraid. But, more than that, Eustace was wretched. He was sad and lonely, but he was also genuinely sorry for being beastly to everyone.

Aslan's "cure" comes in two stages. First, Aslan commands Eustace to undress himself. Eustace tries repeatedly to shed his loathsome skin, but no matter how hard he scratches or claws at himself he can't get deep enough. When he realizes that he can't do it himself, Aslan undertakes the second stage:

> The very first tear he made was so deep that I thought it had gone right into my heart. And when he began pulling the skin off, it hurt worse than anything I've ever felt. The only thing that made me able to bear it was just the pleasure of feeling the stuff peel off. . . . Well, he peeled the beastly stuff right off . . . and there I was as smooth and soft as a peeled switch and smaller than I had been. Then he caught hold of me . . . and threw me into the water. It smarted like anything but only for a moment. After that it became perfectly delicious . . . (VDT, Chapter 7, pp. 474–75)

What Eustace needed was more than the natural remedy of Narnia's moral wealth. He needed to be changed from within. In order for Eustace to continue to grow outside of Narnia he needed what only Aslan could give: an extreme makeover.

Jill's transforming encounter with Aslan comes at the very outset of her first adventure in Narnia. Moments after arriving on Aslan's mountain, she finds an enormous Lion standing between her and a stream from which she desperately wants to drink:

> "Are you not thirsty?" said the Lion.
>
> "I'm *dying* of thirst," said Jill.
>
> "Then drink," said the Lion.
>
> "May I—could I—would you mind going away while I do?" said Jill.
>
> The Lion answered this only by a look and a very low growl
> . . . .

"Will you promise not to—do anything to me, if I do come?" said Jill.

"I make no promise," said the Lion. . . .

"I daren't come and drink," said Jill.

"Then you will die of thirst," said the Lion.

"Oh dear?" said Jill, . . . "I suppose I must go and look for another stream then."

"There is no other stream," said the Lion. (SC, Chapter 2, pp. 557–58)

Jill drinks and is refreshed, but the Lion asks her difficult questions about where her companion, Eustace, is. She confesses that he fell off the cliff because she was showing off. Aslan commends her answer and gives her the instructions she needs to fulfill the mission she was called into Narnia to perform. It takes the example of Puddleglum and plenty of practice to complete Jill's development from being cowardly to being courageous, but the probing encounter with Aslan changes her deeply. The virtues she develops in Narnia will last even when she returns to our world.

In *The Magician's Nephew*, Digory gets up his nerve and asks Aslan for a magic apple that will save his mother's life. Even though Digory had been a sneaky and untrustworthy boy before entering Narnia, he is unable to lie when confronted with Aslan himself. Digory admits that he is responsible for awakening Queen Jadis in Charn and thereby bringing evil into Narnia. The old Digory would have tried to deflect this responsibility, but Aslan's majesty and the beauty of newly-created Narnia makes him sorry for what he has done. Digory tells the truth because he is repentant. He sees that his willfulness has spoiled Aslan's world, and that Aslan above all deserves to hear the truth from Digory.

In each of these three encounters with Aslan, the children feel genuine sorrow for things they have done wrong. The same is true of Edmund's transforming conversation with Aslan in *The Lion, the Witch, and the Wardrobe*, although Lewis doesn't give us the details of what was said (LWW, Chapter 13, p. 174). It is also essential to Lucy's meeting with Aslan when she is reading Coriakin's Book of Spells (VDT, Chapter 10, p. 498). The Lion's majestic presence makes the children mindful of their own self-centeredness. More than that, Aslan works the miracle of healing. Past wrongs are not just forgotten; they are washed away and replaced with a mission that depends upon moving beyond past failures. Deliverance from our old selves and transformation at our core is an extreme makeover. This kind of change is a super-natural gift. In Narnia, that gift is given only by Aslan himself.

Why We Still Need Narnia

Moral development by natural means is back in favor with edu-cational theorists, even if the extreme makeover that Lewis rec-ommends is not. In recent years many schools, both public and private, have come to include "character education" and even "moral virtues" among their educational goals. Much of this has been fueled by concerns about declining moral values, as evi-denced, for example, by rising crime rates, corporate scandals, the breakdown of the family, irresponsible sexual behavior, and an increasingly violent, explicit, and coarsened media. But how-ever it happened that virtue made a comeback, it is now com-mon for schools to plan for the moral development of their students.[8] Despite this, Lewis would probably think that students today need a trip to Narnia just as badly as the children in the *Chronicles* did, because today's character education programs base moral growth on love for self rather than on love for the good.

Character education today aims to encourage students to act ethically: to be respectful, responsible, tolerant, truthful, caring, fair, and so forth. Lots of different lists of good traits (sometimes even called "virtues") have been developed, and almost all have *respect* (especially self-respect) and *responsibility* near the top. Significantly, respect and responsibility are not presented as ends in themselves. Instead, most character education programs pursue these and other traits primarily for the sake of good cit-izenship. Virtue is important because a society in which people are disrespectful, irresponsible, and deceitful is uncivilized, and

---

[8] Many programs of moral improvement have been developed for schools, most under the title of "character education." See, for example, Thomas Lickona, *Educating for Character: How Our Schools Can Teach Respect and Responsibility* (New York: Bantam, 1992); and Kevin Ryan and Karen Bochlin, *Building Character in Schools: Practical Ways to Bring Moral Instruction to Life* (San Francisco: Jossey Bass, 1998). I am indebted to my colleagues Rebecca Pennington and James Drexler for help with the character education literature.

hence undesirable. The purpose of good character is thus pragmatic. The pursuit of virtue doesn't rest on a love for goodness; it rests primarily on a love for oneself that easily becomes self-centered and fails to care for others. Programs that make self-esteem central to character education only make explicit what is implicit in the other programs.

Lewis would not accept today's character education as an adequate imitation of Narnian moral education, but he would concede that it is superior to Experiment House's attempt to do without virtue at all. Today's character education programs recognize that everything we do is motivated by love. We love ourselves; we love our families and friends; many people love God. No one loves Reason or Reality in itself apart from people or God, and this is why serious-mindedness led to moral poverty. Since character education today appeals to love for self or for others, it can avoid producing morally stunted people like the children in the Narnia stories. But it isn't clear whether it can avoid producing viciously selfish people like Uncle Andrew or (worse still) the White Witch and her motley crew of Ghouls, Ogres, Cruels, Hags, Wraiths, Horrors, and people of the Toadstools (LWW, Chapter 13, p. 173; Chapter 14, p. 180).

Boxed in by political taboos, today's character education attempts to teach goodness without any mention of moral reality, that is, without any mention of religion. As Plato notes, it is natural to ask *why* it is wrong to lie if you'll never be caught, or *why* it is wrong to be lazy when you have talents you can use. In Narnia, the answer to these questions is obvious: these actions offend Aslan and rip the fabric of that world. Lewis believes that something like this is true of our world as well. But given currently fashionable dogmas about church-state separation, school officials today can't build programs around such answers because they are religious. Even when school officials agree with Lewis and acknowledge an objective—even a transcendent—moral order, public school programs cannot appeal to religious truths. The place of religion in public discourse is a complicated matter, but for good or ill leaving religion out of the discussion forces educators today to act as if the world is morally neutral. As a result, they must assume that moral claims are either expressions of personal taste or, at best, expressions of community consensus.

This is not very different from the serious-mindedness that Lewis condemns. In his book, *The Abolition of Man*, Lewis attacks the poverty of thinking that all value judgments are expressions of taste or sentiment. Moral education, he argues, depends upon acknowledgement of an objective moral order, a recognition that goodness and beauty are not subject to our wishes or whims. Character education that rests on private taste will result ultimately in selfishness dressed up as virtue. Students who learn their lessons perfectly will be trustworthy, respectful, or responsible only as long as there is a threat of getting caught if they do otherwise. Programs that base the pursuit of morality on love for community will produce whole nations that find it impossible to sacrifice the nation's interests for the sake of something higher. For both sorts of character education programs, there is nothing higher, no overarching moral order. Just as Uncle Andrew couldn't imagine a reason *not* to gratify his desires, students without a Narnia-like moral education will be incapable of genuine self-sacrifice for the sake of some higher good.

It won't be easy to fix today's character education programs. Even if the programs were changed, making devotion to an Aslan-like figure the motivation for pursuing virtue, Lewis would still find them insufficient. This is because we won't truly love Aslan (or his counterpart in our world) unless he first changes us. A morally ordered world like Narnia is sufficient to show us what it means to be virtuous. It even rewards virtue in a way that makes it attractive to be virtuous. But until we have an encounter with the good *one* that remakes us, we will only pursue virtue out of love for ourselves. We all need Narnia (or to realize that Narnia is no mere story); but we need Aslan most of all.[9]

---

[9] I am indebted to my children Amy, Rachel, and Mark for their enthusiastic help with this chapter, and to Joseph Moon for his research assistance.

10

Is It Good to Be Bad? Immoralism in Narnia

JANICE DAURIO

Like his friend, J.R.R. Tolkien, the creator of Middle-earth, C.S. Lewis, the creator of Narnia, believed in an objective moral order, which each showed in his created world. In *The Abolition of Man* (1943) and *Mere Christianity* (1952), Lewis argued the point directly by offering a powerful critique of immoralism—the view that morality is fundamentally a matter of power or superiority, and that many things called "bad" could just as easily be called "good" (and *vice versa*), but perhaps only by an elite few. In *The Chronicles of Narnia*, three characters—Uncle Andrew, Queen Jadis, and the Queen of Underworld—endorse versions of this immoralist ethics. In this chapter we'll see how Lewis critiques immoralism.

Three Immoralists: Thrasymachus, Callicles, and Nietzsche

The fashionable notion that "might makes right" may seem like a uniquely modern idea, but actually it is very old. The *Dialogues* of Plato (428–348 B.C.E.) contain two versions of the idea.

In the *Republic*, where the discussion focuses on what it means to be just, and whether injustice ever pays, Socrates is defending the claim that it is never right to injure another person, when Thrasymachus bursts in and tells Socrates to wipe his nose and quit spouting such childish nonsense. In every society, he says, those with power call the shots, and those without power obey. Justice is "the interest of the stronger"—that is, doing what benefits the strong.[1] Though milksops like Socrates might prattle on about the "virtue" of justice, it's better, for those who are powerful enough to get away with it, to be *unjust* rather than just. Indeed, the best life of all would be that of the successful tyrant, who takes whatever he wants and commits the grossest acts of injustice with impunity.[2]

Callicles, in Plato's dialogue, *Gorgias*, has a similar view. Popular ideas of "right" and "wrong," Callicles claims, are human inventions cooked up by the weak to restrain the strong: "convention" (*nomos*) rather than "nature" (*physis*). An honest look at nature shows "that it is just for the better to have more than the worse, the more powerful than the weaker."[3] A superior individual, if he had sufficient power, would break through conventional moral restraints; "he would trample under foot all our formulas and spells and charms,"[4] and "allow his desires to wax to the uttermost, and not to chastise them; but when they have grown to the greatest he should have courage and intelligence to minister to them and to satisfy all his longings."[5]

Thrasymachus and Callicles, though, are different in one respect. For Thrasymachus, justice is bad; it's doing what the boss man—the guy with power—wants you to do. It's better, Thrasymachus thinks, to be *unjust*—assuming you can get away with it. But for Callicles, justice is a good thing. True justice is natural justice: when the strong subdue the weak. Callicles, unlike Thrasymachus, doesn't think it's bad to be just. Both, however, are immoralists, for both hold that morality is fundamentally a matter of power, and that the good is very different from what most people think it is.

The most famous modern defender of immoralism is Friedrich Nietzsche (1844–1900). While Nietzsche's version of immoralism is different from the crude, self-aggrandizing versions of Thrasymachus and Callicles, they do have something in common.

---

[1] Plato, *Republic*, in *The Dialogues of Plato*, translated by Benjamin Jowett (New York: Random House, 1937), Book I, 338c. All subsequent quotations from Plato are from this edition.

[2] *Ibid.*, 344a–c.

[3] Plato, *Gorgias*, 483d.

[4] *Ibid.*, 484a.

[5] *Ibid.*, 492a.

Traditional Western morality, Nietzsche believes, is doomed. "God is dead," he declares, and the loss of God has left us sailing in a vast uncharted sea with no recognizable ethical landmarks to steer by. Nietzsche paid his enemies the compliment of accepting their belief that without God, we've come to the end of truth and morality as we know it. Without God, people can no longer rationally believe that truth or morality is objective. "We have abolished the real world," he says.[6]

Far from being depressed by this prospect, Nietzsche is rather glad that God is dead. Belief in God is responsible for the illusion of objective morality, and now we are free to be more honest and creative. We can embrace all of life, the good and the bad, not just some of it. If God isn't calling the shots, then we are. Well, *some* of us are calling the shots—in fact, a very small number of us. "The noble type of man experiences itself as determining values; it does not need approval; it judges, knows itself to be that which first accords honor to things; it is value-creating."[7]

The purpose of culture, Nietzsche says, is the production of genius. "A people is nature's detour to arrive at six or seven great men—and to get around them."[8] To provide a fertile soil for the production of such individuals, "the enormous majority must, in the service of the minority, be slavishly subjected to life's struggle, to a greater degree than their own wants necessitate. . . . Slavery is of the essence of Culture."[9]

By contrast, Christianity places a premium on values like humility, kindness, justice, and equality. Like Callicles, Nietzsche believes that these are slavish ideas invented by the weak to protect themselves against the strong. Christian as well as democratic values hinder the will to power and hamper the production of genius. What's needed is a "transvaluation of values"—a radical rethinking of what is considered "good" in light of the

---

[6] Friedrich Nietzsche, *Twilight of the Idols*, translated by R.J. Hollingdale (New York: Penguin, 1968), p. 51.

[7] Friedrich Nietzsche, *Beyond Good and Evil*, translated by Walter Kaufmann (New York: Vintage, 1989), p. 260.

[8] Friedrich Nietzsche, *Beyond Good and Evil*, in *The Portable Nietzsche*, edited and translated by Walter Kaufmann (New York: Penguin, 1976), p. 444.

[9] Friedrich Nietzsche, "The Greek State," quoted in Frederick Copleston, S.J., *Friedrich Nietzsche: Philosopher of Culture*, second edition (New York: Harper and Row, 1975), p. 39.

death of God and the rejection of objective moral standards and objective truth. The best virtues are the aristocratic values of the superior few: strength, boldness, creativity, ruthlessness, and daring. "What is good?—All that heightens the feeling of power, the will to power, power itself in man. What is bad?—All that proceeds from weakness."[10] This is the morality of Nietzsche's "supermen," his "free spirits" of power.

Does this mean that ordinary individuals should give up their "herd morality" and adopt the strong master morality instead? Not at all, says Nietzsche: "It is *immoral* to say that 'what is right for one is proper for another,'"[11] given the real inequalities between people. "The spirit of the herd should rule within the herd—but not beyond it: the leaders of the herd require a fundamentally different valuation for their actions, as do also the independent ones or the beasts of prey, etc."[12] The superior few should follow one morality—the morality of the "beasts of prey"—while the inferior masses should continue to adhere to the servile values of traditional Judeo-Christian ethics and democracy.

Sounds like Thrasymachus and Callicles . . . but Nietzsche's hero must conquer himself. Nietzsche's cultivated, self-over-coming, art-loving "free spirits" aren't the tyrants Thrasymachus and Callicles admired. But Nietzsche's is also a version of immoralism: what Lewis had in mind for Uncle Andrew, the White Witch, and the Queen of Underworld.

---

[10] Friedrich Nietzsche, *The Anti-Christ*, in *A Nietzsche Reader*, translated by R.J. Hollingdale (New York: Penguin, 1977), p. 231.

[11] Friedrich Nietzsche, *Beyond Good and Evil,* in *The Philosophy of Nietzsche*, translated by Helen Zimmern (New York: Modern Library, 1954), p. 524. This may sound like moral relativism, and in fact Nietzsche has often been interpreted as a moral relativist. His considered view, however, seems to have been a kind of *moral anti-realism*—the view that there are no moral truths or moral facts. See, for example, Nietzsche's *Twilight of the Idols*, in *The Portable Nietzsche*, p. 501, and *Beyond Good and Evil* (Kaufmann translation), p. 85. For Lewis's critique of moral anti-realism, see his books *The Abolition of Man* (New York: HarperCollins, 2001), pp. 15–84 and *Mere Christianity* (New York: HarperCollins, 2001), pp. 3–20, as well as his important essay, "The Poison of Subjectivism," in *Christian Reflections* (Grand Rapids: Eerdmans, 1967), pp. 72–81.

[12] Friedrich Nietzsche, *The Will to Power*, I, aphorism 287, quoted in Copleston, *Friedrich Nietzsche*, p. 107.

Coming to a World Near You

Andrew Ketterley, the anti-hero in *The Magician's Nephew*, clearly embraces an immoralist view of ethics. He tells Digory that his fairy godmother, Mrs. Lefay, was imprisoned because she did things that were "very unwise" by the standards of the strong (she got caught), and which the "narrow-minded" call wrong. But "it depends on what you call wrong," says Uncle Andrew with a chuckle (MN, Chapter 2, p. 12). Uncle Andrew thinks that Mrs. Lefay should not be judged by the standards of "ordinary, ignorant people" but by how she treated him, another one of the elite few. "She was always very kind to me."

Uncle Andrew had the power, via some magic rings, to send people out of this world. . . but to where? He didn't know; he needed human guinea pigs who could talk when they returned . . . *if* they returned.

Uncle Andrew shows his immoralist colors after he tells Digory about a promise he broke to this fairy godmother:

> "Well, then, it was jolly rotten of you," said Digory.
> "Rotten?" said Uncle Andrew with a puzzled look. "Oh, I see. You mean that little boys ought to keep their promises. Very true: most right and proper, I'm sure, and I'm very glad you have been taught to do it. But of course you must understand that rules of that sort, however excellent they may be for little boys—and servants— and women—and even people in general, can't possibly be expected to apply to profound students and great thinkers and sages. No, Digory. Men like me, who possess hidden wisdom, are freed from common rules just as we are cut off from common plea- sures." (MN, Chapter 1, p. 15)

Like Thrasymachus, Uncle Andrew believes that one set of moral rules applies to ordinary people (poor saps forced by the powerful to do what is "just"), and another to the rulers. Also like Thrasymachus, he believes that those with power are exempt from ordinary moral rules. But unlike Thrasymachus, Uncle Andrew focuses on *intellectual* superiority ("profound students and great thinkers and sages") rather than sheer power or force.

Consistent with this view, Uncle Andrew can, and does, use a tactic that most people consider to be immoral: deception. He sees that the children are hesitating about being part of his experiment, so he conceals from Polly the truth about the pretty rings he has; he pretends to be innocently making her a gift, when he is actually tricking her into being used for his experiment.

Notice how Uncle Andrew's two-level ethics works. He's not willing to endanger himself for the sake of the experiment, but he is willing to endanger others. Using and deceiving people is okay for him to do to others, but it wouldn't be okay for others to do it to him. Uncle Andrew doesn't follow the Golden Rule of traditional morality, "Do unto others as you would have them do unto you." That rule belongs to conventional morality and applies only to common people.

Uncle Andrew thinks that because he's a Master, it's permissible for him to break a cardinal rule of traditional morality: Don't use people merely as means to your own ends. Like Thomas Anderson (Neo) in *The Matrix*, he believes that he is "special," that "somehow the rules do not apply" to him. Only later, when he encounters Queen Jadis, who wants to use *him*, does he realize how mistaken he was.

Who's Got the Power?

As political philosopher Thomas Hobbes points out in *Leviathan* (1651), there's a problem with banking on power: Eventually, someone shows up with more of it. Uncle Andrew learns this lesson when he meets Jadis, usurping Queen of Charn. Uncle Andrew might lust for the power that comes with knowledge, but Jadis scorns what for immoralists is the merely conventional preference for knowledge over ignorance. She thinks of Uncle Andrew as *her* slave. "Stand up, dog, and don't sprawl there as if you were speaking to your equals" (MN, Chapter 6, p. 46). Jadis wants all the power she can get, in her own world as well as his.

Jadis, like Uncle Andrew, is a big fan of the idea that there are masters and there are slaves. She is very fond of distinctions of rank and the ways in which those distinctions put her above rules that apply to others. When Jadis tells Digory and Polly how she used the Deplorable Word to destroy all living things on Charn, Digory gasps, "But the people."

> "What people, boy?" asked the Queen.
> "All the ordinary people," said Polly, "who'd never done you any harm. And the women, and the children, and the animals."

"Don't you understand?" said the Queen (still speaking to Digory). "I was the Queen. They were all my people. What else were they there for but to do my will? You must learn, child, that what would be wrong for you or for any of the common people is not wrong in a great Queen such as I. The weight of the world is on our shoulders. We must be freed from all rules. Ours is a high and lonely destiny." (MN, Chapter 5, pp. 41–42)

This sounds a lot like Uncle Andrew's two-level morality, but in fact it's more extreme in two respects. First, there is no suggestion that mere intellectual superiority confers any privileged moral status; for Jadis, like Thrasymachus, being a Master is a function of raw power. And second, she claims to be exempt not only from ordinary moral rules but from all constraints of morality—and truth. Unlike Uncle Andrew who thinks of himself and his kind as moral and even noble in a weird and wonky way, in her thirst for power, she dispenses with all the niceties. (She got the throne of Charn by murdering her sister, after all.) She goes beyond morality, beyond good and evil, beyond truth and falsehood. It's as if she somehow sneaked into our world and read Nietzsche: "*To recognise untruth as a condition of life*: that is certainly to impugn the traditional ideas of value in a dangerous manner, and a philosophy which ventures to do so, has thereby alone placed itself beyond good and evil."[13]

To Uncle Andrew and Queen Jadis, anyone with a conscience is a *fool*, one of the *common people* (two of her Majesty's favorite terms). When the Jadis meets Polly and Digory in Charn, her first order of business is to establish the power lines. Completely ignoring the obviously powerless Polly, she first directs her attention to Digory, and then to Uncle Andrew, the "master magician" who sent the children into her world. Utterly lacking what Lewis calls "the taste for the other," she has no interest in people except insofar as they are either potential rivals or potential servants (MN, Chapter 6, p. 47).

In Lewis's devilishly good book, *The Screwtape Letters*, a senior devil, Screwtape, warns a junior devil, Wormwood, about the dangers of letting people see that they can't possess or use other people. The senior devil offers this advice:

---

[13] Nietzsche, *Beyond Good and Evil* (Zimmern translation), p. 384.

> The sense of ownership in general is always to be encouraged. . . .
> We produce this sense of ownership not only by pride but by
> confusion. We teach them not to notice the different senses of the
> possessive pronoun—the finely graded differences that run from
> "my boots" through "my dog," "my servant," "my wife," "my
> father," "my master," and "my country," to "my God." They can be
> taught to reduce all these senses to that of "my boots," the "my"
> of ownership.[14]

For Lewis, via Aslan, the true King of Narnia, in contrast to both
Andrew and Jadis, the usurping Queen of Charn, all created
rational beings are equally subject to objective truth and objective moral values. And according to this true morality, it is
always wrong for some to treat others as a mere means to personal or collective ends.

The immoralist rejection of universal morality is grounded in
the rejection of objective reality. Going beyond good and evil is
accompanied by going beyond truth and falsehood. This
provocative corollary to the immoralist stance is nicely illustrated
in a conversation in *The Silver Chair* between the wicked Queen
of Underland and four prisoners trying to escape her clutches.

The Queen (a.k.a. the Lady of the Green Kirtle) attempts to
talk Prince Rilian and his companions out of their belief in
Overworld, the real world of Narnia. All the longing that they
have for the real world almost completely disappears when they
fall under the spell she casts on them. Rilian's view of that
world, like Plato's, is that the world of goodness and light is
most real: "You see that lamp. It is round and yellow and gives
light to the whole room; and hangeth moreover from the roof.
Now that thing which we call the sun is like the lamp, only far
greater and brighter. It giveth light to the whole Overworld and
hangeth in the sky" (SC, Chapter 12, p. 631). But the Queen of
Underworld laughs at him, and almost convinces him that
Narnia doesn't exist; Narnia is a mere dream or children's story.

But believing doesn't make it so. As the story unfolds, the
Narnians' Overworld triumphs over the Witch's Underworld.
Indeed, it always will, as Lewis is fond of reminding us. We may
not always like it but there is objective reality. "Bemused and

---

[14] C.S. Lewis, *The Screwtape Letters* (New York: HarperCollins, 2001), pp.
113–14.

besotted as we are, we still dimly know at heart that nothing which is at all times and in every way agreeable to us can have objective reality. It is of the very nature of the real that it should have sharp corners and rough edges, that it should be resistant, should be itself."[15]

Gimme That Ol' Time Morality

So what does Lewis think of this immoralism? To quote Trumpkin: "It's all bilge and beanstalks" (PC, Chapter 11, p. 383). Truth is objective, according to Jack (as Clive Staples Lewis insisted on being called from the age of four), and is impervious to our attempts to diddle with it. Ditto for morality. For Lewis, a moral realist, moral laws, like the Golden Rule, are real facts about the world, like gravity.[16] In *God in the Dock*,[17] Lewis agrees with Nietzsche about our *wanting* to be stronger and smarter; but Lewis believes this desire is bad and false. He is convinced that there are such things as goodness and truth.

The immoralist's ethic is impossible to believe in consistently. Although Andrew thinks Jadis is a "dem fine woman" (MN, Chapter 6, p. 49), he constantly complains about her haughty treatment of him. He thinks that it's unfair of her to treat him, a fellow magician, like a slave, and meekly protests her "regrettable violence" in flinging Aunt Letty across the room (MN, Chapter 7, p. 52). Yet on Andrew's own principles, Jadis is exempt from ordinary rules of morality, and so she is not treating him or Aunt Letty unfairly.

Look: say you're a student who has worked hard on a paper and it's really good. You're shocked when you get the paper back with a big fat red "F." The professor says she knows you deserve an "A", but she's giving you the "F" for her own purposes and she has the power to do so. If you challenge the grade, she'll get you kicked out of school. A believer in Uncle Andrew's brand of "clever-people-are-exempt-from-ordinary-moral-rules" ethics wouldn't be able to say to the teacher (either politely or in Howard Sternese) that what she's doing is unfair.

---

[15] C.S. Lewis, *Letters to Malcolm: Chiefly on Prayer* (New York: Harcourt, 1964), p. 76.

[16] Lewis, *Mere Christianity*, p. 20.

[17] Lewis, *God in the Dock*, p. 87.

Moreover, who's to say who's a Master and who isn't? It's human nature for people to think that they're better than they are. "Since most men, as Aristotle observed, do not like to be merely equal with all other men, we find all sorts of people building themselves into groups within which they can feel superior to the mass: little unofficial, self-appointed aristocracies."[18] Uncle Andrew is a prime example. Although he thinks of himself as a towering brainiac, even the children can see that he is a vain, cowardly egotist, blind to even obvious truths. Digory sees that all Uncle Andrew's grand words mean is that "he thinks he can do anything he likes to get anything he wants" (MN, Chapter 2, p. 20). Later in *The Magician's Nephew*, Aslan chooses Frank the Cabby as King of Narnia *because* he's humble and doesn't have a false sense of his own merits.

For Lewis, it's impossible to believe that morality applies to some people but not others. What Lewis calls Natural Law, or "the Tao," is simple and obvious to virtually everyone.[19] However tempting it might be to deny these rules, we continually make clear through our language and our behavior that we accept them as true in an objective sense. To go on to claim that other basic principles are groundless or only relatively true is arbitrary. One cannot pick and choose, for moral laws are part of reality.[20]

Why suppose that superior power or intelligence confers a right to dominate? Although Lewis believes strongly in a divinely ordained hierarchy of creatures,[21] he denies that superiority implies a right of the strong to dominate or exploit the weak.

---

[18] C.S. Lewis, *The World's Last Night and Other Essays* (New York: Harcourt Brace, 1952), p. 41.

[19] Lewis, *Mere Christianity*, p. 5; *The Abolition of Man*, p. 52. Lewis admits that "you might find an odd individual here and there" who doesn't know some elementary moral principle, "just as you find a few people who are colourblind or have no ear for a tune" (*Mere Christianity*, p. 5).

[20] Lewis, *The Abolition of Man*, pp. 54–55; "The Poison of Subjectivism," p. 77. A similar point is made in Lewis's science fiction novel *Out of the Silent Planet* (New York: Macmillan, 1965 [1938]), when the villainous Weston asserts the right to exterminate all Martians based on loyalty to humankind and "the right of the higher over the lower." To this the angelic Oyarsa reply that there are "laws of pity and straight dealing and shame and the like" (p. 138) that all rational creatures know, and that Weston is arbitrarily treating one of these laws—love of kindred—as the be-all and end-all of morality.

Note Lewis's condemnation of slavery (VDT, Chapter 4, p. 451), his lampooning of demeaning caste distinctions in Calormene society ("Way, way, way! Way for the Tarkheena Lasaraleen!") (HHB, Chapter 7, p. 249), and Aslan's command to the Talking Beasts to cherish and treat all lesser animals gently (MN, Chapter, 10, p. 71).

For Lewis, all rational creatures are "free subjects" (MN, Chapter 12, p. 83) and have inherent value that even self-professed "superiors" are bound to respect. In fact, power and authority, far from amounting to a "Get Out of Morality Free" card, imposes additional burdens and responsibilities on their possessors. In *The Horse and His Boy* King Lune explains to Cor that being a king means "to be first in every desperate attack and last in every desperate retreat, and where there's hunger in the land . . . to wear finer clothes and laugh louder over a scantier meal than any man in your land" (HHB, Chapter 15, p. 310; see also MN, Chapter 11, p. 82). In Narnia, as in our world, "to whom much is given, much will be required" (Luke 12:48), and "he who would be first must be last" (Mark 9:35).

Why Can't We Be Friends?

"God is dead," Nietzsche declared, having been killed by our modern ideas. And it's divine genocide we're talking here: Nietzsche's character Zarathustra says that "dead are all gods."[22] Lewis could partly agree: *almost* all the gods are dead: there's just one. And certainly Lewis, like Nietzsche, acknowledges the importance of the will; Lewis just thinks that nature as well as will matters, and that there is more to the will than the will to power. Also, although Lewis can't agree with Nietzsche that *all* there is to a moral claim is what it tells us about the one who makes it,[23] he can, like Nietzsche, be worried about the ulterior motives of the watchful dragons of morality.[24]

---

[21] See Gilbert Meilaender, *The Taste for the Other: The Social and Ethical Thought of C.S. Lewis* (Grand Rapids: Eerdmans, 1978), pp. 70–84, 145–159.

[22] Friedrich Nietzsche, *Thus Spoke Zarathustra*, in *The Portable Nietzsche*, p. 191.

[23] Nietzsche, *Beyond Good and Evil* (Kaufmann translation), section 187.

[24] Blessings of Aslan on Gregory Bassham and Paul Ford, author of *Companion to Narnia*, for their help.

11
Narnia and the Moral Imagination

GAYNE J. ANACKER

The Chronicles of Narnia are loved for many reasons, but one of the most significant is surely their moral resonance. Readers uniformly *love* Lucy for her honesty and transparent integrity, *pity* Puzzle the donkey for his self-deprecating gullibility, *loathe* the White Witch for the purity of her evil, and *admire* the courage and loyalty of Reepicheep. In these memorable characters, readers come to recognize right and wrong, good and bad. They discover compelling role models and their opposites. They see the consequences of good and bad decisions. And they palpably experience both excellent as well as deeply flawed lives in their full texture and extension. In short, *The Chronicles of Narnia* profoundly engage the moral imagination.

What is moral imagination? First consider its absence. In our everyday lives, each of us is caught up in coping with the day-to-day stream of events. In our routines for handling life, the perspectives that we inhabit fill our fields of vision. Under these circumstances, it is difficult to take a fresh look at ourselves, our nation, and our world.

Moral imagination is the ability to consider our decisions, our values, and our lives from fresh and different moral perspectives.[1] These fresh perspectives make it easier to make impor-

---

[1] Similar to the definition found in Patricia H. Werhane, *Moral Imagination and Management Decision-Making* (New York: Oxford University Press, 1999), p. 5.

tant choices and changes that we might not have made if we had remained fixed in our old mental ruts.

Moral imagination can be excited in countless ways. A daydream inspired by a beautiful sight can stir us to imagine the moral fabric of our lives differently and (one hopes) for the better. A tragic accident, a song, a profound loss, a sermon (good or bad!), a child's look—all of these could be catalysts for a personal reconsideration that takes on genuine moral significance.

The Call of Stories

Stories can powerfully contribute to our moral development. It was Plato, long ago in the *Republic*, who urged that education centrally incorporate the recitation of stories (the *right kind* of stories, of course) as a means of developing the desired sort of citizen for the ideal society he envisioned.[2] In recent years, psychiatrist Robert Coles, philosopher Alasdair MacIntyre, and educator William Bennett have strongly re-affirmed the importance of stories in shaping moral character.[3]

Lewis also recognized the importance of stories in the development of children. He saw clearly how an effective story is bracketed by imagination. On the author's side, of course, a good story requires a lively imagination in the creative process. But in Lewis's case, that imagination was harnessed for a purpose, and that purpose concerned the imagination of *the reader*. In a letter written late in his life, he says that it was "the imaginative man" in him that led him "to write the series of Narnian stories for children . . . because the fairy-tale was the *genre* best fitted for what I wanted to say."[4] And his purpose in writing the Narnia stories went far beyond merely creating delightful tales. As he said to George Sayer, his former student and long-time friend, his purpose was to "make it easier for children to accept Christianity when they met it later in life. . . . 'I am aiming at a

---

[2] Plato, *Republic*, 377a–b, 378d–e.
[3] See Robert Coles, *The Call of Stories: Teaching and the Moral Imagination* (Boston: Houghton Mifflin, 1989); Alasdair MacIntyre, *After Virtue: A Study in Moral Theory*, second edition (Notre Dame: University of Notre Dame Press, 1984), Chapter 15; William J. Bennett, *The Book of Virtues* (New York: Simon and Schuster, 1983).
[4] *Letters of C.S. Lewis*, revised and enlarged edition, edited by Walter Hooper (New York: Harcourt Brace, 1988), p. 444.

sort of pre-baptism of the imagination.'"[5] This deep function of imagination partly explains what Lewis meant when he said that "reason is the natural organ of truth, but imagination is the organ of meaning."[6] Imagination does not tell you *what* is true, but it shows you the *real significance and profound implications* of truth. We see this crucial role of imagination played out on every page of the Narnia stories.

Character Types in the Narnia Stories

Stories grab our attention because they are about something that we all find terribly interesting—life: meaning and purpose, how to live, how not to live, how to handle success or failure, what good and bad people look like, and so on. Stories connect us to life viscerally. Whether fiction or non-fiction, stories are real. Gripping and moving stories can be built on almost any facet of life—ambitions, ultimate commitments, fears, important events, passions, hopes, loves, elemental instincts, deep longings—anything that gets deeply at important elements of life.

So how do the Narnia stories provoke moral imagination? Lewis's main device is showing us how certain characters live. It is through seeing them live their lives that our own moral imagination is activated. We can see this by reviewing three broad, morally significant character types found in the Narnia stories:

Type 1: Flawed character repents and overcomes (Examples: Edmund, Eustace, Bree, Jill, and Aravis)

Type 2: Essentially good character endures testings and trials, and overcomes (Examples: Lucy, Peter, Caspian, Tirian, and Polly)

Type 3: Essentially fatally flawed character (Examples: Uncle Andrew, Shift, Rabadash, Jadis, and the Queen of Underworld)

---

[5] George Sayer, *Jack: A Life of C.S Lewis* (Wheaton: Crossway, 1994), p. 318.
[6] C.S. Lewis, "Bluspels and Flalansferes: A Semantic Nightmare," in *Selected Literary Essays*, edited by Walter Hooper (London: Cambridge University Press, 1969), p. 265.

First consider Type 1 characters like Edmund and Eustace. What do we see when we observe their lives? We see how their drives and desires lead them into wrongdoing. We see how their evildoing hurts themselves as well as others. We see how those who manipulate them to do wrong care nothing for them and use them as tools. We see how their wrongdoing ramifies into disastrous chains of events and destroys genuine community among friends and loved ones. We feel the personal hurt of the wrongdoer. We sense the shame and the loneliness of being outside the company of those committed to the good. We sense the longing for wholeness and for release from the burden of having acted shamefully. We feel their sense of personal disaster as they are confronted by one who is wholly good, and wholly for the good—the very being to whom all is owed, and against whom is their real offense. We feel their flood of relief and joy when they realize that the burden of their wrongdoing is not just lifted, but eliminated. We feel the surge of new life and hope as they realize that their lives are not over, but instead have just begun. We feel their gratefulness and sense of renewal as they understand that their new life will be lived to real, satisfying purpose. We feel their joy and happiness as they enter fully into loving relationships with others who serve the good.

I have spent time, here, providing a detailed analysis of the full experience of moral conversion because this experience is at the heart of what Lewis is about in these stories. It is because we feel these moral sentiments with the characters that these stories can have a profound impact on us. We identify with the characters, and their moral development becomes a pattern for our own.

Our identification with Type 1 characters begins with our relating viscerally with the roots of their wrongdoing. Edmund's overpowering desire for Turkish Delight is ours. (And of course we are not just talking about liking candy. We are talking about permitting a desire to overwhelm our commitment to truth, to integrity, and to those we love.) The sense of self-importance Edmund derives from being closely connected to the powerful White Witch is something we know too well. Edmund also enjoys a sense of power through his ability to wound his sister Lucy, and that too is something that we know first-hand in ourselves. Lewis also knows that we are ashamed of these things in ourselves, just as Edmund came to be ashamed, and he knows that we need relief from that shame. The story thus becomes a vehicle for seeking, or re-living, atonement for not only the wrongful deeds we have committed, but more importantly for the self-worship that is at the core of flawed character.

Now let's briefly look at Type 2 characters such as Lucy and Caspian. These are inherently more sympathetic figures, primarily because they are firmly committed to the good, rather than to some extent resisting it. Further, because they are far less self-absorbed than the Type 1 characters, and more resolute against temptation to do wrong, they avoid the fundamental errors that lead to the disasters that befall the Type 1 characters. Lucy, the paradigm for Type 2 characters, deeply loves Aslan and is always terribly eager to see him and enjoy his presence. Because she is leaning forward spiritually, she is the one to whom Aslan grants special communion, and she is the one to whom Aslan first appears in *Prince Caspian.*

Because the Type 2 characters are essentially good people who are generally on the right side of things, we readily like and identify with them. The payoff of this in terms of the moral imagination comes when these essentially good people endure trials and testings.

For example, in *Prince Caspian* Lucy catches a glimpse of Aslan and comes to believe that he wants her and her companions to follow him, but the others don't believe her. Her faith in Aslan is being tested. Will she believe and proclaim that "Aslan is here," even though she is initially belittled and pitied for her "wishful thinking"? She does indeed persevere in her faith, and two good things happen. First, she is rewarded with an ecstatic experience with Aslan among the dancing trees, a picture of joyous spiritual communion. Second, her persistence in following Aslan results in their safely finding their way to Caspian, a picture that perseverance in faith is the only way to find one's true path in life.

In *The Voyage of the "Dawn Treader,"* King Caspian faces a similar spiritual testing. Tempted by a vision of limitless wealth, Caspian claims Goldwater Island as a Narnian possession and threatens to kill anyone who reveals the island's existence. Only Lucy's reproach and a sudden epiphany of Aslan in his glory restores him to his senses (VDT, Chapter 8, p. 484).

Because we identify with Lucy, Caspian, and the other Type 2 characters, we go through their temptations with them, and this causes us to reflect on our own times of testing. As Lucy and Caspian prevailed by doing the right thing, we are encouraged and inspired to prevail ourselves.

Lewis, of course, never intended us to identify with Type 3 characters such as Uncle Andrew or Rabadash. They are present in the Narnia stories because, through the vehicle of fantasy literature, Lewis is telling the truth, and the truth is that there are all too many people like these. Further, their presence is needed in the story for dramatic balance against characters of Type 1 and Type 2. But there is also a *moral* reason for showing us Type 3 characters. We find them fascinating in a way, and we want to understand what makes them so bad. And in examining them through these stories, we can see most clearly the smallness and malignancy of self-absorption. A person devoting his full attention only to himself, seeking only his own interest, is shown to be exceedingly small and crabbed. He's like someone who sneaks into a circus and spends his time grubbing about in the sawdust for loose change under the stands, all the while ignoring the amazing acrobatic feats and exotic sights that surround him. We come to see this self-absorption as a deformity, something that produces a person who is well short of fully human. And since his limitless will is focused upon only himself (an increasingly finite object), the deformity of the soul grows greater and greater, damaging or destroying whatever is near it. We see this smallness and deformity particularly in Uncle Andrew and Shift the Ape. And while we recoil from it, we also are drawn into the moral questions that Lewis intends us to ask ourselves. Am I as self-absorbed as these? Do I look as ugly and small as they? Wouldn't I rather be more like Peter and Caspian? What is it about Peter, Caspian, and Reepicheep that make them so much more attractive than Rabadash, Uncle Andrew, or Shift? These are healthy questions that can lead us toward a fuller and better life.

Virtues, Worship, and Nobility

In addition to the three types of characters just examined, there are many other features in the Narnia stories that bear upon the moral imagination. Let's look at three. First, virtues and vices. The former: self-discipline, compassion, honesty, responsibility, courage, friendship, and loyalty, among others. The latter: lazi-

ness, irresponsibility, cowardice, dishonesty, and so on. A virtue
is a habit of life that makes you *better off* as a person than you
would be if you lacked that habit. And a vice is a habit of life
that makes you *worse off* than if you do not have it. It's clear,
then, that much of what I have said concerning the three types
of characters has a great deal to do with virtues and vices.
Character is the totality of virtues and vices lived out through
one's lifetime. Thus, when we cultivate virtues and combat vices
in our lives, we're engaging in the personal work of attempting
to become more complete, successful, whole persons.
Teachings on virtues and vices are prominently found throughout the Jewish and Christian scriptures. Indeed, the study of
virtues and vices constitutes a great portion of what counts as
morality in most major traditional cultures. Other chapters in
this volume deal centrally with virtues and vices in the Narnia
stories, and so I will not say more about them at this point.

Two additional themes do require comment, however. First,
a truly lovely feature of the Narnia stories is their portrayal of
what I will call *worship*. How can this be, if there is never any
mention of churches, priests, or prayers? The Narnia stories drip
with it, even though it goes in other guise. What I mean by
"worship" in the Narnia stories involves the following elements:
(a) an awareness of another dimension from which this world
derives its existence and its nature; (b) an awareness of a
supreme being who reigns in this other dimension, and who is
to reign in this world as well; (c) a longing for communion with
that supreme being; (d) paying close attention to the expressed
desires and purposes of the supreme being, and letting his
agenda become one's own.

Once the Pevensie children have experienced Narnia, they
long to go back, and speak of it often. Aslan becomes the dominant presence in their daily lives. Lucy is most happy when she
is hugging Aslan and burying her face in his mane. The children
treasure the times when Aslan romped with them in the
meadow. Aslan knows them better than they do themselves, and
they do best when they heed his words. Reepicheep, on board
the *Dawn Treader*, "spends his days far forward, gazing always
to the east."[7] In *The Silver Chair*, Eustace leads Jill in "calling on"

---

[7] Paul F. Ford, *Companion to Narnia* (New York: Macmillan, 1986), p. 346.

Aslan, and they are heard. Aslan then commands them to learn and remember the four Signs that will keep them focused in their mission to save Prince Rilian. When they forget the Signs, they lose their way. Finally, in the concluding scenes of *The Last Battle*, we see that when we pass through the Stable Door into the sunlight, we will be in Aslan's presence, and we will be eager to move "further up and further in."

It's fair to say that the main purpose of the Narnia stories is to draw us into devotion to God, into ordering our lives around his reality. The stories do this by imaginatively reminding us that this world of our everyday lives is not ultimate reality, but only a shadow. The enchantment of the stories helps us see that worship of God is the essence of goodness. And here is where morality and faith come together completely. If there is a God, then worshipping him must be our most important obligation. Everything else is secondary to that.

One final Narnian path to moral imagination deserves discussion. It is difficult to ignore the fact that Narnia is full of kings and queens, princes and princesses (or at least Tarkheenas), knights, lords, and other "nobility." This is reminiscent of the regal and courtly setting of many of the fairy tales of our culture, and represents Lewis's desire to give the Narnia stories that same flavor. The Pevensie children become kings and queens, with Peter the eldest becoming High King. Further, many of the other earthly heroes in Narnia—Eustace, Digory, Polly, Jill—although never coming to be made kings or queens, clearly become ennobled as a result of their triumph in their stories. For Lewis, nobility is extremely important.

Nobility is a tricky topic in our world today, and we are inclined to handle it gingerly. It goes without saying, of course, that Lewis in no way endorses the rapacious egomania or snobby hauteur of so many rulers and aristocrats throughout history. Indeed, Lewis's insistence on nobility, like Tolkien's, can be seen as an attempt to rescue and teach the true notion of nobility.

In the Narnia stories, Lewis's handling of the concept of nobility reveals that those who are noble can be divided into two basic categories: those who deserve their noble distinction and those who don't. The paradigm of the unworthy noble is Miraz, the usurping King of Narnia in *Prince Caspian*. Devious and vicious, he stole the throne by murdering his brother, the true King, and retained his control through lies, deception, and corruption. Miraz receives the honor of being King, but he is not worthy of that honor, and he ultimately pays for his evil ways. Other examples of unworthy nobles include the Tisroc of Calormen and his son, Rabadash in *The Horse and His Boy*, the Governor of Doorn in *The Voyage of the "Dawn Treader,"* and the King of the giants of Harfang in *The Silver Chair*.

Worthy nobility, on the other hand, we see most clearly in Peter, High King of Narnia, who deserves the honor and respect he receives. Why? The most important feature of Peter's nobility is the spiritual dimension. He himself is subject to Aslan, he honors and reveres Aslan, and he rules as Aslan's representative. Thus, Peter's true nobility begins in proper worship. In addition, Peter is honest, fair, respectful, courageous, self-sacrificing, friendly, and loyal. In short, Peter is a truly good man, one whom others find it easy to respect and follow. And the same is true of the other truly deserving nobility: Caspian, Tirian, Rilian, King Frank, Shasta, Aravis, the other Pevensies, and others.

Lewis offers these worthy nobles as role models, and they model the Christian teaching that all who follow Christ have a noble calling. Followers of Christ become children of the most high God, and are thus his royal representatives and ambassadors in the world. Those who live in the light of this noble calling are necessarily changed by it. So it is no accident that Lewis shows his "ennobled" earthly heroes as living and acting nobly upon their return to this world. The Pevensies are changed and empowered, as are Eustace and Jill. The message is unmistakable. Re-orienting our lives toward Aslan in Narnia empowers us to live nobly and virtuously in this world.

In addition to the sheer attractiveness of truly good people living well, Lewis's hook into the moral imagination with regard to nobility centers on courtly respect and deference. Throughout the Narnia stories, we see very good people (and very good Animals) offering respect, service, and obedience to their worthy kings, and we understand intuitively that it is right and just. But now the questions arise *in us* as we read. Am I the sort of person who truly deserves the respect of my children? Do I have the genuine respect of my spouse, my friends, my colleagues, those in my workplace or church? Am I a truly good person whom others find it easy to respect and follow? How could I live better to more truly deserve respect and true honor? How do I become truly *noble*?

Writing and Moral Imagination

Specific features of the Narnia stories make it possible for them to provoke moral imagination. The first is length. The stories needed to be long enough to allow readers to experience the numerous elements of the process of moral development: the source of wrongdoing within people's characters; the seductive attractiveness of evil; the anatomy of temptation; the various unhappy consequences of wrongdoing; the need to re-organize one's life; the commitment to do so; the happier consequences of doing so. The portrayal of comprehensive moral development takes time, and it is a mark of Lewis's genius that he keeps us and our children captivated throughout the portrayal.

A second important feature is the texture of Narnia. It is another mark of Lewis's genius that he created a fantasy world that "feels" real, even more than real. Lewis achieves this in part through the rich texture of the stories. Lewis's depiction of Narnia is so complete, detailed, and delightful that we want to be there, to be part of it. The power of Narnia's attractiveness conditions us for the spiritual and moral challenge contained in the stories.

Third, much of the moral and spiritual power of the Narnia stories resides in the fascinating bivalence of Narnia's being very different from our world, yet morally and spiritually very similar. This complementary *different-yet-like* feature of really good fantasy literature is a big reason why the Narnia stories are able to slip past what Lewis calls the "watchful dragons" of our self-consciousness and strike to the heart of who we are and how we live. When we think theoretically and abstractly about morality and spirituality, our rational consciousness is prepared with the standard intellectual cautions, qualifications, questions, and challenges. But our transport to Narnia disarms our intellectual sentinels (the watchful dragons) and permits the reality of the stories to speak directly to our hearts.

Ethics and Moral Imagination

For at least half a century, philosophers have been aware that there is a crisis in ethics. The crisis has been in the making since the beginnings of the Modern period about three centuries ago. At that point, philosophers began presenting ethical theories that suppose that our main concern in morality is with *actions*: what actions are right, what actions are wrong, and what general principles help us to discern the difference? Many action-based theories have been proposed over these centuries, but none of them has won anything like general acceptance. The moral vacuum created by the successive failures of these ethical theories has created the space in which moral relativism, moral skepticism, and other intellectual diseases have flourished. In the past three decades or so, philosophers have begun to rethink the idea that morality is all about actions. Many philosophers have returned to the moral approach of the ancient and medieval eras, when it was assumed that ethics is centrally concerned with *character and virtue*, not specific actions or duties. This approach to morality is known as *virtue ethics*, and one of the most remarkable developments in recent philosophy is the resurgence of this classic approach to morality.

What role does Narnia play in this important philosophical debate? Lewis's Narnia stories are very effective in helping us (and our children) pay attention to our own moral growth. The central focus of the stories is upon who we are as persons, what we value, who we admire and wish to emulate, what are our habits of response to difficult situations, what sort of life we are leading, what sort of life we wish to lead. All of this is far richer and more subtle than to ask, "Is action X right or wrong?" To be sure, questions of that sort are entirely fair, and they can be answered, but it is a matter of priority and emphasis. Do we focus primarily on *actions*, or on the *character* of the person who acts? Certainly both must be part of an adequate and complete moral theory, but significant moral re-orientation or moral development happens not because a single act or even series of actions is viewed as right or wrong, but because a way of living is recognized as good or bad, healthy or destructive. Morality must be viewed in the context of one's whole life, one's character, all of one's being. The effectiveness of moral imagination, especially as seen in Lewis's Narnia stories, argues strongly that virtue ethics is the proper framework in which to do ethical theory.

A second philosophical implication follows from the effectiveness of moral imagination stimulated by literature such as the Narnia stories. As suggested just above, there is within the world of ideas great concern about how morality is to be understood and justified. And lurking not far behind this concern is a further anxious question: If no ethical theory clearly commands widespread rational respect, how can there be any genuine meaning to terms such as "right," "wrong," "good," and "bad?" Does not morality then simply reduce to what each of us *believes* to be right and wrong? But if so, are there not just as many rights and wrongs as there are persons who have beliefs? In short, does not the chaos of contemporary ethical theory force us to moral relativism or subjectivism?

There are many powerful arguments against moral relativism and moral subjectivism, but for our purposes here, consider just the basic mistake that is being made by those who support relativism or subjectivism in this way. In effect, they are saying that because the theorists cannot reach consensus among themselves on ethical theory, if follows that there can be no objective morality. This is profoundly misguided. It would be like saying that, prior to Newton, since the physicists could not agree on a rationally provable theory of universal gravitation, engineers could not build buildings or bridges. This would force the conclusion that the ongoing contention among the ethical theorists at the theoretical level somehow implies that I cannot recognize that Miraz is evil.

But of course this is absurd. The Narnia stories, along with vast treasures of wisdom literature of all kinds from all lands, count as solid evidence that our understanding of moral goodness does not rely upon the agreement of ethical theorists. The fact that the exercise of moral imagination is effective in leading people to change their lives for the better, even given wide disagreement at the theoretical level, strongly suggests that practical morality—what it means to be a good and excellent person, what it means to live well—is something that is native to us as human beings, and is understood intuitively, at least in great measure, if not always. And although there is wide disagreement within societies as well as between societies on many practical matters of morality, Lewis himself has shown, in his book *The Abolition of Man*, that the moral content of major religious and cultural traditions has far more in common than not.[8] Indeed, far from ethical theory justifying practical morality, it is the other

---

[8] C.S. Lewis, *The Abolition of Man* (New York: Macmillan, 1965), pp. 95–121.

way around. An ethical theory has significance only to the extent that it satisfactorily accounts for what we know to be right and good about how to live.

If a critic were to suggest that we suspend our judgments about morality until the ethical theorists come to consensus, a common sense argument can be made in reply. The critic has the job of convincing us that something that *seems* an ordinary and essential part of our daily lives (moral choice) is so misguided as to require suspension of judgment. This burden of proof is not light. It is very heavy. Here is the standard: the reasons provided by the critic have to be more sure or certain to us than are the moral judgments he wants us to suspend. It is a matter of rational balance. If our practice of moral judgment seems reasonable and, for practical purposes, *necessary for life*, we should not surrender the practice unless the reasons against the practice are rationally more compelling that the moral practice itself. To give up something rational because of something less rational would be to turn rationality on its head. But no argument has ever been presented (to my knowledge) that would convince me that I am making some kind of mistake in judging that Miraz is an evil man. What could possibly be clearer?

Lewis expects that we will be attracted to the goodness of Lucy, impressed by the nobility of Peter, thrilled with the courage and honor of Reepicheep, and repelled by the self-absorption of Uncle Andrew. And he knows that our encounter with these characters will draw us into significant reflection upon our own lives. In this way, as Gilbert Meilaender remarks, the *Chronicles* "serve to enhance moral education, to build character."[9] Few works of fiction have done it better.[10]

---

[9] Quoted in Ford, *Companion to Narnia*, p. xxxi.

[10] I have the great fortune of living with two Narnia experts, my lovely wife, Karen Lee Anacker, and my lovely daughter, Rachael Lee Anacker. I am grateful to both for their suggestions and corrections.

12

Beasts, Heroes, and Monsters: Configuring the Moral Imaginary

WENDY C. HAMBLET

C.S. Lewis's *Chronicles of Narnia* present a fascinating narrative site for an examination of the effects of children's stories on young audiences. The tales that we share with our youngsters not only reflect our deepest cultural and ethical traditions; they also feed the mythic imaginations of the young, and help to shape their value systems in ways that remain doggedly faithful to the traditional beliefs of the group. Children's stories provide the valiant models for children's emulation, and the frightful monsters they must learn to dread and shun. The battles and triumphs of fantasy heroes teach the most esteemed standards of conduct, the grand ideals of heroic souls, and the glories of honorable enterprise.

Even noble failures set examples for emulation. In the tradition of the Homeric epic, the timeless tales of adventures sketch the triumphs and losses of the noblest actors and communicate to their audiences that the short-lived glory of the war-torn hero is preferable to the long-lived mediocrity of the commoner. On the other hand, the wickedness of the villain provides examples of monstrous behaviors to be recognized as vicious and appropriately avoided. For many people, the "identity politics" that will determine what kind of human being they will become is initiated in the nursery, under the thrall of the earliest fantasy tales.

Philosopher Alasdair MacIntyre argues that the narratives shared within a culture wield such prodigious power that they compose "intellectual prophecies" that eventually come to fulfillment as "social performance."[1] This is plausible with respect to broadly accepted cultural myths and ethnic folklore, which often claim an exclusive status as "the people's story" or as "human truth," and these pseudo-histories are often deemed more reliable than the political memories of states, or the entries in history books. The latter are invariably decided by the victors of history's battles, whereas "people's histories" are emblazoned in the mythic narratives of the culture.

We rarely entertain the possibility, however, that children's fiction and fantasy stories may wield an equally persuasive power over social attitudes and performance. Fairy tales hardly seem to be the stuff from which cultural truth is crafted. Monsters, elves, and ogres are clearly creatures of fiction, so it seems unlikely that tales involving them will be mistaken for "truth." However, it is precisely because children's tales are not served up as serious, that they hide their persuasive power behind a mask of playful pretense. Moreover, since they are taken up in fun, and the characters are utterly fantastic and their valiant deeds are quite fictitious, the "truths" communicated in childhood tales may retain a power over the mythic imaginations of the young. The subliminal messages of fantasy tales can seep down into the psyches of young listeners and eventually lodge in the truth assumptions of the culture. Their hidden "truths" may persist in having a direct influence on the beliefs and behaviors adopted by the society.

One might argue that, in modernity, with its scientific, secularized worldview, there is a clear distinction between the "certain" data (*logos*) of empirical experience and the irrational claims of fantasy stories (*mythos*), so that the risk of blurring the boundaries between the two is no longer a realistic danger. Critics may argue that the "mythic"—with its larger than life symbols, its fantastic imagery and its paradoxical logic—no longer has the power to control the imaginations of reasonable people.

However, as philosopher Dudley Young has argued, the seductive power of narrative is actually heightened precisely *because* the emotive ("mythic") aspect of existence is largely missing from the modern world. In *Origins of the Sacred*, Young

---

[1] Alasdair MacIntyre, *After Virtue* (Notre Dame: University of Notre Dame Press, 1984), p. 85.

cites this lost dimension of reality (historically nourished and satisfied by religious festival, ritual frenzy, and celebratory feast) as a dangerous impoverishment of the emotional depth and quality of human existence. That impoverishment, claims Young, makes people perilously susceptible to the seductive manipulation of demagogues.[2]

The phenomenon of the Hitler Youth provides a frightening example of "mythically impoverished" folk swept away in a frenzied collective madness by the words of a charismatic leader. Even the philosopher Martin Heidegger, so sensitive to the morally precarious arrogances of traditional metaphysics, was, in the early days of National Socialism, seduced by Hitler's mythic glorifications of Germany's past and his promises of its grand destiny (themselves grounded in metaphysical assumptions). Under this seduction, Heidegger could interpret the early excesses of the Fuehrer (for instance, banning his Jewish colleagues from university teaching) as reasonable within the "superior wisdom" of the "god [that might] save us now" from a decadent modernity.[3]

Veiled and hazy, the symbols and logic that confront the reader—especially the young reader—in fantasy tales can prove powerful indeed, especially in modern times with the impoverishment of people's cultural, familial and spiritual worlds. The "truths" communicated in children's tales can remain insidiously functional, determining thoughts and behaviors in their audience. At best, the borders between reality and fiction remain blurred for most young children. Even grown-ups may be incapable of raising a conscious, rational challenge to the moral and political messages hidden deeply between the lines of seductive tales they read.

For these reasons, as Plato claims, it is crucial that we take great care with the tales we tell our young. Convinced that gymnastics, melodic harmonies, and the "music" of fictional tales can

---

[2] Dudley Young, *Origins of the Sacred* (London: Little, Brown, 1991), Introduction.

[3] Heidegger rages against the impoverishment of modernity in *An Introduction to Metaphysics* when he states, "The spiritual decline of the earth is so far advanced that the nations are in danger of losing the last bit of spiritual energy that makes it possible to see the decline . . . and to appraise it as such" (London: Yale Press, 1959, pp. 37–38).

mold a person's character, Plato censors even the nursery stories in his city in *logos* described in the *Republic*.[4] The younger one is, the slimmer the gap in one's mind between truth and fiction, the more easily one can mistake the illusory for the real. And the more this happens, the more power these stories can hold over one's ideas and behaviors.

The Modern Framework for Truth and Ethics

The Western world as we know it began with our ancient Greek ancestors. Our ancestors were culturally born when Indo-European warrior tribes, like marauding Calormenes, descended from the Russian steppes, slaughtered their way across the continent and settled around the Mediterranean Sea. Hyper-masculine and male-sky-god worshipping, these warrior heroes butchered those in their path. But, in time, they came to settle down and assimilate the earthy, mother-goddess-worshipping indigenous folk of the sea lands. Together, the two combined to form a new culture—one that worshipped war but also wisdom, that celebrated the war god (Ares) but also had a special relationship with the god of love (Eros) and hailed the goddess of the hearth (Hestia), who defended families from harm.

The ancient Greeks were thus a far more complex people than is generally acknowledged. They settled in the mountain valleys and worked the soil, but worshipped the heavens and loved the seas. They elevated their warrior-heroes but also revered their philosophers and their statesmen. Like Reepicheep, they proved their valor in daring sea adventures and in contests of battle. But they also advanced the arts and the sciences and developed the first universities. Our ancestral culture celebrated the excellences of spirit that made for colonial adventure and war. But they also prized other, more ethereal excellences; beauty, wisdom, temperance and justice served as the overriding "truths" of the ancient Greek world. *Hybris*—the overblown arrogant pride that was thought to be mercilessly punished by the gods—was regarded as the worst of human faults.

The special mixture of warrior and philosopher that composed the "best" of the ancient world is imaged in the patron

---

[4] This second city is generally translated "ideal city" but it would be more rightly interpreted as "the city [constructed] of ideas."

goddess of Athens, Athena, goddess of wisdom but also of war. It is also manifest in the ancient Greek worldview that understood the being of beings in terms of the delicate balance between opposing forces (*enantioi*) come together as a holistic, harmonious universe. In the ancient Greek view, the universe is coherent, cooperative, and purposeful. God or Nature (*physis*) is good, healing, and orderly.[5] In the ancient worldview, justice composes the inner balance that simultaneously guarantees the integrity of each individual thing and that thing's harmonious relations with reality as a whole.

In the seventeenth century, however, the humble and reverent ancient Greek metaphysics lost its grip to new, "modern" ideas. Philosopher René Descartes (1596–1650), widely considered the Father of Modernity, offered a new account of the nature of reality that diminished the significance of the material world and elevated human reason to divine heights. Descartes laid the framework for modern understandings of self and world that still rule in the West. In his *Discourse on Method* (1637), he sets forth the only correct method for investigating the nature of things: the brave adventurer into the unknown need only break complex problems down into smaller units until we arrive at the simplest truths, and then put these simple truths into order and link them to their natural consequences. Thus may all things be successfully probed, penetrated, ripped asunder, and reconstructed into clear and distinct ideas.

With Descartes, modern arrogances of knowledge replaced the ancient wisdom of humility. Gone are the gods from the liveliness of things; gone is the internal balance of nature, its inner justice, its seductive *telos*, its inherent healing properties. Gone is the mystery of Being and beings. Only the intrepid warrior-scientist remains to expose the naked secrets of nature in the marketplaces and battlefields of the world.

Narnia and Modern Militarism

At first glance, the symbols and imagery of the Narnia *Chronicles* follow a conservative pattern—a pattern now widely recognized as dangerous to our impressionable young, a pattern

---

[5] Plato, *Phaedrus*, 246a.

that fosters an ideology of war instead of ideals of justice and harmony. The characters of Narnia emerge in stark moral garb— good guys and bad guys, heroes and monsters. Uncomplicated heroes like Rilian and Tirian march fearlessly into danger— courageous, intrepid, undaunted by threat of death. Crusades are launched and battles are fought, good men (and bears, horses, and Centaurs) fall in noble defeat, and are mourned and celebrated by their survivors. Finally, victims are rescued, the wicked are expunged from a vulnerable world, and all is put right through moral action that finds its highest expression in the gallantries of war.

As in many fantasy tales, the ethic that undergirds the Narnia stories is openly militaristic. The virtues celebrated in the Narnia tales are those of the warrior—brazen courage, fortitude in bat- tle, (blind) obedience to the commander—rather than the bal- anced spectrum of inward excellences that Plato heralds as necessary to the life of virtue—temperance, justice, and courage under the yoke of a wise reason. Courage and perseverance against all odds drive the wearied king ever onwards in his quest to save his threatened world. The good powers are mostly powerful male images (from Aslan to the various kings of Narnia); the evil ones (for example, the swarthy Calormenes and the black dwarfs) tend to be menacing and dark. The old clichés (white is good; dark is evil) that drove modern imperialisms continues to hold sway in the *Chronicles*. Aslan, the ruling force of Narnia, symbolizing the ruling deity in the tales, is repeatedly said to be "not a tame lion" (LB, Chapter 2, pp. 677, 679; Chapter 3, p. 682; Chapter 7, p. 707). The very image of the lion signifies raw masculine power. The lion is lauded as King of the Jungle, nourished and served by his female counterpart in real jungles of the world.

Aslan represents the voice of reasoned goodness, yet his rules can also be troubling. Aslan declares that the animals and trees *with voices* are not to be harmed, while killing the voice- less creatures is acceptable (LB, Chapter 2, p. 677). This recon- firms an old political prejudice that has historically been rallied to elevate the interests of the home group over those of strangers and foreigners. It communicates that the members of the linguistic community—politically franchised, legitimate members of the dominant group—are "naturally" more worth-y than those that are linguistically alienated. The latter are excluded from the dominant discourse, silenced "in their very nature" by the ruling force that created them.

Aslan is also a transcendent ruler. Just as the god of the Judeo-Christian world does not intercede to prevent the sufferings and degradations of lands and peoples, Aslan is absent throughout most of the Narnia histories, retiring after a glorious creation spectacle and reappearing only sporadically until the end of decaying time. The god of Narnia does not linger within the things of creation but, as in modernity, stands over them as a distant figure of might in a universe that is power-driven and deeply hierarchical in its very nature.

Battles still decide the winners and the losers in the *Chronicles*, as in the imperialist era, and the battles are largely confrontations between conflicting truths. Wars decide what is true and who has moral entitlement to power, thus re-instituting the dangerous idea that might establishes right. Consistent with the most troubling ethnocentric adventurisms of the imperialistic era, the Narnia tales claim that it is knowledge that establishes moral legitimacy and rightful power. Roonwit the Centaur, the valiant servant of the king of Narnia, reminds us that a "noble death is a treasure which no one is too poor to buy" (LB, Chapter 8, p. 717). It is this belief that continues to motivate many a wide-eyed soldier to the frontlines of modern battles, as well as many a terrorist youth to strap explosives to his belly and walk into an innocent crowd.

Lewis versus Modern Militarism

On a closer reading, however, the *Chronicles* display many traits that work to undermine the militaristic ethic and to disarm the violence-legitimating features characteristic of many fairy and fantasy tales. Many of the characters—Aravis, Susan, Eustace, Edmund, Tumnus, Emeth and the duped animals in *The Last Battle*, to name only a few—are neither wholly good nor wholly evil. The clear white of goodness and dark of evil that are raised as paradigm images in *The Magician's Nephew* come to be complicated and undermined by the images of the White Witch and the Green Witch in other Narnia tales.

Moreover, the Narnia tales clearly condemn unjust and unnecessary violence. As his characterizations of Miraz, Jadis, Gumpas, the Green Witch, and the Calormenes illustrate,

Lewis is quick to condemn aggression and despotism as responsible for much of the evil in the world. Even the good King shares in the warrior's unfortunate tendency to grab too quickly for a weapon when feeling threatened (LB, Chapter 2, p. 680). Lewis demonstrates that heroes are very brave, but often foolishly so. He also shows how to redeem oneself from this flaw: when heroes are too quick with their swords, they must, as Tirian does in *The Last Battle*, bravely admit their error and accept the "justice of Aslan" for their misdeeds (LB, Chapter 3, p. 682).

Lewis does not condemn all violence in the *Chronicles*, however. He leaves room for notions of "righteous indignation" and "just war," as do most peace-loving philosophers. Where good cause can be shown for taking up the sword, one must not flinch at one's duty to protect the innocent and fight the good fight. The good violence of self-defense against the Calormenes, the just war of liberation against the White Witch, the slaying of the Green Witch, and the retributive violence against the bullies of Experiment House serve as examples of good violence that must be suffered if good ends are to be brought about.

Though the *Chronicles* may, on the surface, seem to serve the same god of war to which many a crusading epic ministers, Lewis punctuates the battles with moral struggles and refusals of violence. Many subtle moral messages against wanton violence, victimization, and unnecessary force are embedded in the tales. The complications he introduces in the characters and plotlines of the stories frustrate any facile moralizations about purely good or purely evil things and people. Moreover, the tales culminate in an unanticipated outcome so deep in its Platonic symbolism as to defy any simplistic either/or dichotomies.

The figure of Aslan serves as a paradigm, a ruling divine image of goodness. That image haunts every story, although Aslan himself comes and goes from the tales. His presence and absence could be argued to symbolize the various stages of religious belief and to reflect the historical waverings of human beings and their relations with the god-image throughout history. Now immanent, now transcendent, the god is present in people's lives and minds even in his absence from the current history. Ultimately, the disappearances of Aslan attest that, when the god is absent from his creation, little remains sacred. Life becomes cheap and humans fabricate their own gods and declare their own "goods" and values. In short, might becomes right in the absence of an overriding moral force. The treacheries of Shift, Ginger, and the Calormenes in *The Last Battle* provide a glaring demonstration that when the god is missing from the earth, the unscrupulous can co-opt the god's power and manipulate the trusting masses to fulfill their evil designs.

The *Chronicles* overturn another dangerous legacy of Western religion and politics. The myth of the primal fall from paradise, a myth common to almost every religious system, has supported a pervasive popular assumption that humans are fundamentally fallen, flawed, and decadent. This myth, I have argued elsewhere,[6] is responsible for a ubiquitous and lingering sense of guilt, loss and unworthiness that undermines a healthy worldview and positions people for resentment and violence. The conviction that human nature is fundamentally corrupt is a frequent underpinning of the ideology of *Realpolitik.* The former belief (that human nature is essentially corrupt) counsels violence against evil "others," while the latter belief (that all nations are pitted in a war of all against all) counsels war against other nations. Lewis re-appropriates the original goodness and innocence of the human world and undercuts the demoralizing effects of the "myth of the fall" by glorifying Adam and Eve as the venerated ancestors of the human world (LB, Chapter 16, pp. 164–65).

In addition, the *Chronicles* clearly expose the dangers of blind allegiance and the folly of trusting corrupt leaders. The political rhetoric that serves wicked leaders' designs is revealed as powerfully manipulative and seductively deceptive, even where clearly empirically false. For example, Queen Jadis tells Polly and Digory that, with a single word—"the Deplorable Word"—she wiped out all her subjects and destroyed their entire world. Lewis implies here that words in the mouths of the pow-

---

[6] Wendy C. Hamblet, *The Sacred Monstrous: A Reflection on Violence in Human Communities* (Lanham: Lexington, 2004), Chapter 4. Lewis himself accepted the traditional Christian doctrine of the Fall, though he emphasizes that the doctrine need not be understood in ways that conflict with modern scientific views of human origins. See Lewis, *The Problem of Pain* (San Francisco: HarperSanFrancisco, 2001), pp. 63–85.

erful can do great harm to innocent people. When the children, shocked, wonder aloud what sort of justice could permit innocent subjects to be killed by their own queen, the Queen responds: "Don't you understand? I was the Queen. They were all *my* people. What else were they there for but to do my will?" (MN, Chapter 5, p. 42).

From this declaration, the reader is shown the folly of trusting blindly in authority. All leaders must prove their worthiness to rule by promoting the common good. From the mouths of these innocents, who were trying to make sense of the world of power and politics, emerges the question that challenges the status quo of all power relations: do the powerful care about justice at all? Lewis urges the reader to ponder: Is the duty of the good statesman to serve as the caretaker of the flock, or are the powerful simply tyrants over the helpless masses?

The Queen, however, denies innocence a voice in political matters. She concludes the discussion by declaring, "I had forgotten that you are only a common boy. How should you understand reasons of State?" (MN, Chapter 5, p. 42). This pronouncement forces the reader to recall that the power elitisms that compose political hierarchies also determine *moral* classifications within the society. "Reasons of state" have always been cited by leaders to justify oppression. In the early centuries of the modern era, colonialism, imperialism, and the slaughter of hundreds of millions of innocent peoples was carried out in the name of god and country. The reader is made to recall that many of the evil designs of leaders have, historically, been cloaked in the secrecy and false legitimacy of "reasons of state." In the revealing light of hindsight, those historical "reasons of state" have proven as unjust and un*reason*able as those of the Evil Queen.

Humans need moral inspiration from on high, but human leaders can lead them far astray from justice and goodness and into the dark night of worldly battle. Just as the god of the Jews and the Christians and the Muslims has receded into the transcendent clouds in the modern era, so does Aslan fail to "turn up . . . nowadays" in Narnia to correct people's false assumptions and lead them aright (LB, Chapter 1, p. 674). As a result, the beasts among us get bad ideas. Leaders lead us along terrible paths. Lewis warns what fate will ensue when this happens: all worlds draw to an end as they decay.

"It's All in Plato"

Lewis employs Platonic images and themes throughout the *Chronicles*. Like Plato, he hopes to seduce the reader into a deeper analysis of the personages and events staged in the stories in order to lure the reader toward ethical reflection on established certainties. The allusions to Plato finally become explicit at the close of the *Chronicles*, where worlds are seen to be simply microcosmic stages on which we act out our living fantasies—caves within caves, worlds within worlds within worlds (LB, Chapter 16, p. 765). As in Plato's allegory of the cave, Lewis depicts the worlds of politics and economics as microcosmic worlds that emerge and disappear into forgotten histories. All too often, the "truths" we take for granted are false and dangerous ideologies of war and oppression, false images paraded by unscrupulous leaders before commoners who are mentally blinded by the ruling propaganda. Lewis, with his fantasy stories, may be likened to the enlightened Platonic philosopher who returns to the dark cave to dispel the false "truths" of evil politicians and to disseminate the changeless eternal truths hidden in the heavens.

Eternal truth is laid up in the heavens because wisdom and justice in their purest form do not fluctuate with the conveniences of worldly affairs or with the whims of evil leaders. Truth is the property of the gods alone, eternal, enduring, changeless. The sun knows when it is truly right to rise and set; the seasons can be counted upon to arrive at the right time and in the proper order. Stars never lie; men and beasts do (LB, Chapter 2, p. 677). The good is eternal, intangible and always beautiful; it cannot be replaced by the false "goods" of the cave.

In the *Chronicles*, Lewis presents a compelling critique of modernity. With fantastic characters and unlikely plots, he challenges the reader to meditate upon the dangerous militaristic traditions in the West and to confront the histories of violence perpetrated in the name of god and country. Warnings against the seductive words of unscrupulous leaders are emblazoned in the image of the devastated land of Charn. Worlds can be destroyed by a single deplorable word from a power-drunk ruler. A foreboding alarm sounds from the many dried-up pools of forgotten worlds that dot the Wood between the Worlds.

Lewis closes the many chapters of the many books chronicling the many adventures of children and beasts, kings and queens, Englanders and Narnians by illuminating the fundamental nature of the world in which these adventures had been played out. That world is revealed to be simply one of a great many possible worlds—"like an onion: except that as you continue to go in and in, each circle is larger than the last" (LB, Chapter 16, p. 765). This prediction, rendered in the midst of the destruction of familiar things and lands, militates against the hopelessness of the hyper-rational techno-world that constantly threatens mass destruction of all that we know and love. Worlds will come and go, just as warriors and great rulers and grand empires will come and go. And yet, if we hearken to the lessons embedded in the Narnia tales, there is hope that new chapters of new histories in new worlds will be better than the violent past chapters recorded in the histories of our species.

13

No Longer a Friend of Narnia: Gender in Narnia

KARIN FRY

There are strong female characters throughout *The Chronicles of Narnia*, like Lucy, Jill, Aravis, and Polly, but part of their strength is attributed to the fact that they are more interested in "masculine" pursuits, such as going on adventures or fighting in battles. The character of Susan, however, suggests some interesting points about gender in Narnia, because Susan isn't like the other heroines of the *Chronicles*. Susan is "pretty" rather than good at school, she doesn't like to ride to war, and she is given the title "Queen Susan the Gentle" in the early days of Narnia. Susan is the most "feminine" and gentle of the heroines, and her beauty is stressed throughout the books. However, by the end of the *Chronicles*, Susan is the only main character who is not invited into the country beyond the Shadowlands, and she is described in *The Last Battle* as being "no longer a friend of Narnia" (LB, Chapter 12, p. 741). Is there a connection between Susan's feminine qualities and her exclusion from eternal happiness with Aslan? Or to put the question more pointedly, is Narnia unfriendly to femininity?

The Female Heroes

Like Jo in *Little Women*, the typical female heroine in the *Chronicles* is frustrated with female gender roles, and surpasses the conventional limitations of her sex by bending the gender rules. Gender theorists largely view gender roles as culturally constructed because what is appropriate behavior for males and females differs throughout the world and throughout time. Children's books become interesting sites for gender studies because they sometimes provide models for what girls and boys *should* be like in a given culture. Because Narnia is connected to Christian morality, whatever is said about gender has value implications, serving as an example of "proper" gender roles to the young reader. Rather than merely describing behavior, the story suggests a right and a wrong way to be "male" or "female."

Lewis's choices for the gender roles of his characters are more sympathetic than the stereotypical norms of his day, but there are certainly places throughout the *Chronicles* where traditional roles dominate. For example, in *The Lion, the Witch, and the Wardrobe,* Father Christmas gives gender-specific gifts to Peter and the girls. While Peter gets a sword, Susan is given a horn to "call for help" and a bow and arrow that is not to be used in battle. Lucy is given a curative cordial and a small dagger, which is also not to be used in battle, and only in great need. When Lucy shows interest in fighting because she thinks she could be brave enough, Father Christmas tells her that "battles are ugly when women fight" (LWW, Chapter 10, p. 160). Since Father Christmas is a good character whose opinion is to be trusted by the average child, it appears that the "true" gender role for women in Narnia excludes them from battle. Female combat is ugly. However, this gender rule is not entirely straightforward. The most admired girl heroes attempt to do as much as they can, even if they are not allowed to fight themselves. Lucy challenges this norm, and wishes she could fight in battles, as do most of the other female protagonists in the *Chronicles.*

Many female characters in the *Narnia* stories break traditional female stereotypes. Aravis, in *The Horse and His Boy,* boldly runs away from her father in order to avoid a loveless arranged marriage, and prefers masculine pursuits like archery, playing with horses and dogs, and swimming (HHB, Chapter 7, p. 251). Aravis is a "queer girl" because she is not interested in dresses, boys, or marriage, but she is also a lauded character that sets an example for others by saving Narnia from invasion (HHB, Chapter 7, p. 252). Jill Pole—though she sometimes "prattle[s] and giggle[s] (SC, Chapter 9, p. 607) in a girlish way— is also adventurous and deviates from typical female stereotypes by showing more courage than Eustace, when she sneaks into the stable of the false Aslan against orders (LB, Chapter 6, p. 703). King Tirian declares that if she were a boy, she would have been whipped, but since she is a girl, he notes her unusual bravery in addition to her disobedience (LB, Chapter 6, p. 703). Lucy, perhaps the greatest female hero in all the Narnia tales, is said to be "as good as a man, or at any rate as good as a boy" because she is interested in going to battle (HHB, Chapter 13, p. 290).[1] The most sympathetic female characters in the *Chronicles* are consistently the ones who question the traditional roles of women and prove their worth to Aslan through actively engaging in the adventures just like the boys.

Because the most admired girls are those who challenge the typical gender roles associated with their sex, it would be a mistake to say that the Narnia stories are entirely sexist. Girls have the freedom to go beyond traditional gender roles and are capable of being just as good as boys in the adventures and in their devotion to Aslan. Masculinity is not overly praised either, because even though the boy characters describe girls with negative attributes, like a tendency to sulk (LWW, Chapter 3, p. 123), or gossip (MN, Chapter 4, p. 36), or having a bad sense of direction (MN, Chapter 4, p. 36; SC, Chapter 1, p. 552), the girls also describe the boys in derogatory terms (PC, Chapter 9, p. 370; SC, Chapter 1, p. 550). When Prince Caspian and Edmund clash over who's in charge, Lucy complains about boys acting like "swaggering, bullying idiots" (VDT, Chapter 8, p. 484). The characters have positive and negative things to say about both male and female characters, suggesting an equality between the sexes. However, the problem is that many of the positive qualities of the female characters seem to be those by which they can rise above their femininity.

Because Lucy is "just as good as a boy," she succeeds in living up to a masculine standard, which suggests that being a girl isn't quite good enough. These girl role models are heroes just like the boys, but only because they are just as good as boys. Feminist philosopher Simone de Beauvoir (1908–1986) has

---

[1] Lucy, too, is sometimes portrayed in stereotypically feminine ways. For instance, when Lucy first meets Aravis, we're told that "they liked each other at once and soon went away together to talk about Aravis's bedroom and Aravis's boudoir and about getting clothes for her, and all the sort of things girls do talk about on such an occasion" (HHB, Chapter 15, p. 305).

commented on the problem of having a sexed standard.[2] If women seek only to measure up to men, this suggests that there is something wrong with "femaleness" that needs to be over-come. The standard for what a character should be like in Narnia is a masculine standard that some girls can approximate because they are interested in "boy" adventures, but others, like Susan, cannot. Susan does have some masculine strengths. She is a good archer and a good swimmer. However, unlike her brother Edmund, she doesn't enjoy showing off her talents if it means beating someone who is already down (PC, Chapter 8, p. 365). While the other girls want to actively participate in the adventures like the boys, Susan does not. Given a choice, Susan does not ride to battle, and avoids fighting altogether (HHB, Chapter 13, p. 290).

The Girly Girl

Susan is clearly the most "girly" of all the main characters in Narnia, and she has many stereotypically feminine qualities. First, Susan is a mothering character. In fact, our first introduction to Susan in *The Lion, the Witch, and the Wardrobe*, is a quick con-frontation between Susan and her younger brother Edmund. When Susan suggests that it's time for Edmund to go to bed, he insists that he doesn't have to listen to his older sister because she's not his mother (LWW, Chapter 1, p. 111). Susan's tendency to be mothering is usually described as a negative trait, because she is overly protective, seeking to limit the behavior of her sib-lings without the right of an actual mother. The irony of this spat between Susan and Edmund, however, is that there is a notable absence of mothering (and fathering) throughout the *Chronicles*. Most of the adventures occur when the parents are away and have left the children with relative strangers. Perhaps Lewis is remembering his own childhood, when his mother died of can-cer and he was sent to a boarding school at the age of nine. Yet, Susan is not entitled to give orders or to treat her younger sib-lings in a motherly way. Her maternal sense of worry is out of place, and causes her to always be a "wet blanket" whose opin-ions should be ignored (PC, Chapter 9, p. 370).

---

[2] Simone de Beauvoir, *The Second Sex* (New York: Vintage, 1989), p. xxi.

In addition to being a mother hen, Susan is more cautious than the other children. Rather than actively joining in with the adventures, Susan is often passive and fearful. Several times in *The Lion, the Witch, and the Wardrobe*, Susan wishes that they had not come to Narnia at all, and she suggests that they leave once they discover that Mr. Tumnus's house has been destroyed (LWW, Chapter 5, pp. 131–32; Chapter 7, p. 139). Susan's excessive caution does not change after "years" in Narnia either, because even at the end of the first story, she is the only character who doesn't want to follow the white stag (LWW, Chapter 17, p. 196). Her anxiety worsens in *Prince Caspian*, where she is reproached by her siblings on several occasions. When Peter offers his hand to help Susan down a steep gorge, he tells her to buck up and stop grousing because even a baby could get down from there (PC, Chapter 11, p. 385). Even Aslan suggests that Susan should not listen to her fears, and he breathes on her to make her braver (PC, Chapter 11, p. 386). Susan shrinks from the adventures, or wants to go at a slower pace, and she is often ignored by the other children as a nag who wants to spoil the fun. Feminine stereotypes suggest that girls are typically more fearful, but in Narnia, the other girl characters usually rise to the occasion. Only Susan shows a lack of bravery.

Susan's less aggressive nature is reflected in her gentleness. Susan's title in Narnia is "Queen Susan the Gentle," which can be contrasted to Lucy's more active title, "Lucy the Valiant" (LWW, Chapter 17, p. 195). Lucy valiantly rides into adventures, but Susan does not. Unlike the other female characters, Susan doesn't like to fight, she is tender hearted and doesn't like to kill things (PC, Chapter 8, p. 365; Chapter 9, p. 371). She also doesn't like to watch others fight (PC, Chapter 8, p. 364). In fact, Susan is so bothered by violence that when a bear is killed for food, she wants to sit a long way off from those who are skinning and preparing it (PC, Chapter 9, p. 371). One would suspect that a gentle nature would be a positive trait in a Christian fable, but in Susan's case, it adds to her tendency to spoil the fun by not wanting to join in. Susan's tenderness is often connected to her cowardice and her overall negative attitude that rejects the spirit of adventure and service in Aslan's cause.

Finally, Susan has stereotypically feminine interests in comparison to the other girls. As the stories progress, Susan becomes increasingly interested in things like boys, parties, and fashion. Susan's interest in boys first appears in *The Horse and His Boy*, where Susan is an adult in Narnia in the process of accepting offers for marriage. The only other character in the *Chronicles* that has a similar interest in the attention of suitors is Lasaraleen, and she is clearly a foil to the main character, Aravis, who is trying to escape an arranged marriage. Lasaraleen is a shallow woman, talks too much, has a tendency to giggle, and is primarily interested in "clothes and parties and gossip" (HHB, Chapter 7, p. 251). She thinks that Aravis should accept her arranged marriage merely because the man is rich (HHB, Chapter 7, p. 251). Unlike Lasaraleen, Aravis is not interested in fashion or parties, and she is nearly driven "mad" by having to listen to Lasaraleen's long speech about which dress to wear (HHB, Ch. 7, p. 251). Similarly, Susan is criticized for being interested in "nylons and lipsticks and invitations" (LB, Chapter 12, p. 741). The superficial nature of these stereotypical female interests is condemned. Susan is interested in dates, fashion, and in getting married. She is also motherly, cautious, gentle, and doesn't wish to go on adventures. She is embedded within traditional femininity, and it is these character traits that foreshadow the fact that Susan will be excluded from the Narnian equivalent to heaven. But there is one more female trait that is ascribed to Susan that plays into her exclusion. Susan is also beautiful.

Beauty and the Beast

In *The Voyage of the "Dawn Treader,"* Susan is not part of the story because she is with her parents on a trip to America. However, the reader learns that most grown-ups think that Susan is "the pretty one of the family and was no good at school work (though otherwise very old for her age)," and that her parents think she will get more out of the trip than her younger siblings would (VDT, Chapter 1, p. 426). The suggestion is that Susan is favored by her parents and possibly by others because of her beauty. As an adult in Narnia, Susan is described as tall and gracious, with long black hair, and her beauty is so well known that kings from other lands seek her hand in marriage (LWW, Chapter 17, p. 194). Prince Rabadash, for example, is so captivated by her beauty that he claims that he "must have her. I will die if I don't get her" (HHB, Chapter 8, p. 256). Likewise, when Shasta sees Susan for the first time, he calls her the most beautiful lady he has ever seen (HHB, Chapter 4, p. 233).

The only characters who surpass Susan's beauty are the evil Witches. All the Witches are beautiful, linking feminine beauty to evil, where conniving women use their beauty to get what they want from the men or boys. One obvious example of this is the Green Witch from *The Silver Chair* who transforms herself into a serpent to kill Prince Rilian's mother and then seduces the Prince through her enchanting beauty. She distracts him from his quest to avenge his mother's death with her beauty, and enslaves him in Underland. The first time Rilian sees this beautiful witch in her thin green garment he is "like a man out of his wits" (SC, Chapter 4, p. 576). Rilian thinks she is "the most beautiful thing that was ever made" (SC, Chapter 4, p. 576). Her beauty is so seductive that he almost loses his mind, and ultimately, her beauty causes him to forget who he is, and he becomes her slave for ten years. Only for a short period each night, when he is bound to her silver chair, does he remember who he is. But then, of course, he is unable to do anything about it.

The connection between the plight of Prince Rilian and the expulsion of Adam and Eve from Paradise cannot be overlooked. The story of the Fall is a tale in which Eve, through beauty and charm, seduces Adam into a life of sin by tempting him to eat the apple, just like the Green Witch seduces Prince Rilian and condemns him to a life in the dark world of Underland. Except that in the Narnian version of the story, the woman and the snake are one and the same. Luckily, with the help of the children, Prince Rilian escapes from his curse and is able to kill the Witch in her serpent form. This is fortunate since it would not have suited Rilian's heart or honor to kill a lady, but killing the snake is much easier (SC, Chapter 13, p. 634). Perhaps part of the reason why he finds it easier to kill the snake is that the physical beauty of the Witch doesn't get in the way. Like all witches, the Green Witch uses her beauty, and connives in order to get what she wants, turning men away from the Christian cause of Aslan.

The case of Prince Rilian is emblematic of how evil functions in Narnia. Typically, there is a beautiful woman who is wicked, and she seduces the boy or man to do evil. As in the Genesis story of the Fall, the woman leads men towards sin. The beautiful White Witch tempts Edmund with a maddening desire for Turkish Delight, as she had earlier tempted Digory to take an apple from the Edenic garden in Narnia to cure his sick mother (MN, Chapter 13, p. 94). Unlike Adam, Digory succeeds in resisting the temptation, and is rewarded by Aslan with permission to take a curative apple for his mother. Interestingly, the girls are not as easily corrupted by the Witches. Lucy immediately believes what the animals have told her about the wickedness of the White Witch and is not fooled by her. Polly knows that Jadis is bad right away, and dislikes her from the first. The boys, however, are much more likely to be affected by the beauty of the Witches, and often succumb to their evil plans.

Evil is not always portrayed in a female form in Narnia, because some of the male characters are clearly "bad guys." However, these characters fail to have magical powers and have no supernatural traits. Uncle Andrew is a bad man, but has no true magic, and can only rely upon the magic rings that were given to him by a woman who had fairy blood (MN, Chapter 2, pp. 19–20). The corrupt Calormenes are portrayed as treacherous and power-hungry, as is Shift, the wicked Ape, but again, none of them has magical powers. Ultimate evil in Narnia is always a woman with supernatural power over men. The motivation for these Witches is usually world domination, which under better times would reside with the masculine Aslan. Picking up from the Judeo-Christian tradition, it is Eve who causes humanity to be expelled from Paradise, it is women who seduce others toward sin, and it is women who seek power and wish to destroy the male God. Perhaps the real reason that Susan cannot survive in Narnia is that she has some feminine power through her beauty and is secretly a threat to the prevailing power structure. Though she never uses her beauty for gain, she is condemned nevertheless.

I Dream of Jinn

Perhaps the most important allusion to the Fall in the *Chronicles* is the passage in *The Lion, the Witch, and the Wardrobe* describing the lineage of the White Witch. The White Witch is a descendant of Lilith, a female demon regarded in some strands of rabbinic literature as Adam's first wife, prior to Eve. The figure of Lilith reconciles an apparent conflict between the two biblical accounts of the creation of humanity, one which tells of Adam and his wife being created at the same time (Genesis 1:27), and another in which Eve is described as being created after Adam, from his side (Genesis 3:21–23). To reconcile these conflicting narratives, Lilith was thought to be Adam's first wife, who was excluded from Eden due to her sin, which may have been to say God's name. Similarly, Jadis, who later becomes the White Witch, destroys all of Charn by saying an evil word, much like her ancestor, Lilith. In Jewish folklore, Lilith becomes a she-devil who mates with demons and is responsible for everything from killing newborns and causing miscarriages, to causing men to have nocturnal emissions due to her influence in their dreams.[3] The White Witch isn't related to Eve, and doesn't have "a drop of real Human blood," but she is related to the beautiful, evil, and even more corrupting Lilith (LWW, Chapter 8, p. 147). Lilith is also described as one of the Jinn (LWW, Chapter 8, p. 147). The Jinn (a.k.a. genies) derive from Islamic tradition, and are spirits that have supernatural powers and can be either good or bad. When evil, the Jinn seduce and tempt humanity towards sin. In fact, in this tradition Satan is a Jinn who was expelled from heaven for refusing Allah's request to bow before Adam, and took revenge by tempting Adam and other humans to sin.[4] Though there is no historical connection between the Jewish "Lilith" and the Islamic "Jinn," Lewis has merged the two into one.

Putting aside the problematic link between evil and Jewish and Islamic culture, there is certainly a troubling connection between the feminine and evil in the lineage of the White Witch. Evil originates with woman, not just with Eve and the apple, but also with Lilith. Lewis adopts the sexist position of many strands of Christianity that makes women responsible for original sin. In Narnia, the model of corruption mirrors the Fall, where Eve is condemned for tempting Adam to eat the apple, just as the Witches seek to seduce the children towards sin. All women in Narnia are connected to this biblical history, since female humans are called "Daughters of Eve." This terminology

[3] Jocelyn Hellig, "Lilith as a Focus of Judaism's Gender Construction," *Dialogue and Alliance* 12 (1998), pp. 40–47.
[4] Mustansir Mir, *Dictionary of Qur'anic Terms and Concepts* (New York: Garland, 1987), p. 113.

associates women with Eve's behavior and shame, and distances them from whatever traits could be inherited from Adam. But at least the girls are not descended from Lilith, as the White Witch is. Whatever the problems with Eve, Lilith is clearly worse.

The world that Lewis creates finds femininity suspicious, deceptive, and closer to evil because it seduces and beguiles men, and indeed, has some power over them. Female beauty is condemned, and the women who happen to be beautiful or interested in their physical appearance are reproached. Oddly enough, Susan is never described as being overly interested in her own beauty. In *The Voyage of the "Dawn Treader,"* Lucy is said to be jealous of her sister's beauty, but Susan herself is never described as being vain, unless a connection can be made between her beauty and her interest in boys, parties, and fashion. Luckily, Lucy doesn't succumb to her desire to be beautiful, but one cannot help but wonder if Susan is somehow condemned for her beauty. Perhaps the problem with Susan is that she gets led astray by her own beauty, even though she is never described as conceited. What leads her astray is an interest in grown-up things and in boys, and these superficial interests harm her spiritual life.

The Feminine Excluded

Susan has many stereotypically feminine traits, but throughout the *Chronicles* feminine attributes are suspect. While many of the heroic characters have flaws, Susan is the only one who is not forgiven or given the opportunity to work out her problems. Most of her flaws are connected to negative female stereotypes that go against Aslan's morality, and unlike the other girls, Susan is not interested in rejecting feminine roles. Susan does not do anything as evil as Edmund does. She does not betray the children to the White Witch, and she does not lie. Susan is not, like Eustace, blatantly self-centered or mean to other children, and she is often tender towards others. Yet, she is consistently described in negative terms as a wet blanket, and she is the only one of the Narnian heroes who is excluded from Aslan's country at the end of the novels. As Paul Ford notes in his *Companion to Narnia*, "adventure" in Narnia is a metaphor for "life at its highest realization," and acting "grown up" is a clue to wrong thinking.[5] Susan dislikes adventure and is too "grown up," so there are hints throughout the *Chronicles* that Susan is on the road to ruin. Even the fact that Lucy is the High King Peter's favorite sister (PC, Chapter 11, p. 384) is a clue to some of the problems with Susan.

The events that prevent Susan from enjoying eternal bliss with the others happen outside of Narnia. Peter reports that Susan no longer believes in Narnia and Aslan, and this is why she cannot return. In Christian terms, Susan is an apostate. She doesn't believe in Narnia or Aslan any longer, and so is eternally condemned. However, other factors come into play. As Lucy explains, Susan is too preoccupied with superficial feminine interests like "nylons and lipsticks and invitations" (LB, Chapter 12, p. 741). Clearly, Lewis has issues with these kinds of interests, which may in fact be a very feminist position. Many feminists would agree that there is something wrong with encouraging women to be interested in such frivolous concerns. However, Susan's feminine interests are used as evidence that she no longer deserves to be in Narnia.

The exclusion of Susan doesn't seem so bad on the face of it, and it is glossed over as something that Susan brought upon herself. However, it shouldn't be forgotten that the reason that everyone can journey to this heavenly land at the end of the novels is because the characters have died and will now live out their true and more real spiritual lives in a heaven-like place. Susan's parents and all of her siblings have died in a train crash and will spend eternity with Aslan (LB, Chapter 16, p. 767). Susan won't be allowed to join them, and she must be miserable in England surrounded by such total grief. This fact is never mentioned. The tone of Susan's exclusion suggests that she is more interested in getting dates anyway, so she will not grieve for her siblings or parents for very long. She failed to believe in Narnia, and has dug her own grave.

Focusing on the gender traits of Susan reveals a somewhat negative picture of femininity and stereotypically feminine traits, to the point where the feminine is to some degree excluded from Narnia. The feminine is removed because corruption and

---

[5] Paul F. Ford, *Companion to Narnia*, fourth edition (San Francisco: Harper and Row, 1994), pp. 1–2.

evil have a feminine face. While the other heroic girl characters overcome their femininity and reject its corrupting aspects, Susan is unable to. Even though Aslan says that "once a king or queen in Narnia, always a king or queen" (LWW, Chapter 17, p. 194), Susan is dethroned. While there are some feminist aspects to the way in which the other girls are able to succeed, Susan is excluded because she is too feminine. Like the Witches, she may have too much feminine power, or has allowed her femininity to corrupt her in some way. Generally speaking, the picture of the ideal believer in Narnia is a masculine one, where the female characters need to get over their femininity in order to succeed like the boys. Because Susan remains in her stereotypically feminine role and possesses all the worst aspects of being a woman, she cannot progress on the spiritual path, and so is excluded from the heavenly land of Aslan. In these respects, the *Chronicles* are indeed "unfriendly" to the feminine.

Part III

Further Up and Further In

Exploring the Deeper Nature of Reality

14

Plato in Narnia

GARETH B. MATTHEWS

Near the end of *The Last Battle*, Digory mutters under his breath, "It's all in Plato, all in Plato" (LB, Chapter 15, p. 759). What does he mean? Is Lewis saying that *The Chronicles of Narnia* are a simply a retelling of something to be found in Plato? If so, what is the story in Plato that is retold in the Narnia tales? Or is he suggesting that the key to understanding the *Chronicles* is to be found in Plato? If so, what is the key in Plato, and how does it unlock the meaning of the Narnia stories?

Digory and Socrates

Readers of the complete Narnia tales will know that the Lord Digory of *The Last Battle*, who says "It's all in Plato," is actually the Professor in *The Lion, the Witch, and the Wardrobe*. Could it be that the Professor teaches his students Plato? Perhaps. We have no way of knowing. But here is a more intriguing question: Is Digory meant to be a figure out of one of Plato's dialogues? Some readers have thought so. Indeed, some have thought that the Professor of *The Lion, the Witch, and the Wardrobe* is meant to be a Socrates figure. But how could that be? Here is a suggestion. Socrates in the dialogues of Plato, especially in the early ones, tends to ask questions rather than give answers. In fact, he is especially good at asking questions and refuses to answer those questions himself. His questions make the people he is questioning reflect on something puzzling that they hadn't puzzled about before. In some cases they come up with answers they didn't know they would be able to give. And they come up with these answers, not by looking in a book, but by just thinking about the questions Socrates poses. This method of questioning has come to be called the "Socratic method."

Many teachers today use the Socratic method. It's a way of encouraging students to figure out things for themselves, rather than simply accept, on the authority of the teacher, the answers that the teacher gives.

Plato's greatest work, the *Republic*, is taken up with the question of what justice is, both justice in a state and justice in a single individual. In Book 1 of that dialogue Socrates uses his characteristic question-and-answer method to see if his conversation partners can figure out for themselves what justice is. Cephalus, an old "no-nonsense" sort of person, says that justice is simply telling the truth and paying your debts. That's all there is to it, he says.

Socrates encourages Cephalus to think the suggestion through. He does this by asking another question: "Would it be just to return a weapon to someone who has, in the meantime, gone mad?" Everyone who thinks about Socrates's question soon realizes that, despite its initial attractiveness, Cephalus's proposal cannot be accepted. It wouldn't be just to return a weapon to an owner who had gone mad. And so, whatever justice or fairness is, it is not simply telling the truth and paying your debts.

Is what the Professor does in *The Lion, the Witch, and Wardrobe* similar to what Socrates does in this exchange with Cephalus in the *Republic*? Up to a point. But let's think about the comparison a little more.

Edmund, who had been with Lucy in Narnia, decides when he gets back to tell Susan and Peter that he and Lucy had only been pretending when they said they had visited another world. He tells them that Lucy's story about Narnia was, in fact, all nonsense. When Edmund says this, Lucy, of course, is simply devastated. Peter and Susan, who have always found Lucy to be trustworthy, don't know what to think. So they decide to ask the Professor for help.

What the Professor does is to ask Peter and Susan questions. He begins by asking them how they know that their sister's story isn't true. When Susan says that it is Edmund's report that has convinced them, the Professor asks them whether their experience with Lucy in the past had led them to believe in Lucy. They agree that it had. But they were afraid that she might have gone mad. The Professor then assures them that one can tell by looking at Lucy that she is not mad.

Peter then offers other reasons for doubting Lucy's story. The last and strongest reason is that, although Lucy reported being in this other world for hours, she had returned from the wardrobe in less than a minute. To him this difference between the time Lucy reported being in Narnia and the time she had been missing from our world is enough to make her story incredible.

The Professor replies that if there really were such a place as Lucy describes, then it would likely have a separate time of its own. He adds: "However long you stayed there it would never take up any of *our* time" (LWW, Chapter 5, p. 132). Moreover, he continues, a girl of Lucy's age would be unlikely to make up the idea that there is another world with a time of its own, a time not even correlated with our time.

There is, indeed, something Socratic about what the Professor does in this incident. What he does is, we could say, a little Socratic, but not entirely so. One thing that makes it a little Socratic is that the Professor wants the children to think the issue through for themselves, just as Socrates wants those around him to think for themselves about what justice is. In another of Plato's dialogues, Socrates asks his conversation partners what courage is. In a third, he asks what temperance is. Socrates is always interested in figuring out, through questioning other people, what some virtue is.

The Professor has a different sort of aim. He wants to help Susan and Peter figure out whom they should believe: Edmund or Lucy. Determining whether someone is trustworthy who claims to have witnessed something very important, say, a traffic accident, or a murder, is difficult to do. Police have to learn how to do this. And trial lawyers have to be good at convincing the members of a jury that one witness is lying and another is telling the truth. But helping people figure out which witnesses are reliable is rather different from helping people think about what justice or bravery is.

In some of Plato's dialogues, Socrates suggests that we all know what justice and bravery are, but we may need someone to ask us questions so that we can come to say what we already know. By contrast, the Professor has certain maxims for weighing evidence, principles that he hopes Edmund and Susan, if they think about them, will also accept. Here is one:

> *Maxim 1*: If we think two people, A and B, have both witnessed roughly the same thing but report having seen very different things, we should believe the one whose reports have been more reliable in the past.

This maxim seems to be a good one. If you and I think about it, we might well come to accept it as well. But consider this maxim, which the Professor also puts forward:

> *Maxim 2*: If someone reports having visited another reality altogether, we should tend to believe the reporter, if, according to the report, the time in that other reality does not match up with the time in our reality.

This maxim is certainly an interesting one. But we might have reasons for doubting it. We might, for example, be skeptical about whether there is such a thing as another reality. If we don't think there is such a thing, then we won't think it's important to determine whether somebody has ever been there. Moreover, we might reason that a memory of having had an extraordinary experience that cannot be coordinated with the time in our ordinary experience must be more like dreaming than taking a real trip to another world. I can, for example, fall asleep for a very short time and yet, while asleep, have a dream of having done something that took a very long time. But then I don't suppose that the trip I dreamed about was real.

The Professor clearly expects that Susan and Edmund, when they think about the matter, will come to accept his maxims and to disbelieve Edmund. In a somewhat similar way, Socrates, in the *Republic*, expects that Cephalus and the others, when they think about the matter, will come to reject Cephalus's suggestion that justice is telling the truth and paying your debts.

Still, the question Socrates asks ("What is justice?") is a very different kind of question from the one the Professor asks

("Should we believe Lucy or Edmund?"). The Professor is discussing grounds for believing someone who claims to have had a very unusual experience. Socrates is discussing the nature of justice. Any thoughtful person should have some idea of what justice is. But very few of us have any idea of how to determine whether someone who claims to have visited another world is telling the truth. So, the Professor is only partly a Socrates figure.

The Allegory of Underworld

There is, however, something more like Plato in *The Silver Chair*, where we find an image quite like one in Plato's *Republic*, the famous Allegory of the Cave.[1] In presenting it, Socrates tells a story about prisoners being chained to their places in a cave, where the only things they can see are shadows of objects cast on the cave wall by the light of a fire inside the cave. The prisoners, unable to see the objects themselves, take the shadows to be their reality.

A prisoner who gets unchained may be able to leave the cave altogether and emerge to see real objects lighted by the real sun. Anyone who has seen real objects outside the cave, according to Socrates, will not want to return to the cave. But it will be the released prisoner's obligation to return to the cave and enlighten the prisoners so that they, too, will want to be unchained.

In *The Silver Chair*, Jill Pole, Eustace Scrubb, and Puddleglum the Marsh-wiggle find their way into "Underworld," a realm of its own, without a real sun—a world that lies under "the Overworld" of Narnia. There are many parallels between Underworld and the Cave that Socrates describes in the *Republic*.

The basic idea Plato wants to put across with his Allegory of the Cave is the contrast between appearance and reality. Plato thinks of the physical world we experience through our senses as an image or shadow of the real world of eternal and unchangeable realities—the Good itself, Beauty, Justice, Wisdom, and other such timeless essences, or "Forms." Insofar as you or I might be good or wise, it is, Plato insists, only by

---

[1] Book 7, 514a–517c.

"partaking in," or imitating, the Form of Goodness and the Form of Wisdom that we are good or wise.

The Allegory of the Cave is meant to make vivid Plato's idea that many of us (perhaps most of us) live our lives in the world of mere appearances or illusions. Most of us, most of the time, passively accept what we're told by our parents, teachers, politicians, and the media.

According to Plato's Allegory, we may be released from our cave of ignorance by philosophy and led by reason outside the cave to view true realities lighted by the real sun, which, for Plato, is the symbol of the highest reality, the Good itself. The objects that a philosophically enlightened person can see in the light of the Good are the Forms. Once we have been liberated from the cave and have seen true realities, we will not want to return to the cave, Socrates says. Nevertheless, it is our duty, he thinks, to return and help free the prisoners from their world of illusion.

The picture of Underworld we get in *The Silver Chair* is also a world dimly lit by its own inferior light of only partial comprehension. The chief prisoner of Underworld, Prince Rilian, is tied to a silver chair, much as Plato's prisoners are chained in place. But he is also kept in the thrall of the Queen of Underworld by the thrumming sound of a musical instrument and by a sweet-smelling fume that dulls his mind.

When Prince Rilian is freed from his chair and is able to confront the Queen, she tries to re-enchant him and convince him that Narnia, the Overworld, is not real, but only imaginary. Jill tries to fight off the Queen's efforts to enchant her:

> Jill couldn't remember the names of the things in our world. And this time it didn't come into her head that she was being enchanted, for now the magic was in its full strength; and of course, the more enchanted you get, the more certain you feel that you are not enchanted at all.
>
> She found herself saying (and at the moment it was a relief to say): "No. I suppose that other world must be all a dream."
>
> "Yes, it *is* all a dream," said the Witch, always thrumming. (SC, Chapter 12, p. 630)

The enchantment idea is Lewis's addition to Plato's Allegory of the Cave. Yet it is fully in the spirit of Plato. And it is surprisingly appropriate to our experience today. I remember attending a meeting in which the proceedings were picked up by a closed-circuit television camera and displayed on monitors positioned around the room. To my astonishment, the participants in that meeting kept turning to the monitors to see themselves and others at the meeting, rather than looking directly at the people who were talking. They were so enchanted with the images of the meeting that they found those images more worth attending to than the speakers themselves.

Lewis embellishes Plato's Allegory in another way. In one passage, the Queen of Underworld tries to undermine her visitors' belief in Aslan and Narnia by convincing them that they are merely projections of their own imaginations:

> The Witch shook her head. "I see," she said, "that we should do no better with your *lion*, as you call it, than we did with your *sun*. You have seen lamps, and so you imagined a bigger and better lamp and called it the *sun*. You've seen cats, and now you want a bigger and better cat, and it's to be called a *lion*. Well, 'tis a pretty make-believe, though, to say truth, it would suit you all better if you were younger. And look how you can put nothing into your make-believe without copying it from the real world, this world of mine, which is the only world. But even you children are too old for such play." (SC, Chapter 12, p. 632)

The Queen here is playing Aristotle to Lewis's Plato. Aristotle criticized Plato for, as he supposed, simply making up a distinct thing, the Form of Beauty, in addition to all the beautiful things in the world—beautiful flowers, beautiful pictures, beautiful sunsets, and so on. In a similar way, the Queen criticizes the Narnians for making a grand and utterly perfect form of Underworld (namely, Narnia) and for making up Aslan as a large and perfect cat.

Later, we come to a fascinating further development in the story. Puddleglum claims that, even if he and his friends have made up Aslan and Narnia, still, this ideal world and this ideal being are better and, in the end, more important than what can be found in Underworld.

> Suppose we *have* only dreamed, or made up, all those things— trees and grass and sun and moon and stars and Aslan himself. Suppose we have. Then all I can say is that, in that case, the made-up things seem a good deal more important than the real ones.

Suppose this black pit of a kingdom of yours *is* the only world. Well, it strikes me as a pretty poor one. And that's a funny thing, when you come to think of it. We're just babies making up a game, if you're right. But four babies playing a game can make a play-world which licks your real world hollow. That's why I'm going to stand by the play-world. (SC, Chapter 12, p. 633)

Not surprisingly, there is a line of thinking in Plato's *Republic* that is similar to this speech of Puddleglum's. Socrates says to his friend, Glaucon, "Suppose a painter had drawn an ideally beautiful figure complete to the last touch, would you think any the worse of him, if he could not show that a person as beautiful as that could exist?" Glaucon agrees that he would not. Socrates continues: "Well, we have been constructing in discourse the pattern of an ideal state. Is our theory any the worse, if he cannot prove it possible that a state so organized should be actually founded?"[2] Glaucon agrees with Socrates that it would not be a worse picture, even if nothing completely like it could ever actually exist.

The Real Narnia

Plato, of course, thought the ideal state was real anyway, whether or not it could be actualized in the world we see around us. And here we come to the most Platonic aspect of the Narnia *Chronicles*. Near the end of *The Last Battle*, after Narnia has been destroyed, Peter, Edmund, and Lucy find themselves in a place where, as Edmund notes, the mountains seem very similar to those in Narnia. "They're different," Lucy says. "They have more colours on them and they look further away than I remembered and they're more . . . more . . . oh, I don't know . . . ." "More like the real thing," adds Lord Digory. He explains:

You need not mourn over Narnia, Lucy. All of the old Narnia that mattered, all the dear creatures, have been drawn into the real Narnia through the Door. And of course it is different; as different as a real thing is from a shadow or as waking life is from a dream. . . ." His voice stirred everyone like a trumpet as he spoke these words: but when he added under his breath "It's all in Plato, all in

---

[2] *Republic*, Book 5, 472d–e.

Plato: bless me what *do* they teach them at these schools?" the older ones laughed. It was so exactly like the sort of thing they had hear him say long ago in that other world where his beard was gray instead of golden. (LB, Chapter 15, p. 759)

In this ending to the *Chronicles* we have a picture of what we can call "Christian Platonism." The idea of there being a realm of perfect things in which the things of our earthly life partake by resembling them is genuinely Platonic. It is the idea that our present life is really a hall of mirrors, or a "Shadowland," as Lewis puts it in *The Last Battle*. The idea that we, or some of us anyway, may someday reach a world of perfection is certainly Christian. Yet it is also to be found in Plato, especially in the myths that Plato used to supplement the reasoning in his dialogues.

In one myth Plato tells us near the end of the dialogue *Phaedo*, we learn that people who have lived very holy lives will be "freed and released from the regions of the earth as from a prison." They will make their way to "dwelling places it is difficult to describe clearly."[3] One reason for the difficulty in describing them seems to be their unqualified beauty.

After telling us this myth of an afterlife, Plato adds an important warning. It is a warning Lewis might well have been willing to append to the *Chronicles*:

> No sensible man would insist that these things are [exactly] as I have described them, but I think it is fitting for a man to risk the belief—for the risk is a noble one—that this, or something like this, is true about our souls and their dwelling places, since the soul is evidently immortal, and a man should repeat this to himself as if it were an incantation, which is why I have been prolonging my tale.[4]

Admittedly, nothing quite like the Christ figure, Aslan, is to be found in Plato—not even in Plato's myths. And Plato's idea that philosophy offers the best route, perhaps the only route, to eternal bliss is not really Christian. So, there are important differences between Plato and Christian thought, even as that thought is reflected in the Narnia stories. Still, there are very

---

[3] *Phaedo*, 114b.
[4] *Ibid.*, 114d.

important respects in which Lord Digory's comment, "It's all in Plato," is quite correct. The *Chronicles*, like Plato's own myths, do present a story version of Plato's theory of reality.

In several respects Lewis develops further Plato's idea of a "heaven of Forms" to which our souls, or some of them, may journey, as a kind of homecoming. Readers of Plato have sometimes taken the Forms to be abstract objects that individual objects in "our world" of coming to be and passing away have in common. But Plato also suggests that each Form is a perfect exemplar of itself. Thus, the Form of Beauty would be something perfectly beautiful, and the Form of Mountain would be itself a perfect mountain.

A famous difficulty with his theory that Plato himself points out (the difficulty is called the "Third Man Argument") is this. If the Form, Beauty, is itself beautiful, then it seems there would be something the Form and all the beautiful things in this world—paintings, vases, sunsets, and so on—have in common, something that makes them all beautiful. This "something" would be another Form of Beauty over and above the first one. And, assuming that it, too, is beautiful, there would be still another, and so on indefinitely.

The Narnia tales seem to embrace such a succession in a strikingly Platonic vision of nested levels of being or reality. Thus, near the end of *The Last Battle*, Lucy says:

> This is still Narnia, and more real and more beautiful than the Narnia down below, just as *it* was more real and more beautiful than the Narnia outside the Stable door! I see . . . world within world, Narnia within Narnia . . . .
>
> "Yes," said Mr Tumnus, "like an onion: except that as you go in and in, each circle is larger than the last." (LB, Chapter 16, p. 765)

Lewis's idea that there are worlds within worlds, instead of worlds *over* worlds, as Plato suggests, might make us think of Russian dolls—ever smaller dolls within ever smaller dolls. But Lewis saves us from thinking that this succession dwindles into insignificance by making each world bigger on the inside than it is on the outside.

There is another development of Plato's ideas that should be appreciated. Plato seems to leave us with the idea that there will be nothing for our souls to do in heaven except eternally contemplate the Forms, including the Form of the Good, which Christian Platonists identify with God. But Lewis suggests that heaven is still a life of exploration and adventure. Even if we have explored one Narnia fully, there is always another one to explore. The "Great Story which no one on earth has read" is one which "goes on for ever: in which each chapter is better than the one before" (LB, Chapter 16, p. 767).

When, at the conclusion of the *Narnia* tales, Lucy expresses the fear that she and the others will be sent back to their former world, Aslan calms her fears. "The dream is ended," he says; "this is the morning" (LB, Chapter 16, p. 767). Thus, in a fittingly Platonic reversal of the idea that paradise may be only a desperate dream of our own imagination, Aslan assures Lucy and the others that it was their earthly life that was the dream. What now awaits them is true reality.

15

Different Worlds, Different Bodies: Personal Identity in Narnia

TIMOTHY CLEVELAND

Change is a constant in our world. Traffic lights turn. Clouds come and go. It rains, then it shines. Bread turns to toast. The stock market swings up and down. But change is not only a feature of our world, for we also constantly change, most often in small and hardly noticeable ways. We start small and gradually grow taller. Our hair grows and grays. We slough off a layer of cells as we shower. Trivial memories fade. We forget what we had for breakfast two weeks ago. We gain a pound, then we slim down. More significantly, we can change in some drastic and sudden ways too. A religious conversion, plastic surgery, or a serious automobile accident can change us almost instantly in ways immediately obvious to everyone. Through changes large and small we cope and continue with our lives.

But however dramatically we may be changed, we are never transformed in the extraordinary ways some of the characters in *The Chronicles of Narnia* are. The Pevensie children—Peter, Susan, Lucy, and Edmund—step from the wardrobe in England into the land of Narnia where they grow up to be Kings and Queens, only to return home as children again. Eustace turns into a dragon (VDT, Chapter 6, p. 464). Aslan transforms himself from a lion into an ordinary house cat (HHB, Chapter 6, p. 245) and possibly into an albatross (VDT, Chapter 12, p. 511). Aslan changes Rabadash into a donkey (HHB, Chapter 15, p. 307). The Green Witch morphs into a giant serpent (SC, p. 633). Dwarfs are transformed into Monopods (VDT, Chapter 11, p. 502). Caspian dies, old and decrepit, and is restored to life as a vigorous young man (SC, Chapter 16, p. 661). In *The Last Battle*, all the Narnian heroes except Susan are reunited and miraculously restored and transformed. These radical changes are the stuff of magic and miracle. Nonetheless, we easily recognize the characters as the same persons in spite of such changes.

This odd aspect of reading *The Chronicles of Narnia* raises some interesting philosophical questions. How are we able to recognize these characters as the same persons when they undergo such drastic changes? What makes Eustace the same person who is later a dragon? How can the Green Witch and a giant serpent be the same individual? Underlying these questions is a more fundamental one: what is a person anyway? As time passes, we all change. What makes us the same person throughout all those changes? These questions have troubled philosophers for centuries and have come to be known as "the problem of personal identity." This problem is not simply an academic issue for philosophers. Intelligent and insightful answers are important to all of us. "What or who am I?" is a question that affects some of life's deepest concerns. How we answer these questions concerning personal identity determines what we think about important moral issues such as when a human life begins and ends. It is also common to think of persons as having rights and responsibilities. Any confusion or obscurity in our concept of a person will infect our thinking about rights and responsibilities. So, the problem of personal identity ought to command our most careful attention.

You may be convinced the problem is important. You may be less confident the characters in the *Chronicles* have anything to teach us about *our* identity. They inhabit an imagined world of magic and fantasy. We live in the real world of physics, biology, and genetics. There are great differences between our world and Narnia. At least this important similarity exists, however. We, like the people depicted in the *Chronicles*, all continue to be who we are through changes great and small. Their changes just happen to be much more drastic than ours. But it is just these extraordinary changes that bring the real issue into focus. Let's see how the wondrous imaginings of C.S. Lewis can shed new light on the philosophical problem of personal identity.

Who's on First? Distinguishing Cor from Corin

Talk of personal *identity* can be confusing. We use the words "identical" and "same" in two very different ways. Sometimes we say things such as, "I have the *same* car as you do" and "My copy of *Prince Caspian* is *identical* to yours." These are perfectly straightforward expressions and create little confusion. We know what they imply. Your car is the same make and model as mine, perhaps the same color as well. Your copy of *Prince Caspian* is the same edition, has the same words on each page, and has the same cover as mine. Notice what is the same—make, model, color, edition, words, cover. Your book and my book, your car and my car, are distinct things with identical characteristics or qualities. This use of the word "identical" is said to refer to *qualitative identity*. Two things are qualitatively identical when they are exactly alike, when they have identical qualities.

This kind of identity is the basis of much of the plot in *The Horse and His Boy*. In this story, Shasta, the adopted son of the Calormene fisherman, discovers that he looks just like the Archenland prince, Corin. Recall the episode when he first encounters Corin. "'I'm nobody, nobody in particular, I mean,' said Shasta. 'King Edmund caught me in the street and mistook me for you. I suppose we must look like one another'" (HHB, Chapter 5, p. 241). Later Corin introduces Shasta to Edmund and Lucy. "'Don't you see, Sire?' said Corin. 'It's my double: the boy you mistook me for at Tashbaan.' 'Why, so he is your double,' exclaimed Lucy. 'As like as two twins. What a marvellous thing'" (HHB, Chapter 12, pp. 287–88). The marvelous thing is that they turn out to be identical twins long separated and happily reunited by the end of the story. Identical twins are good examples of qualitative identity. They are almost exactly alike.

We must be careful, however, not to confuse qualitative identity with personal identity. There are two distinct twins, Corin and Shasta. They are not, nor can they be, the same person. They simply look alike to the point of being indistinguishable. Shasta does discover who he is in the end. "'Apparently King Lune is my father,' said Shasta. 'I might really have guessed it, Corin being so like me. We were twins, you see. Oh, and my name isn't Shasta, it's Cor'" (HHB, Chapter 14, p. 300). He doesn't discover that he is Corin, though he looks just like him. He discovers that he is *one and the same person* as the boy they call

"Cor." Shasta isn't simply qualitatively identical to Cor. Shasta is Cor. In this case, Shasta is said to be *numerically identical* to Cor. They are one and the same individual. The question of personal identity is, then, a question of *numerical* identity, not *qualitative* identity.

Confusing the two kinds of identity can create serious difficulties when thinking about personal identity. The problem of personal identity concerns how we remain the same even through changes. At one time we have certain qualities. At other times we have different qualities. If something changes, then it is no longer exactly the *same* thing. How, then, can the later thing be identical to the earlier thing? Well, they can't be *qualitatively* identical. But they can be earlier and later stages of *numerically* one and the same thing. Think of the little person depicted in your first-grade class picture. Think of yourself now. These two stages are not exactly alike in qualities. One is much larger than the other, and probably has more teeth. They are, however, stages that make up the very same person—you. We must keep in mind that the problem of personal identity is about numerical identity as time passes: When is an earlier stage part of numerically the same person as a later stage?

Identity and Fantasy

A few years ago I had my very long hair cut short. I don't look the same. I hope I look better. In any case, I am the same person I was. One person didn't go out of existence with my haircut and another person come into existence. We might say that my long hair wasn't *essential* to me. But this implies that something is essential. The philosopher Aristotle (384–322 B.C.) can help us here with his distinction between *accidental* and *essential* properties. An accidental property is a characteristic that a thing *can* lose while remaining the same thing. My having long hair was an accidental property of me. An essential property is one that a thing *cannot* lose and continue to exist as the same thing. A square has four sides. It cannot lose a side and continue to be a square. Having four sides is essential to a square. With respect to persons, the question becomes, what properties can one lose while still remaining the same individual? It is this question of the essence of a person that brings the problem of personal identity into focus.

Notice that the issue of essence and accident is put in terms of what *can* or *cannot* happen. "Can" and "cannot" are words for possibility and impossibility. When thinking about essence we don't have to consider what is actually the case. We only have to reflect on certain possibilities. I actually have hair, but I can imagine being bald. It's possible that I could become bald. I would still exist even though I became bald. Having hair is therefore not essential to me. Going bald is something we are familiar with. It occurs frequently enough. But could I turn into a dragon as Eustace does in *The Voyage of the "Dawn Treader,"* while retaining my personal identity? This possibility seems ridiculous. Only in fantasy and science fiction do such strange things happen. This possibility, fantastic as it is, is nonetheless relevant to the question of personal identity.

Consider an example having nothing to do with personal identity. The idea of a bachelor implies the idea of an unmarried male. Even in fantasy or science fiction a bachelor cannot be married. It is unimaginable. A bachelor could be bald, or eighty-feet-tall, or possess magical powers, and still be a bachelor. But a bachelor cannot be married, not even in a fantasy world. We know this because we understand the idea of a bachelor. A married bachelor contradicts the definition of "bachelor." A married bachelor would have to be both married and not married at the same time. This situation cannot happen in our everyday world, nor can it happen in the world of fantasy and science fiction. It is *logically impossible*. The essence of being a bachelor involves being unmarried.

When we think we clearly understand a concept, thinking about fantastic cases can help us test that understanding. Writers of fantasy stories, like Lewis and his friend J.R.R. Tolkien, describe possibilities for maintaining personal identity that we might miss if our reflections remain tied to our ordinary experiences. While these fantastic scenarios couldn't happen in our world, they don't seem to contradict the idea of a person either. That is, if we correctly understand what a person is.

Dragons and Donkeys

What is a person? Usually we *identify* a person by outward appearance. I *recognize* the checker in the grocery store by his looks. This might lead us to think that a person is *identical* to his or her body, but this would be a mistake. People *identified* me by my long hair, but my long hair was not essential to my personal *identity*.

It's easy to see why a person is not identical to his or her body. Our bodies change all the time, but we remain the same persons throughout the change. Our bodies change gradually and in imperceptible ways. We may not notice that many of the characteristics of our bodies could be different, that they are not essential to who we are. Lewis's stories, by contrast, involve characters that change bodily properties so drastically we can't help but notice. Nevertheless, we recognize Eustace even when he has changed into a dragon just as we know Rabadash is the same person as a donkey that he was as a human. These fantastic possibilities make it obvious that a person is not identical to his or her body.

Less fantastic episodes in Lewis's tales make the same point. Peter, Susan, Lucy, and Edmund, like the rest of us, were once children with children's bodies. They grow up to have adult bodies with very different characteristics from their childhood bodies. Unlike us, by some magic, they become children again. Some childhood stages of their lives are later than some adult stages. Though their bodies change, they continue to exist. So these possibilities in the *Chronicles* imply we are not identical to our bodies.

Persons and Souls

Reflecting on the bizarre possibilities of life in Narnia, some may be tempted to think of a person as something completely non-physical. After all, Rabadash changes so much that he is no longer a human being. There is apparently nothing physical about Rabadash that remains. It seems to follow, therefore, that the essence of Rabadash must be his mind or soul. One may think that this is the conclusion Lewis wishes us to draw. Perhaps that is the only way to make sense of all the strange transformations in the *Chronicles*.

The famous philosopher René Descartes (1596–1650) argues that a person is not identical to anything physical. Reduced to its bare bones, his argument is as follows.[1] If I can imagine

---

[1] See René Descartes, *Meditations on First Philosophy*, Meditation 6. The bare bones argument is from W.D. Hart, *The Engines of the Soul* (Cambridge:

existing without my body, then it's possible for me to exist without my body. If it's possible that I exist without my body, then I'm not identical to my body. I can imagine existing without my body. So, it follows that I'm not identical with my body—I must be some immaterial stuff, a soul. One might think this theory best explains the extreme physical makeovers in Narnia. Souls persist through all the strange changes.

The soul theory, however, raises more questions than it answers. What makes a soul the same soul over time? Answering this question seems more difficult than the one about persons. Also, just as the physical stuff that you are made of changes over time, why couldn't the immaterial stuff that you are made of? Rabadash has different bodies at different times. Why can't he also have different souls at different times? Since we never see the soul, how do we know how many it takes to sustain a person? Whether we are thinking of physical or non-physical stuff, it seems we can imagine it changing while the person remains the same person. Perhaps it is a mistake to think that persons are identical to any particular bit of stuff.[2]

Much the same can be said about the identity of other things. Consider King Caspian's ship, the *Dawn Treader*. On its voyage to the End of the World, the ship is attacked by a Sea Serpent and the ship's carved stern gets broken off (VTD, Chapter 8, p. 480). Later, the Magician Coriakin magically repairs the damage (VDT, Chapter 11, p. 505). So, the material of the *Dawn Treader* is no longer identical to its original material. The voyage was long and we can imagine that various parts of the ship wore out and had to be replaced. In fact, it's easy to imagine that all the original sails, planks, rigging, and nails were replaced before the ship returned to Narnia. It seems that Caspian returned in the same ship he left in, the *Dawn Treader*. Yet none of the material is the same. So what is the ship anyway? Identity over time is beginning to look mysterious indeed.

Cambridge University Press, 1988), Chapter 1. Hart provides a sophisticated and detailed defense of a contemporary soul theory.

[2] C.S. Lewis, being an orthodox Christian, is of course committed to *talk* of "souls." However it is far from clear that anyone who takes talk of souls seriously must be committed to the metaphysics of the soul theory. By "soul," Lewis may only intend whatever is essential to the "self." See the last section of this chapter, especially footnote 4.

Identity and Memory

If a person is not some particular kind of stuff, then what is left for it to be? When someone asks us who we really are, we may well answer by describing our personality traits and things we most value. This answer doesn't identify us with any kind of stuff, physical or non-physical. But although our personality and values are important, they don't seem essential to who we are. A person can undergo great changes in personality and overhaul his or her deepest values. Edmund and Eustace come to mind at once. Both have what we might call "conversions" after encounters with Aslan. After listening to Eustace's confession, Edmund comforts him. "'That's all right,' said Edmund. 'Between ourselves, you haven't been as bad as I was on my first trip to Narnia. You were only an ass, but I was a traitor'" (VDT, Chapter 7, p. 475). The chapter concludes by noting that from that day on Eustace "began to be a different boy" (VDT, Chapter 7, p. 476). One must be careful here. Eustace is still Eustace. It's his personality that's different, so personality will not account for personal identity.

Think of the *Dawn Treader* again. What makes it the same ship if all its parts are gradually replaced? It's not the material. Perhaps it's the function the material serves that makes it the same ship. All the different material preserves the constant function of a sailing ship. It's not the material that makes it a ship but how the material is organized. Perhaps identity is a unity of function or organization. So, what kind of unity would a person be? One influential suggestion comes from the English philosopher John Locke (1632–1704).[3] The unity that makes up a person is *consciousness*. What unites consciousness as time passes? Locke's answer is memory. Only I can have my conscious states. Conscious states are linked over time by memory. For Locke, memory is the key to personal identity. His criterion is simple. A person *A* at one time is the *same person* as person *B* at an earlier time if *A* has memories of *B*'s experiences. Since a person can have conscious awareness of only his own experiences, if *A* shares some of *B*'s memories, *A* must be a later stage of the same person as *B*.

---

[3] John Locke, *An Essay Concerning Human Understanding* (1690), Book 2, Chapter 27.

This theory will certainly explain many of the puzzles about persons in Lewis's *Chronicles*. Eustace, even as a dragon, remembers how beastly he was as a boy. Peter, Susan, Lucy, and Edmund, even after their return from Narnia, can recall their adventures as grown up kings and queens. Is memory the link that unites the different stages of a person over time? Though this explanation is certainly better than the body or the soul theory, it is not without its problems. It follows from this theory that a person exists only as far back as his or her memory extends. Does this mean that with total amnesia or Alzheimer's disease a person ceases to exist? Also, if I only extend as far back in time as my memory goes, then it doesn't seem that I am identical to the small child my parents called by my name. That could be a little unsettling. In *The Horse and His Boy*, Shasta has no memory of his real father or his true origin. He will never remember having early experiences of his father or brother before his exile. But the whole glorious ending of the story is that he comes to realize that he is the same person as that boy who was exiled. That story was *his* story. This ending would not make sense if a person exists only as far back as his memory extends.

Another problem for the memory theory is apparent if we consider the story of Prince Rilian in *The Silver Chair*. Though he later remembers who he is, he loses his memories while under the spell of the Queen of Underworld. "'Ten years!' said the Prince, drawing his hand across his face as if to rub away the past. 'Yes, I believe you. For now that I am myself I can remember the enchanted life, though while I was enchanted I could not remember my true self'" (SC, Chapter 11, p. 627). The memory theory cannot make sense of Rilian's statement. This last stage of Rilian, after the spell is broken, can remember being the earlier enchanted person as well as being the child of King Caspian. Now the memory theory would say these are stages of the same person, Rilian. Yet the enchanted person, while under the spell, cannot remember being the child of Caspian. So, the memory theory must say the enchanted person is not the same person as the child of Caspian. Thus, the memory theory is forced to conclude that the enchanted person both is Rilian and is not Rilian! This situation is obviously impossible. The memory theory cannot coherently explain what makes Rilian the same person who experiences all those changes.

If that's not bad enough, the memory theory faces yet another problem. We can't always trust our memories. Just because we think we remember something doesn't mean that we actually had the experience. Memories can be false as well as true. For example, we sometimes remember what we want to believe happened instead of what really happened. In *The Last Battle* we discover that Susan is "no longer a friend of Narnia" (LB, Chapter 12, p. 741). As a grown up she does not believe she or her siblings ever were in Narnia. Their memories are all fabrications of childhood fantasies. Eustace says that "whenever you've tried to get her to come and talk about Narnia or do anything about Narnia, she says, 'What wonderful memories you have! Fancy your still thinking about all those funny games we used to play when we were children'" (LB, Chapter 12, p. 741). How can we distinguish a true memory from a false one? A true memory is caused by the actual experience. But memory alone cannot determine its own cause. A memory always seems to be of the actual experience. The only way to know if the memory is a true one is to know if the person who had the memory is the same person who had the actual experience. But now the memory theory is chasing its own tail in a tight circle.

The memory theory has ways to break out of the circle. Outside evidence could establish that a memory is probably true. In that case, we could trust that the person with the memory is *probably* the person who had the earlier experience. But that means we can only trust our own identity over time on the basis of outside evidence. That I exist over time is at best only probable. Don't I know myself better than that?

Persons and Point of View

To be conscious is to have experiences. We navigate through the world based on our experiences. We don't trip over the curb because we see the curb coming. To achieve that we must be able to interpret our experiences. We must order our experiences in time and space. As time passes, the curb is experienced as coming closer and closer. Closer to what? To the person having the experience. These considerations show that understanding the flow of experience presupposes a *point of view*. To judge that the curb is three feet away assumes it is three feet away from *me*. Understanding experiences seems to presuppose a *first-person perspective.*

The pronouns "I" and "me" are first-person pronouns. "He" and "she" are third-person pronouns. Other than Elmo and former presidential candidate Bob Dole, almost everybody refers to themselves in the first-person. This fact about the way we talk is important, but having a *first-person perspective* is more than the ability to refer to oneself as "I." It is the ability to think of yourself as an "I" independently of any name or description. For example, I think, "I said I would do that," instead of "Tim Cleveland said Tim Cleveland would do that." When Rilian was enchanted he could not remember himself as Rilian, but he still had many first-person thoughts. "'Friends,' he said, 'my hour is very near. I am ashamed that you should see me yet I dread being left alone'" (SC, Chapter 11, p. 623). This ability lasts even through total amnesia. Suppose I suffer from complete memory loss. I can still think, "*I* have forgotten who *I* am." Having a first-person point of view is essential to having experiences, but memory continuity isn't essential to having a point of view. A person is something with this capacity for a first-person perspective. This capacity is something all the persons in the *Chronicles* possess. They are each particular first-person points of view sustained through time.

You might think of "point of view" and "first-person perspective" as simply other words for a soul, an immaterial thinking thing. This is not so. For human beings and non-human animals such as Reepicheep that are candidates for being persons, having a first-person perspective depends upon having a body. Why? A point of view is the focal point of experiences. It has a location. The best candidate for that location is within the bounds of a body. A point of view that is located nowhere in particular is nothing. So being a person depends upon having a body.[4] That does not mean a person is identical to his or her body. The *Dawn Treader* continued to exist even though

---

[4] Taken in isolation this statement implies that any agent without a body, such as God, is not a person. To avoid confusion let me reiterate that I am speaking here of human beings and non-human animals, what we might call "creatures," that are persons. A person is something with a first-person perspective. God is a person because God has first-person thoughts. The view is that having a first-person perspective does not have to be sustained by an immaterial substance or soul. In the case of humans and other creatures, their first-person perspective is constituted of a body, not by anything immaterial.

its parts changed. That does not mean it could exist with no parts. If we disassembled the *Dawn Treader* and scattered all its parts, the parts would still exist but not the *Dawn Treader.* It's *constituted* of its parts but not *identical* to them. In the same way, a person is constituted of a body but not identical to a body. A person's body can change, but one is never without a body. A person is a first-person point of view constituted by a body.[5]

One might propose the following objection to the first-person perspective theory, however. Suppose in the afterlife one encounters two persons that look exactly like Reepicheep. They both have the same memories, personalities, and both claim to be him. Which, if either, is the real Reepicheep? Can the first-person perspective theory say anything except: if the person thinks he is Reepicheep, then he is? But then two different persons would be identical to the original Reepicheep. That is impossible. So, an objector will claim that something must be wrong with the first-person theory. Consider how the soul theory would handle these duplication cases. The real Reepicheep is the one with his soul. If one of the duplicates has his soul, then he is Reepicheep. If neither has it, then both are imposters. Of course, we may never be able to *know* which one, if either, is Reepicheep. But there is nonetheless a *fact of the matter,* says the soul theorist. Thus, the duplication cases do no harm to the soul theory. So, perhaps the first-person theory should be aban-

---

[5] In *The Problem of Pain,* Lewis seems to articulate a theory of the self that sees first-person perspective as what is essential to personhood. Discussing the difference between creatures that have a self and those that have only awareness or "sentience," Lewis says of the merely sentient creatures that experience two pains: "[T]here are, indeed, two pains: but there is no co-ordinating self which can recognize that 'I have had two pains.' Even in a single pain there is no self to say 'I am in pain'—for if it could distinguish itself from the sensation—the bed from the stream—sufficiently to say 'I am in pain,' it would also be able to connect two sensations as *its* experience. The correct description would be 'Pain is taking place in this animal'; not as we commonly say, 'This animal feels pain', for the words 'this' and 'feels' really smuggle in the assumption that it is a 'self' or 'soul' or 'consciousness' standing above the sensations and organizing them into an 'experience' as we do." Lewis, *The Problem of Pain,* (San Francisco: HarperCollins, 2001), p. 136. Note that Lewis is obviously equating soul with whatever is essential to self or consciousness, and what he seems to suggest is essential is the ability to have first-person thoughts.

doned, and the soul theory reconsidered.

Such a conclusion would be much too hasty. The first-person theory implies we may never *know* which is the real Reepicheep, if either is. There is no third-person criterion for determining which "duplicate" preserves Reepicheep's first-person point of view. Nonetheless, the first-person theory also implies that there is a *fact of the matter.* Reepicheep is identical to his first-person perspective. If one of the duplicates preserves his first-person perspective, then he is Reepicheep. If neither preserves it, then both are mistaken. That both think they are Reepicheep is irrelevant. Some people falsely think they are Napoleon. So, Reepicheep's duplication does no more harm to the first-person point of view theory than it does to the soul theory.

The first-person point of view theory best explains how the characters in *The Last Battle* survive their deaths. What survive are their particular first-person points of view. But they are never without bodies. Their bodies are simply restored. This restoration is miraculous. But if we understand the idea of person correctly we can see that the afterlife Lewis describes is possible. A person can survive death if his or her first-person perspective continues in some kind of body. It may be a resurrected earthly body or a new heavenly body. In either case, the afterlife Lewis describes is perfectly consistent with what a person is. Careful reflection on Lewis's *Chronicles* may reveal not only insight into the idea of a person but room for hope as well. It all depends on your point of view.[6]

---

[6] For a beautifully worked out version of constitution and the first-person theory, see Lynn Rudder Baker's masterful *Persons and Bodies* (Cambridge: Cambridge University Press, 2000).

I am thankful to Gregory Bassham and Jerry Walls for their comments on an earlier version of this paper. I am especially grateful to Jean-Paul Vessel for numerous helpful suggestions.

16

Why Eustace Almost Deserved His Name: Lewis's Critique of Modern Secularism

ANGUS MENUGE

"There was a boy called Eustace Clarence Scrubb, and he almost deserved it" (VDT, Chapter 1, p. 425). Lewis doesn't say this merely because Eustace is an insufferable prig. Eustace is Lewis's portrayal of the thoroughly modern secularist, someone who views the world as a storehouse of physical stuff which science can use for human progress, but who rejects or ignores the ideas of spiritual reality and objective moral values. Unimaginative and closed to the supernatural, Eustace is a chronological snob (someone who thinks that new ideas are necessarily superior to old ones) who reads books that have "a lot to say about exports and imports and governments and drains," but are "weak on dragons" (VDT, Chapter 6, p. 464). Eustace's character and worldview reflect his "progressive" parents, Harold and Alberta, who are "very up-to-date . . . and wear "a special kind of underclothes" (VDT, Chapter 6, p. 425). Harold and Alberta see to it that Eustace goes to a modern "scientific" school, "Experiment House," where bullies are viewed as "interesting psychological cases" (SC, Chapter 1, p. 549) and Bibles are "not encouraged" (SC, Chapter 1, p. 551). It'as an environment that produces "men without chests,"[1] people who use their heads to satisfy their bellies, quite unchecked by the

---

[1] Lewis uses this term explicitly in *The Abolition of Man*. It is a reference to Plato's three-part model of the soul, in which the head represents the reason, the belly the appetite, and the chest the seat of moral virtue.

moral virtues that can lead one to sacrifice one's immediate wants for the greater good of the community.

Eustace is but one of several characters in the Narnia stories that embody modern secularism. The philosophy is critiqued throughout the *Chronicles*. This is not only because modern secularism conflicts with Lewis's own orthodox Christian worldview, which affirms spiritual reality and objective morality. Lewis was also concerned that, due to modern educational trends, all too many children growing up in the West were uncomfortably like Eustace. He witnessed this firsthand when he took evacuees from London into his Oxford home, the Kilns, during the Second World War: the children were fixated on the immediate world of the senses and on utilitarian projects, as if life had no higher meaning than transient experience and gaining material goods. Lewis himself had espoused modern secularism, but came to believe that this philosophy was both pernicious and intellectually flawed. After Lewis became a Christian, he wrote several works addressing modern secularism, exposing its dangers (for example, *The Abolition of Man*) and refuting its central claims (for example, *Miracles*). Lewis's critique of modern secularism takes the same two-pronged approach in *The Chronicles of Narnia*.

It's the Power, Stupid

We first encounter the philosophy of modern secularism in the person of Uncle Andrew, a reclusive figure who has found a way to travel to other worlds. Readers may be surprised that Uncle Andrew is described as both a scientist and a magician. This is quite intentional on Lewis's part. Lewis argues that experimental science, like magic, is liable to corruption by the lust for power.[2] When Digory (Uncle Andrew's nephew) and Polly (a neighbor) stumble into Uncle Andrew's laboratory, he sees the children as just the experimental subjects he needs: "This is too good an opportunity to miss. I wanted two children. . . . [A] guinea-pig can't tell you anything" (MN, Chapter 1, p. 16).

Like Eustace, Uncle Andrew is a man without a chest, quite willing to use other people to take the risks he lacks the courage

---

[2] This is an important theme in Lewis's science-fiction novel, *That Hideous Strength* (1945). See especially Chapter 9, Section 5 of that book.

to face himself. Viewing value as mere usefulness for a given end, he has no basis for granting that anything, even another person, has any inherent value or worth. On the other hand, people may have great instrumental value for the one thing Uncle Andrew does care about, scientific knowledge that he can use to make himself powerful, famous, and fabulously wealthy. On seeing the creation of Narnia by Aslan, Uncle Andrew is particularly struck by the fact that part of a lamp-post (brought into Narnia from London) grows into a brand new one.

> "The commercial possibilities of this country are unbounded. Bring a few old bits of scrap iron here, bury 'em, and up they come as brand new railway engines, battleships, anything you please. They'll cost nothing, and I can sell 'em at full prices in England. I shall be a millionaire." (MN, Chapter 9, pp. 67–68)

Although modern secularists like to emphasize the prestige of science, Lewis suggests they often have a rather low view of truth. This is not surprising. If nothing has intrinsic value, then even truth is not valuable for its own sake. What matters are only useful truths, truths that grant power. And because a secular framework provides no basis for objective morality, the strong can pursue power free from obligation to the weak. Lewis thereby argues that modern secular assumptions lead to a Nietzschean "master morality" in which power becomes the ultimate good.[3]

We see cruder expressions of the same philosophy in *The Voyage of the "Dawn Treader."* When King Caspian arrives, the Lone Islands are home to slave-traders who capture the landing party. Slavery depends on denying that all people have equal dignity and worth. While the rights of free people are protected, slaves have value only so far as they serve the interests of others. An unwanted slave, such as the hapless Eustace, has no value at all. Although Caspian abolishes slavery on the Lone Islands, he is himself tempted to reduce value to material gain. When Caspian discovers a magic pool that can transform any object into solid gold, he seeks to claim the island for Narnia so that he will become the richest king in the world (VDT, Chapter 8, pp. 483–84). Caspian does not learn from the fate of the

---

[3] For more on this theme, see Chapter 10 in this volume.

Narnian lord, transformed into a golden statue at the bottom of the pool. We may lose the value we really have by placing it in a material substitute. Only when Aslan appears is Caspian awakened from his enchantment, restoring a divine perspective on value.

Openness to the Transcendent

Modern secularism not only devalues human beings, it closes off the realm of the spiritual or supernatural—what philosophers call the transcendent. When the Pevensie children first visit the Professor's house, all except Lucy have a prejudice against possibilities that transcend their everyday experience. When Lucy claims to have found another country through the back of a wardrobe, they immediately suppose that she is either lying or deranged. They assume that these are the only possibilities even though all their actual evidence counts against both of them (Lucy is very honest and perfectly coherent). They do not seriously consider a third possibility, that Lucy is telling the truth, even though it better fits the evidence, for given their background philosophy such a thing "couldn't be true" (LWW, Chapter 5, p. 131). The Professor protests that their philosophy has closed their minds to the true logic of the situation. Lewis is arguing that modern secularism leads to a mind-set that dismisses claims for the transcendent (the existence of God, objective morality, miracles, "intelligent design"), even if they are well-supported by facts and logic. When the Professor complains, "Why don't they teach logic at these schools?" (LWW, Chapter 5, p. 131), Lewis thereby suggests that modern education is to blame.

An inadequate emphasis on critical thinking is not the only problem. Lewis argues that the secularization of education leads to a built-in bias against the transcendent. This is an important theme in *Prince Caspian*. When Miraz usurps the throne, he is eager to start a line of kings independent of Aslan. Rejecting Aslan's authority, he seeks to suppress all the stories that connect him to Narnia's history. Since Aslan is the Christ-figure of the *Chronicles*, Miraz's program is one of secularized revisionist history of the sort attempted in the Soviet Union. Miraz requires teachers to reject the old stories of Aslan as myths, no matter how well-attested. When Miraz discovers that the young

Caspian's nurse has told him of the great Lion, Miraz responds with Orwellian censorship: "never let me catch you talking—or *thinking* either—about all those silly stories again. . . . [T]here's no such person as Aslan. And there are no such things as lions" (PC, Chapter 4, p. 335). The nurse is summarily dismissed. An educational system that only presents secular accounts of reality inherently favors modern secularism over religious perspectives. Since students are only allowed to think along secular paths, they will easily, though erroneously, identify rationality with secular thought. The abstract logical possibility of the transcendent will not suffice to gain it a fair hearing.

We learn that a centralized educational system can be highly effective at promoting a secular bias. Miss Prizzle, one of Miraz's loyal teachers, taught "'History' that was . . . duller than the truest history you ever read and less true than the most exciting adventure story" (PC, Chapter 14, p. 408). When brought face to face with Aslan, Miss Prizzle, and all of her class except Gwendolen, preferred flight from transcendent reality to an acknowledgment of its existence (PC, Chapter 14, p. 408). As Lewis argues in *Miracles*, evidence alone will not settle the question of the supernatural, because for any experience, no matter how remarkable, the materialist can maintain that there must be some natural explanation, even if all those available are extremely improbable. This is why when Uncle Andrew hears Aslan sing Narnia into being, "he tried his hardest to make believe that it wasn't singing and never had been singing—only roaring as any lion might in a zoo in our own world. . . . Now the trouble about trying to make yourself stupider than you really are is that you very often succeed" (MN, Chapter 10, p. 75).

In our world, scientific progress has produced far more impressive results than those of medieval Narnia,[4] and many hastily conclude that naturalistic science[5] is the only source of knowledge (a view known as *scientism*). This has affected both the content of the curriculum and the understanding of the educational process itself. As Nancy Pearcey argues in her recent

---

[4] Upon hearing the *Dawn Treader* praised as a fine Narnian sailing ship, Eustace boasts of the technological superiority of our "liners and motorboats and aeroplanes and submarines" (VDT, Chapter 2, p. 437).
[5] By "naturalistic science" I mean science that will admit only natural causes for natural phenomena.

book, *Total Truth*,[6] modern secularists have claimed that only naturalistic science makes objective, cognitive claims. In disputed questions such as the origin of the universe and of life, this means that religious answers are treated as subjective preferences that could not amount to knowledge, and which therefore do not belong in the classroom. This is why the Bible is not encouraged at "Experiment House." For the same reason, ethics can neither be taught nor enforced. The pupils of the school are treated as experimental subjects, devoid of intrinsic value, who are conditioned to be useful to society. Like Miss Prizzle, the Head of Experiment House cannot accept the transcendent in front of her face: "when she saw the lion and the broken wall and Caspian and Jill and Eustace . . . she had hysterics and . . . began ringing up the police with stories about a lion escaped from a circus, and escaped convicts who broke down walls and carried drawn swords" (SC, Chapter 16, p. 663). She said this even though the police found no evidence to support her story and even though her own crazed behavior suggested she did not believe it herself, but was desperately repressing what she really knew.

By relegating issues of ultimate meaning and ethics to a private, subjective realm, modern education creates "men without chests," people who lack any credible basis for putting the needs of others before themselves. This is illustrated in secular, totalitarian societies where people are required to serve the State not because it is right, or because it is a calling from God, but simply so that they may play a useful role in the human machine. As various communist experiments have shown, this approach does not work, because no amount of conditioning really convinces people that they should give ultimate allegiance to the State. Having denied an objective basis for the moral authority of anything, modern secularism provides no reason to respect State authority. If power is the only prerogative, people will serve the State only when coerced, and will otherwise do as they please. But modern secularism gives no particular meaning to one's personal projects either. Can one really enjoy life if nothing ultimately counts as success, because life has no inherent value or purpose? We see the depressing fallout of modern

---

[6] Wheaton: Crossway, 2004.

secularism most clearly in the gnomes of Underland who were brainwashed into thinking that the Witch's dark world and quest for power were the only realities that mattered: "We didn't know who we were or where we belonged. We couldn't do anything, or think anything, except what she put into our heads. And it was glum and gloomy things she put there all those years" (SC, Chapter 14, p. 642). By "liberating" human beings from God, modern secularism allows the strong to enslave the weak for amoral purposes. When the illusory authority of the State's conditioners and usurpers is revealed, only nihilism, the view that nothing really matters, remains.

Is There Nothing More?

To call attention to the regrettable consequences of modern secularism falls short of a refutation. If the modern secular worldview is true, then we are stuck with these consequences and our preference for alternatives only shows our proneness to illusion. Indeed secular thinkers offer debunking explanations of our beliefs in transcendent realities, such as God or objective morality. For example, psychologist Sigmund Freud claimed religious beliefs were masks for childish wishes and repressed sexual desires, and the philosopher Michael Ruse and the scientist E.O. Wilson argue that "ethics as we understand it is an illusion fobbed off on us by our genes to get us to co-operate (so that human genes survive)."[7] But Lewis does not stop with exposing the unsettling fall-out of modern secularism; he uses the *Chronicles* to mount an effective critique. He argues both that modern secularism is inconsistent and that its debunking approach to transcendent realities is fatally flawed.

One of Lewis's arguments (developed at greater length in *The Abolition of Man* and *Miracles*) is that modern secularism is inconsistent in its treatment of human beings. The inconsistency is evident in those secularists who believe that human beings can be experimented on ("conditioned") for the sake of social progress. For these same secularists also assume that that some human beings (educators and scientists) are autonomous agents

---

[7] Michael Ruse and E.O. Wilson, "The Evolution of Ethics," *New Scientist* 108: 1478 (17th October, 1985), pp. 51–52.

who cannot be experimented on, even though they can experiment on others. Thus, Uncle Andrew is quite happy to use
Digory and Polly as talking guinea-pigs, to find out about other
worlds. But he exempts himself from trying the magic rings on
the grounds that he is a scientist.

> "I am the great scholar, the magician, the adept, who is *doing* the
> experiment. Of course I need subjects to do it *on.* . . . No great wis-
> dom can be reached without sacrifice. But the idea of going myself
> is ridiculous. It's like asking a general to fight as a common sol-
> dier." (MN, Chapter 2, p. 22)

The inconsistency is clear. Officially, the modern secularist
thinks all human beings can be shaped to promote progress,
and if that is so, Uncle Andrew has no basis, other than arbitrary
power, for claiming a privileged status for himself. Uncle
Andrew acts as if he alone has the special dignity and value of
a person, exempting him from being experimented on, but
allowing him to do experiments on others. But if Uncle Andrew
is such a person, then his secular view of human beings is false,
and there is no reason to deny that other human beings are persons as well. It follows that if it is wrong for experiments to be
done on Uncle Andrew, it is equally wrong for him to do those
experiments on others. Through his inconsistent philosophy of
human beings, Uncle Andrew is violating what philosophers call
the Principle of Relevant Difference. According to this principle,
it cannot be right to treat one person in a certain way and wrong
to treat another person in that way unless there is a relevant difference between the two people. Sometimes there are relevant
differences, which is why we can incarcerate criminals but not
law-abiding citizens, and why traffic cops are free to exceed the
speed limit but the rest of us are not. But there is no such relevant difference between Digory and Polly, on the one hand, and
Uncle Andrew, on the other, just because he is a scientist, while
Digory and Polly are not. This difference is not sufficient to support the claim of Uncle Andrew that he has distinctive personal
rights that set him apart from others.

More generally, Lewis believed that modern secularism is
incoherent because it assumes that the conditioners (scientists
and educators) have capacities that are incompatible with that
philosophy. Uncle Andrew and the teachers of "Experiment

House" think of themselves as rational beings with free will, since they believe they can design experiments and curricula and can choose whether or not to implement them. Yet they treat the subjects of these experiments and curricula as passive objects, to be shaped like the clay in a potter's hand. Either everything is merely a passive subject of the forces affecting it, in which case the conditioners have no more rationality or free will than their subjects, or there really are autonomous agents, in which case there is no good reason to say conditioners belong to this class but their subjects do not. In the first case, modern secularism undermines the rationality of education and science, because no one, including the conditioner, can make rational choices. In the second case, the conditioners have abandoned secularism by recognizing the transcendent value of persons. Either way, modern secularism is false.[8]

Debunking the Debunkers

Lewis also responded to the debunking strategies of secularists. As early as *The Pilgrim's Regress* (1933), an allegorical spiritual autobiography Lewis wrote shortly after his conversion, Lewis discerned a common logical pattern to the debunkers' theories. Debunkers always claim that transcendent ideas (such as the ideas of God, eternity, absolute truth, and objective morality) derive from mundane material causes. But, following Plato and Descartes, Lewis realized that one can think of an idea as a sort of copy, and its cause as the original. In that case, we should ask whether the original proposed by the secularist (a mundane material cause) is adequate to explain the copy (a transcendent idea). Lewis's argument is that the content of transcendent ideas could not derive from material causes. The most dramatic expression of this argument is found in *The Silver Chair*.

Prince Rilian is captured by the Witch of a dark, subterranean world called Underland, and placed under an enchantment that makes him forget who he is. Each night the enchantment abates and he is bound in a silver chair. Eustace (now reformed by his encounter with Aslan), Jill, and Puddleglum free the prince and

---

[8] For a more careful version of this argument, see my *Agents Under Fire: Materialism and the Rationality of Science* (Lanham: Rowman and Littlefield, 2004), especially Chapters 1–3.

are about to escape when the Witch returns. She tries to convince them that their departure is futile because Underland is all there is. One can view Underland as what the world is really like if modern secularism is true. The children, Rilian and especially Puddleglum all protest that Underland cannot be everything because they have ideas of an Overworld above, including its sun and Aslan. These can be read as the ideas that appear to transcend the secular.

Given this interpretation, we can see the Witch as a classic secular debunker. The Witch uses a heavy enchantment to make the others believe that what they can immediately see exhausts reality. This expresses Lewis's view that secularism appeals to our "favoritism for the familiar," our bias in favor of what we can directly experience. But Puddleglum still remembers the sun, comparing it to a lamp in the room. The Witch exploits the fact that the lamp is visible but the sun is not and argues that the idea of the sun derives simply from the lamp, which is all there really is. The same strategy is applied to the idea of Aslan himself, which must have been copied from a cat in Underland. The Witch triumphantly asserts a general principle for debunking transcendent ideas: "'you can put nothing into your make-believe without copying it from the real world, this world of mine, which is the only world'" (SC, Chapter 12, p. 632).

The enchantment is almost complete when Puddleglum counteracts it by stamping on the Witch's fire and replying to her debunking philosophy:

> "Suppose this black pit of a kingdom of yours *is* the only world. Well, it strikes me as a pretty poor one. And that's a funny thing, when you come to think of it. We're just babies making up a game, if you're right. But four babies playing a game can make a play-world which licks your real world hollow." (SC, Chapter 12, p. 633)

The argument is left rather implicit, but Lewis is clearly attacking the intelligibility of the debunkers' claim that our ideas of "higher" things can derive from "lower" sources. How can the idea of something great derive from something lacking that greatness? Could the idea of eternity arise from the materialist's temporal world? Could the ideas of infinity and perfection derive from the finite, imperfect world of the secularist? Could the idea of a necessary being like God derive from the secularist's contingent universe? There is a good case to be made that material causes do not account for the content of these ideas.

Fundamentally, modern secularism must claim that the ideas of eternity, infinity, perfection, and necessary existence are no more than illusions thrown up by a temporal, finite, imperfect, and contingent world, even though nothing in the causes of the ideas explains their content. But surely there is another possibility. The secularist assumes that we begin with matter and everything that seems to transcend matter must somehow be reducible to it. What if, instead, we begin with a being who actually is eternal, infinite, perfect and necessary? This original would surely suffice to explain anything else in the universe that is less than itself, but it would also explain how we have transcendent ideas, since they are copies of transcendent originals. Lewis suggests that the world around us is "shadowlands," a shadow or a copy of heavenly realities. At the end of *The Last Battle*, Narnia comes to an end and there is a new heaven and a new earth. Lord Digory explains:

> "[T]hat was not the real Narnia. That had a beginning and an end. It was only a shadow or a copy of the real Narnia which has always been here. . . . And of course it is different; as different as a real thing is from a shadow or as waking life is from a dream." (LB, Chapter 15, p. 759)

Lewis here turns the tables by suggesting that the material world is not the bedrock of reality, but only a copy of a divine original.

Beyond Shadowlands

Eustace Clarence Scrubb almost deserved his name because he had been taken in by modern secularism, a philosophy that Lewis argues is dangerous, inconsistent, and unable to explain transcendent ideas. But just as Eustace's mind was changed by his encounter with Aslan, Lewis suggests that a philosophy that affirms the reality of the transcendent can overcome the problems that beset modern secularism. Amazingly, he communicated all this through books ostensibly for children. But then Lewis saw the very idea of "children's books" as reflecting a condescending, progressive picture of education that derived from the very secularism he was combatting.

17

Time Keeps On Ticking, Or Does It? The Significance of Time in *The Chronicles of Narnia*

MICHAEL and ADAM PETERSON

In a deceptively simple way, Lewis weaves into the tales of Narnia many complex ideas that are widely discussed in the intellectual arena. One of these is the concept of time, which is a recurring motif throughout the *Chronicles*. As we shall see, Lewis's ideas about time lead us into philosophical reflection on extraordinary scientific findings, difficult metaphysical problems, and profound theological themes.

Toto, We're Not in Kansas Anymore!

Several of the Narnia books begin with the children conversing about time, trying to get their orientation to time—or perhaps we should say *dis*orientation! Eustace calls it "the usual muddle about times" (LB, Chapter 5, p. 693). The problem arises when Lucy first returns from the wardrobe. She thinks she has been gone for hours, but Peter and Susan say that only moments have passed:

> "What do you mean, Lu?" asked Peter.
> "What I said," answered Lucy. "It was just after breakfast when I went into the wardrobe, and I've been away for hours and hours, and had tea, and all sorts of things have happened."
> "Don't be silly, Lucy," said Susan. "We've only just come out of that room a moment ago, and you were there then." (LWW, Chapter 2, p. 120)

Contemporary fiction, fantasy, and film are no strangers to concepts such as time travel or crossing over into another dimension. Who can forget when Dorothy woke up in her bed in Kansas claiming that she and her dog, Toto, had many adventures in the Land of Oz? But her family and friends assured her that she had just been unconscious from a bump on the head!

It's not just that there are different times but that the "passage" or "flow" of time is different between this world and Narnia. Peter, Susan, Edmund, and Lucy became kings and queens in Narnia, aging, growing, and changing. We learn that Peter "became a tall and deep-chested man and a great warrior" (LWW, Chapter 17, p. 194). The most interesting change, though, is that Aslan appeared bigger as the children grew in Narnian time. Curious about this effect, Lucy asks Aslan if he really is bigger, and he replies: "I am not. But every year you grow, you will find me bigger" (PC, Chapter 10, p. 380).

Regardless of time spent in Narnia, when the children return to their normal world, they have not aged. Although they reigned "for years and years" in Narnia, when they came back through the door to England again, it all seemed to have taken "no time at all" (PC, Chapter 1, p. 317). When Edmund and Lucy meet Prince Caspian, we are told outright: "Narnian time flows differently from ours. If you spent a hundred years in Narnia, you would still come back to our world at the very same hour of the very same day on which you left. And then, if you went back to Narnia after spending a week here, you might find that a thousand Narnian years had passed, or only a day, or no time at all. You never know till you get there" (VDT, Chapter 1, p. 429; see also MN, Chapter 15, p. 103).

In addition, Narnian time flows at unpredictable rates.

> "And that means," continued Edmund, "that once you're out of Narnia, you have no idea how Narnian time is going. Why shouldn't hundreds of years have gone past in Narnia while only one year has passed for us in England?" (PC, Chapter 3, p. 330)

This unpredictability is behind Peter's remark that returning to Narnia after 1303 Narnian years had passed was as if they were "Crusaders or Anglo-Saxons or Ancient Britons or someone coming back to modern England" (PC, Chapter 3, p. 330).

Discrepancies over time occur in several of the tales. When the children come back to Narnia after being away for a year at boarding school, Caspian says they have been absent "exactly three years" in Narnian time (VDT, Chapter 2, p. 432). And King Tirian tells Jill that what she perceived to be the passage of a week in her world was a "scarce ten minutes in his world." He adds: "The time of your strange land is different from ours" (LB, Chapter 5, p. 693; compare to Chapter 16, p. 765). Interestingly, Lewis speculates that time in other worlds might have "thicknesses and thinnesses" in addition to linear directionality.[1]

Philosophical problems arise concerning both the subjective perception and objective reality of time. Clearly, Lewis's treatment of time in Narnia is completely appropriate to tales of fantasy, reflecting the child's less settled, less reflective sense of time as well as all of the wonderment of passing between the normal world and an imaginary world. After all, when children are having fun, time seems to pass too quickly; but time drags when they're bored. Similarly, Pink Floyd's "Time" from *Dark Side of the Moon* comments on how adult perception of time is different from that of youth: "You are young and life is long . . . and then one day you find ten years have got behind you. . . . Every year is getting shorter."[2] Although the subjective sense of time can vary between this world and Narnia, the *Chronicles* also claim that there is such a thing as objective time in each of the two realms, although it cannot be readily calibrated between them. And that claim deserves further discussion.

Does It Take an Einstein?

Sir Isaac Newton (1643–1727) advanced the classical objectivist view of time: "Absolute, true, and mathematical time, of itself and from its own nature, flows equably without relation to anything external, and by another name is called duration."[3] Even today, this is probably the instinctive view of the ordinary person—that there is cosmic time, regular and measurable,

---

[1] "Thickness" occurs "whenever we learn to attend to more than one thing at once." C.S. Lewis, *Letters to Malcolm: Chiefly on Prayer* (San Diego: Harvest, 1991), pp. 109–110. In the Great Dance in *Perelandra*, persons have "thicker" cords of time than do flowers and insects. C.S. Lewis, *Perelandra* (New York: Macmillan, 1968), p. 219. Also, eternity has "width," but chronological time has only "length." C.S. Lewis, *The Problem of Pain* (New York: Collier, 1962), p. 123.

[2] Capitol, original release March 24th, 1973.

[3] Isaac Newton, *Principia Mathematica*, (1687), Book I.

although persons might differ for various reasons in their perception of it.

Our understanding of time was revolutionized, however, by Albert Einstein's (1879–1955) special theory of relativity. Contrary to the traditional assumption that time is absolute, Einstein showed that "every reference body (co-ordinate system) has its own particular time."[4] Simply put, scientists have found that gravitational fields of massive bodies (such as the earth) and high speed motion (even approaching the speed of light), have amazing effects on time. Stephen Hawking (born in 1942) considers the effects of motion by recounting the famous Twins Paradox. Suppose that

> one of the twins went for a long trip in a spaceship at nearly the speed of light. When he returned, he would be much younger than his brother who stayed on Earth. . . . [T]here is no unique absolute time, but instead each individual has his own personal measure of time that depends on where he is and how he is moving.[5]

The astronaut's clocks—atomic and biological—have registered fewer hours and years than the clocks on earth have done. Amazingly, Einstein's theory implies the possibility of time travel (forward, not backward) and rejects absolute simultaneity (because there is no absolute time governing different frames of reference). Although different observers moving relative to each other will assign different times to the same event, no particular observer's measurement is more correct than any other's.

So, relativity theory lends plausibility to the idea that weeks and years pass for the children in Narnia while only a very short time passes in their normal world. This is possible given different frames of reference. Relativity also implies that any observer can calculate precisely what time and position any other observer will assign to an event, provided she knows the other observer's relative velocity. This makes rough sense of comparisons between times in Narnia and the ordinary world which Lewis provides in "An Outline of Narnian History."[6] In most recorded instances, Narnian time passes *more quickly* than time in England, although

---

[4] Albert Einstein, *Relativity: The Special and the General Theory*, translated by Robert W. Lawson (New York: Holt, 1920), p. 27.

[5] Stephen Hawking, *A Brief History of Time* (Toronto: Bantam, 1988), p. 33.

[6] Lewis MS 51 in Walter Hooper, *Past Watchful Dragons: A Guide to C.S. Lewis's*

the flow of time in Narnia is not uniform (for example, 1,303 Narnian years pass between the English years 1940 and 1941 but only a few Narnian years pass between 1941 and 1942). So the relationship between Narnian time and English time is more complex than we initially might have imagined.[7] Based on relativity, we might even speculate that Narnian time flows at unpredictable rates because of erratic changes in velocity, but this strains even the bounds of children's fantasy.[8]

Contemporary science might even tempt us to compare the wardrobe as a magical passage between our world and Narnia to "worm holes" (time warps in astrophysics) that allow travel between time frames in distant parts of the universe. Digory makes a similar point about the Wood between the Worlds, comparing it to the tunnel between their houses back home: "Mightn't this wood be the same?—a place that isn't in any of the worlds, but once you've found that place you can get into them all" (MN, Chapter 3, p. 28).

Popular culture is no stranger to such ideas. Traveling across the "space-time continuum" is a key theme in the Michael J. Fox film *Back to the Future*. And *The Santa Clause*, with Tim Allen, has little Charlie referring to the "space-time continuum" to explain to his skeptical mother and her husband how Santa can visit all the houses in one night. These astounding facts about time reflect a new scientific vision of the universe as holistic, dynamic, and interconnected, a theme that Lewis uses to great advantage.

Aslan Just in Time?

Perhaps the most enigmatic reference to time is Aslan's response to Lucy as he is leaving the children to visit Trumpkin the Dwarf. Aslan tells Lucy that they "shall meet soon again."

Chronicles of Narnia (London: Fount Paperbacks, 1980), pp. 50–53. See also Paul Ford's chart, entitled "A Comparison of Narnian and Earth Time," showing the curvilinear nature of Narnian time in his *Companion to Narnia* (New York: Macmillan, 1994), pp. 454–55.

[7] In all recorded instances of someone returning to England from Narnia, Narnian time appears to go faster than English time. But from the perspective of someone returning to Narnia, the relationship is unpredictable, almost always seeming that Narnian time goes more quickly but in one instance more slowly. We are grateful to Devin Brown for making this point so perspicuously.

[8] In *Perelandra* (p. 220) Lewis speaks of changing "waves of time."

"Please, Aslan," said Lucy, "what do you call *soon?*"
"I call all times soon," said Aslan. (VDT, Chapter 11, p. 499)

All times soon? Incredible!

Relativity theory allows us say that Aslan inhabits a different frame of reference but doesn't explain how "all times" from all frames of reference can be immediately present to any observer. This is because the transmission of information anywhere in the universe cannot be faster than the speed of light (186,000 miles per second). It takes billions of years, for example, for light to reach earth from remote galaxies.

For everyone except Aslan—the characters in the story and all of us—there is such a thing as time. There is the need to measure, and be measured by, time. So, what are we to make of Aslan's claim that his relation to time is not like Lucy's or anyone else's? That for him all times—and therefore all events in all times—are immediately present? This claim is tantamount to the assertion that Aslan is not limited by any frame of reference or the speed of light, but that he can simultaneously encompass all other frames of reference. The very best in contemporary science has no categories to explain this!

Now our discussion of time has moved into the territory of metaphysics, the branch of philosophy that addresses the big questions of ultimate reality that lie beyond the reach of empirical science. And we can't take this discussion very far without factoring in Lewis's metaphysical commitment to theism—the belief that there is an all-powerful, all-knowing, all-good being who is the eternal, personal creator and sustainer of the world. This makes it plausible to interpret Aslan's statement—"I call all times soon"—as expressing the view that God is timeless.

The theistic tradition affirms God's eternity, but theists disagree over whether God's eternity is "timeless" or "everlasting." The *timelessness* position asserts that God does not experience the world moment by moment as we finite persons do, but rather that he experiences the world's history all at once. The medieval philosopher Boethius (A.D. 480–525) says that God possesses an endless life which has neither past, nor present, nor future, which he embraces as a "simultaneous whole" in an "eternal present."[9] Lewis sides with this position: "Almost certainly," he

---

[9] Boethius, "God is Timeless," in Peterson *et al.*, eds., *Philosophy of Religion:*

writes in *Mere Christianity*, "God is not in Time." Since our
human life "comes to us moment by moment," we instinctively
assume that this is the way things are for God, except endlessly
so. But Lewis says that every moment from the beginning of the
world is "always the Present for Him."[10] Unlike us, God doesn't
have to wait billions of years to find out what's going on in
some remote part of the universe!

Some theists hold an alternative position: that God is *everlasting* through time and not outside of time. They argue that
timelessness—as held by Lewis and many other theists—reflects
ancient Greek thinking that God is static and unchangeable. At
stake in the disagreement is whether we can coherently think of
God as a *personal agent*. Conceptually, we take agents and their
actions to be in time. The biblical description of God as one who
plans, responds, and redeems entails that God changes, and that
these changes have beginnings and endings. So, surely, in some
significant way, God is in time. In support of this point, philosopher Nicholas Wolterstorff (born in 1932) argues that "any being
which changes is a being among whose states there is temporal
succession."[11] Theists holding the *everlastingness* position
believe that it appropriately preserves important characteristics of
God: that God is still distinct from finite creatures in that he has
no beginning and no ending, that his own existence is in himself, and that he is sovereign over his creation.

Although we cannot pursue this intriguing debate further, it's
clear that Lewis rejects *everlastingness* and proceeds as if *timelessness* is no obstacle to God's being an agent. In *The Horse and His
Boy*, the Large Voice of Aslan discloses that he was the hidden
influence always working on Shasta's behalf—as the cat who com-
forted him among the Tombs, as the lion who gave the Horses new
strength, and so on (HHB, Chapter 11, p. 281). This account typi-
fies Lewis's understanding that God's providence timelessly inter-
acts with events in the temporal world, including free choices.[12]

Selected Readings, second edition (New York: Oxford University Press, 2001),
pp. 137–38.

[10] C.S. Lewis, *Mere Christianity* (New York: Simon and Schuster, 1996), p. 146.

[11] Nicholas Wolterstorff, "God Is Everlasting," in Peterson, *Philosophy of
Religion*, p. 140.

[12] C.S. Lewis, *Miracles* (San Francisco: HarperCollins, 2001), Appendix B. See
also *The Great Divorce* (San Francisco: HarperCollins, 2001), pp. 139–144.

Aslan's Limitation

Lewis acknowledges that metaphysical theories about God's relation to time are matters about which thoughtful people, including Christian believers, legitimately disagree. However, he also recognizes that the theory one holds must fit coherently with one's other views. So, in his philosophical writings, he is careful to explain how his own theory of God's timelessness fits with a number of key concepts, such as petitionary prayer and the incarnation of the Son of God in a human being, Jesus of Nazareth.[13] But Lewis is also concerned to explain how time-lessness does not violate human free will.

Some philosophers think that God's timeless knowledge negates free will—that is, the power to do otherwise than one in fact does. The *Chronicles*, however, confidently combine Aslan's timelessness with portrayals of the characters' free choices. Aslan says he can do nothing with Uncle Andrew, the Magician, for "he has made himself unable to hear my voice" (MN, Chapter 14, p. 98). When Lucy asks Aslan to save Edmund, Aslan replies, "All shall be done," but it may be "harder than you think" (LWW, Chapter 12, p. 169). Aslan even warns Rabadash to put aside his pride and accept "mercy" so that he may avoid certain doom, but Rabadash freely chooses destruction (HB, Chapter 16, 306–07). So, truly free choices are not determined by Aslan's timeless knowledge or by any other capacity of Aslan.

When Tirian and the Seven Kings and Queens meet inside the Stable and discover the Dwarfs huddling together, they soon perceive that they are not really in a stable but in a beautiful, open place. But the Dwarfs cannot perceive this, complain about the cramped conditions, and cannot even recognize Aslan when he appears. When Lucy asks Aslan to help them see, he answers: "I will show you both what I can, and what I cannot do" (LB, Chapter 13, p. 747). First, Aslan growls, but the Dwarfs hear it as a gang in the Stable trying to intimidate them (compare to MN, Chapter 14, p. 98). Then Aslan makes a glorious feast appear, and even though they eat, they complain that it is distasteful stable food.

---

[13] Respectively, *Miracles*, Appendix B, and *Mere Christianity*, p. 148.

"You see," said Aslan. "They will not let us help them. They have chosen cunning instead of belief. Their prison is only in their own minds, yet they are in that prison; and so afraid of being taken in that they cannot be taken out." (LB, Chapter 13, p. 748)

Not even Aslan can override the Dwarfs' free will. In the same vein, *The Great Divorce* tells us that Hell is the creature shutting itself up "within the dungeon of its own mind."[14]

Lewis's book *Mere Christianity* contains an explicit argument for the compatibility of God's timeless knowledge and free choice:

> [I]f God *foresaw* our acts, it would be very hard to understand how we could be free not to do them. But suppose God is outside and above the Time-line. In that case, what we call "tomorrow" is visible to him in just the same way as what we call "today." All the days are "Now" for Him. . . . He does not "foresee" you doing things tomorrow; He simply sees you doing them: because, though tomorrow is not yet there for you, it is for Him.[15]

Time's Up!

Gaining a complete understanding of how time is used in the *Chronicles* requires more than exploring the science of relativity and the metaphysics of timelessness. It requires an examination of the theological significance of Aslan's timeless life and purposes. As Lewis says in *Mere Christianity*, our life is "dribbled out moment by moment"; but of God he says, "His life is Himself."[16] The Bible depicts God speaking to Moses from the burning bush: "I am that I am"—that is, I am the Ever-living One (Exodus 3:14, KJV).

Theologically, this means that the inhabitants of time—persons, animals, and objects—and indeed time itself are created things, not self-existent. Aslan, by contrast, is in complete con-

---

[14] Lewis, *Great Divorce,* p. 70.
[15] Lewis, *Mere Christianity,* p. 149; see also *Miracles,* pp. 176–77. For a critique of this argument, see Gregory Bassham, "The Prophecy-Driven Life: Freedom and Foreknowledge at Hogwarts," in David Baggett and Shawn E. Klein, eds., *Harry Potter and Philosophy: If Aristotle Ran Hogwarts* (Chicago: Open Court, 2004), pp. 220–21.
[16] Lewis, *Mere Christianity,* p. 148.

trol of time, the great framework of our finite, contingent existence. This is clear when Aslan culminates history in the great Battle at the Stable (LB, Chapters 9–12, pp. 718–741) and calls Time itself to an end (LB, Chapter 13, pp. 748–751). Since time bounds our existence, what we creatures do with the time we have takes on tremendous significance: the choices we make, the actions we perform, the things we love, the aims we pursue.

In other words, time is filled with opportunity that we either grasp and use to the fullest or let slip through our fingers. Edmund, who himself was in peril of turning against good, chose to resist the sinister White Witch, and succeeded in destroying her wand and turning the fortunes of a fierce battle (LWW, Chapter 17, p. 192). However, the Dwarfs chose not to know Aslan as he really is. *The Great Divorce* aptly describes those who refuse the ultimate opportunity: "There is always something they insist on keeping even at the price of misery. There is always something they prefer to joy—that is, to reality."[17]

Opportunity for curing their self-imposed blindness melts away as the Dwarfs persist in the darkness of their own perceptions. Aslan roars: "Now it is time!" then louder, "Time!"; then so loud that it could have shaken the stars, "TIME". The Door flew open (LB, Chapter 13, p. 748). Through the open doorway, Tirian, the children, and the others see the great giant, Father Time, awaken from his sleep. Aslan says: "While he lay dreaming his name was Time. Now that he is awake he will have a new one" (LB, Chapter 14, p. 749).

The Last Battle conveys the theme that Time will be transcended, and only those creatures who have loved and followed Aslan in time can share in the transformation that is to come. Creaturely time—and opportunity in time—ends in Aslan's judging the truth of hearts as all rational creatures great and small, one by one, come through the Door. The very sense of time is confused in the description of this event: "This part of the adventure . . . seemed rather like a dream . . . . Especially, one couldn't say how long it had taken. Sometimes it seemed to have lasted only a few minutes, but at others it felt as if it might have gone on for years" (LB, Chapter 14, p. 751). Here Lewis won't let anyone's perception of time be normal. How could he,

---

[17] Lewis, *Great Divorce*, p. 71.

with all creaturely worlds and therefore all times coming to an end?

As the children observe the terrible apocalyptic spectacle through the doorway, they see Dragons and Giant Lizards destroying Narnia, only themselves to die and whither, swept away by the perishing of time itself. Then Aslan says to Father Time, "Now make an end." The giant quenches the sun and all is darkness. Aslan then instructs Peter to close the Door, which he locks with a golden key (LB, Chapter 14, p. 753). Time is no more. But this ending is also a beginning. The children realize that they are in a beautiful country with blue sky and flowers and towering green mountains in the distance. They see laughter in Aslan's eyes as he turns and shoots away toward the mountains, saying, "Come further in! Come further up!"

Where Is Aslan's Country?

This is Aslan's country. But how is it related to Narnia and the children's England? The children don't have a geography—or a chronology—to grasp it. Following Aslan westward into the high mountains, Peter, Lucy, and the others discuss whether it's wrong to mourn for Narnia (LB, Chapter 14, p. 753). When they begin to recognize features of Narnia along the way, they are puzzled over how they previously could have witnessed its destruction. In temporal life, once things are destroyed, they do not return. Peter wonders aloud why Aslan told them they would never return to Narnia, because they obviously had returned. How should they think about this new place, Aslan's country?

Digory explains that Aslan meant they could not return to the Narnia of their finite, temporalized understanding: "[T]hat was not the real Narnia. That had a beginning and an end." He continues, saying that the Narnia and England they knew were just faint copies or shadows of the real Narnia and the real England (LB, Chapter 15, p. 759). Both time and what the children loved in time are contrasted to fuller, richer existence in Aslan's country. "All of the old Narnia that mattered, all the dear creatures," have not perished but are more real than ever (LB, Chapter 15, p. 759). Even the flowers have "more color," and every rock and blade of grass looks as if it "meant more" (LB, Chapter 15, pp. 759–761). Using similar images, *The Great Divorce* pictures both persons and things as more solid in Heaven.

Jewel the Unicorn cries out, "I have come home at last! This is my real country. I belong here. This is the land I have been looking for all my life, though I never knew it till now. The reason why we loved the old Narnia is that it sometimes looked a little like this" (LB, Chapter 15, p. 760). Jewel here articulates the theological principle of the inherent value of temporal creaturely life, damaged but not destroyed by sin. So, it is entirely appropriate, as we spend the time of our lives, to love the truly good things and wish they would not end.[18] Indeed, we find ourselves wishing with Jill that Narnia "might go on for ever" and not be subject to the inevitable destruction of time (LB, Chapter 14, p. 753). As it dawns on Jewel that he is in exactly that place which he had always desired, he squeals to everyone with the sheer delight of total self-abandonment: "Bree-hee-hee! Come further up, further in!"

Aslan's timeless country is thus the context in which persons find their ultimate fulfillment. "Great joy" characterizes those who love Aslan and pass through the Door. After the Door is shut, the children feel deep satisfaction and their "hearts leapt" as a "wild hope" arises within them that they might stay with Aslan forever (LB, Chapter 16, pp. 766–67). Their joy is increased when they find that their friends Roonwit the Centaur, Farsight the Eagle, and many others who had died are among "the happy creatures" filling Aslan's timeless kingdom. When we are related to God, Lewis says, we become "more truly ourselves."[19]

Life with Aslan

Time in the *Chronicles* allows Lewis to say both what Aslan's country is and what it is not. It *is* a condition of full reality that is *not* subject to decay, destruction, and death. Now if "time-lessness" sets Aslan apart from all else, we may ask, What is the unique nature of Aslan such that there is an unsurpassable quality of experience in his country?

---

[18] See Lewis, *Great Divorce*, p. 105: "Every natural love will rise again and live forever in this country."

[19] Lewis, *Mere Christianity*, p. 190; see also *Great Divorce*, p. 132: "Everything becomes more and more itself" in Heaven.

Subtle clues—the "laughter" in Aslan's eyes (LB, Chapter 14, p. 753), Aslan's gently touching Emeth's forehead with his tongue (LB, Chapter 15, pp. 756–57)—suggest that joy, love, and peace characterize the life of Aslan. Joy, love, peace, and the personal beings that are created to experience them are meant to last forever, beyond the ravages of time.[20] In *Mere Christianity*, Lewis writes:

> If you want joy, power, peace, eternal life, you must get close to, or even into, the thing that has them. . . . Once a man is united to God, how could he not live forever? Once a man is separated from God, what can he do but wither and die?[21]

We should not be surprised, therefore, that when Tumnus the Faun surveys the new land with Peter, Edmund, and Lucy, he explains: "that country and this country—all the *real* countries—are only spurs jutting out from the great mountains of Aslan" (LB, Chapter 16, p. 766). Connectedness in the country of Aslan is a metaphor for our participation in the life of God.

And God is Love. "Christians believe," Lewis writes, that "the living, dynamic activity of love has been going on in God forever and has created everything else."[22] The wonderful literary portrayal of this idea is that Narnia is created by Aslan singing, "Narnia, Narnia, Narnia, awake. Love. Think. Speak" (MN, Chapter 9, pp. 64–70). God is not a static thing, Lewis explains, but a dynamic, pulsating activity, a life, almost a kind of drama or dance. Specifically, the God, who is above mere time, is essentially personal-social-relational life—or, as classical Christianity teaches, a Trinity, Three Persons in one Being. The *Chronicles* help us understand that we creatures of time must become related to what is beyond time. There is no other way to the happiness for which we were made.[23]

The fascinating tales of Narnia—in which time, different times, and what is beyond time figure so prominently—captivate

---

[20] Lewis says that we long to emerge from the "unilinear poverty" of time. *Reflections on the Psalms* (San Diego: Harvest, 1986), p. 137.

[21] Lewis, *Mere Christianity,* p. 153.

[22] *Ibid.*, pp. 152–53.

[23] "The humans live in time, but our Enemy destines them to eternity." Lewis, *The Screwtape Letters* (New York: Collier, 1982), pp. 67–68.

children, pushing all of their buttons with talking animals, evil witches, Father Christmas, dragons, and a struggle to save a strange but charming land. No doubt the story appeals to the child in all of us. But it also touches the adult in all of us—the adult who has struggled with pain and disappointment, longed for enduring good, and who realizes deep down that the true meaning of it all, which we seek in time, cannot be a human creation and therefore must lie outside of time.

Interpreted theologically, the tales of Narnia are about the offer to finite creatures to allow a new world to be born in each of us and to let it come to full fruition in God's kingdom. We could state Mr. Tumnus's earlier point more precisely and say that the *connectedness* of everything to the mountains of Aslan is what *makes* them truly *real*. The imagery of connectedness suggests that God's purpose is to bring about a great community or society or, indeed, a family. *The Chronicles of Narnia* paint an inviting picture of a relational universe whose whole destiny—sidetracked by doubt, struggle, and evil within the domain of creaturely time—is back on track toward its timeless source. No wonder, as we read it, as child or as adult, we seem to hear at our own level a voice beckoning to us: Come further in and further up!

Part IV

The Deepest Magic

Religion and the Transcendent

18

Aslan the Terrible: Painful Encounters with Absolute Goodness

ERIK J. WIELENBERG

> Some people talk as if meeting the gaze of absolute goodness would be fun. They need to think again.
>
> —C.S. Lewis, *Mere Christianity*

When Peter, Susan, and Lucy first encounter Aslan in *The Lion, the Witch, and the Wardrobe*, the meeting is not an easy one:

> People who have not been in Narnia sometimes think that a thing cannot be good and terrible at the same time. If the children had ever thought so, they were cured of it now. For when they tried to look at Aslan's face they just caught a glimpse of the golden mane and the great, royal, solemn overwhelming eyes; and then they found they couldn't look at him and went all trembly. (LWW, Chapter 12, pp. 168–69)

Puzzling. How can something be good *and* terrible at the same time? Like roundness and squareness, or Paris Hilton and Saturday night bingo, the two just don't seem to go together.

As any Philosophy 101 student can attest, however, apparent incompatibility often yields compelling philosophy. According to Lewis, not only are goodness and terribleness compatible, their combination lies at the core of all genuine religious experience.[1] In this chapter we'll explore Lewis's views on "trembly" experi-

---

[1] C.S. Lewis, *God in the Dock: Essays on Theology and Ethics*, edited by Walter Hooper (Grand Rapids: Eerdmans, 1970), p. 175. Lewis, following Rudolf Otto, calls this combination the "Numinous."

ences of the divine, and see how they can help us understand why a good God allows bad things to happen to good people.

Hume's Challenge

Starry skies. Sunlight dancing on the surface of a mountain lake. A child's smile. Ours is a universe of great goodness and beauty. It is also a universe of great pain and suffering—of wasting diseases, devastating natural disasters, senseless accidents, and barbaric concentration camps. The goodness and beauty seem to point to a wise, loving, and powerful Creator. The pain and suffering suggest a world of blind and indifferent natural forces. "The heavens declare the glory of God," sings the Psalmist. "Reality bites," is the Buddha's blunt reply.[2] Who's right? How can the universe be in the hands of a good God and also contain so much suffering? This is a thorny puzzle philosophers call "the problem of pain." One of the most famous and powerful skeptical treatments of the problem is found in David Hume's *Dialogues Concerning Natural Religion* (1779).

In the *Dialogues*, Hume raises the problem of pain by way of two characters, Demea and Philo. Demea offers the following Puddleglumian description of life on earth:

> The whole earth . . . is cursed and polluted. A perpetual war is kindled among all living creatures. Necessity, hunger, want stimulate the strong and courageous: fear, anxiety, terror agitate the weak and infirm. The first entrance into life gives anguish to the newborn infant and to its wretched parent: Weakness, impotence, distress attend each stage of that life. And it is at last finished in agony and horror.[3]

Demea is clearly not the sort of chap one wants working on suicide hotline! For most creatures on earth, he thinks, life is short, nasty, fearful, and painful. Philo agrees with Demea about the rottenness of life and ultimately concludes from this that there isn't a good God running things after all.

---

[2] A loose translation of Buddha's First Noble Truth: "Life is suffering." An alternate translation might be: "Shit happens. A lot."

[3] David Hume, *Dialogues Concerning Natural Religion*, second edition (Indianapolis: Hackett, 1998), p. 59.

It is precisely the suggestion that the ills of the world disprove God's existence that Lewis is out to refute in his book *The Problem of Pain*. To do this, Lewis tries to explain why a good God would allow so much suffering. Philosophers who discuss this sort of thing often draw a distinction between *moral* evil (wrong choices by human free will that often lead to suffering) and *natural* evil (destruction and suffering that is caused by other things, like natural disasters). Lewis suggests that about four-fifths of the suffering in the world falls into the first category. But what of the remaining one-fifth? This is where things get interesting. If God exists, then He is the ultimate cause of all the natural suffering in the universe. So, to explain this sort of suffering, Lewis really has to answer the following brain-buster: Why would a good God hurt His creatures?

God's Megaphone, Aslan's Claws: The Transformations of Edmund and Eustace

One reason God might hurt us is to let us know that we are doing something wrong and to allow us to see our evil in its true light:

> [P]ain insists on being attended to. God whispers to us in our pleasures, speaks in our conscience, but shouts in our pain: it is His megaphone to rouse a deaf world. A bad man, happy, is a man without the least inkling that his actions do not 'answer', that they are not in accord with the laws of the universe.[4]

In the Christian universe, God is in charge; in Narnia, Aslan is in charge ("he seems to be at the back of all the stories") (HHB, Chapter 14, p. 302). As Puddleglum, the pessimistic but insightful Marsh-wiggle sagely notes, "[t]here *are* no accidents. Our guide is Aslan" (SC, Chapter 10, p. 620). And Aslan often uses pain as his megaphone.

Edmund is the first character in the *Chronicles* to be roused by Aslan's megaphone. After Lucy returns from her initial visit to Narnia by way of the wardrobe, Edmund teases her mercilessly: "He sneered and jeered at Lucy and kept on asking her if she'd

---

[4] C.S. Lewis, *The Problem of Pain* (New York: HarperCollins, 2001 [1940], p. 91.

found any other new countries in other cupboards all over the house" (LWW, Chapter 3, p. 121). Upon his own arrival in Narnia, Edmund quickly falls under the spell of the White Witch and her magically delicious Turkish Delight. Afterwards, to spite Lucy, he refuses to tell Peter and Susan that Narnia is real. And, of course, it's Edmund who betrays the others to the White Witch in hopes of becoming King of Narnia and obtaining all the Turkish Delight he can eat. Edmund, in short, is an ethically challenged boy—at least initially.

Edmund's rousing begins as soon as he sneaks away from dinner with Mr. and Mrs. Beaver and goes to the Witch's palace in order to betray his siblings. There is no Turkish Delight in the offing; instead, Edmund is forced to travel by sledge in the Narnian winter without a coat—"And oh, how miserable he was!" (LWW, Chapter 11, p. 162). His suffering soon forces him to face the truth about the Witch: "All the things he had said to make himself believe that she was good and kind and that her side was really the right side sounded to him silly now" (LWW, Chapter 11, p. 162).

But the crucial transformation occurs when Edmund finally thinks of someone other than himself. It is selfishness that underlies all his nastiness, and he is fully roused only when he is cured of this. The important moment arrives when Edmund and the Witch stumble across a group of animals enjoying a meal given to them by Father Christmas. The Witch is so enraged by Father Christmas's return to Narnia that she turns the creatures to stone, despite Edmund's protests. Edmund is roughly treated for his objections:

> "As for you," said the Witch, giving Edmund a stunning blow on the face as she re-mounted the sledge, "let that teach you to ask favour for spies and traitors. Drive on!" And Edmund, for the first time in this story, felt sorry for someone besides himself. It seemed so pitiful to think of those little stone figures sitting there all the silent days and all the dark nights, year after year, till the moss grew on them and at last even their faces crumbled away. (LWW, Chapter 11, p. 163)

Edmund learns from his suffering, and he becomes a better person as a result. Later, when he encounters the Witch after his rescue, he is no longer under her spell: "Edmund had got past thinking about himself after all he'd been through. . . . It didn't seem to matter what the Witch said" (LWW, Chapter 13, p. 175). In the ensuing battle against the Witch, Edmund smashes her wand and is nearly killed in the process. His suffering has made him into a hero.

Eustace undergoes a similar transformation in *The Voyage of the "Dawn Treader."* But his case is different from Edmund's in interesting ways. Like Edmund, Eustace starts off as, in the words of the now-reformed Edmund, a "record stinker" (VDT, Chapter 1, p. 426). He is thoroughly selfish and believes himself superior to everyone else. He has an awful time during his first days on the *Dawn Treader*; everything about the voyage is "beastly" or "ghastly," and everyone around him is stuck-up, incompetent, or both. Whereas Edmund's misery during his journey on the White Witch's sledge almost immediately began to rouse him, Eustace's misery on board the *Dawn Treader* only seems to make him worse. He becomes increasingly resentful and selfish. The reason for this, I submit, is that Eustace's initial character is worse than Edmund's. It's true that Edmund's *actions*—particularly the betrayal—are worse than those of Eustace. But keep in mind that Edmund was under the influence of evil magic, and that Eustace was never presented with the opportunity to commit the sort of betrayal that Edmund committed. Moreover, unlike Eustace, Edmund was never entirely deceived about the morality of his own actions. Even as he was carrying out his act of betrayal, "deep down inside him he really knew that the White Witch was bad and cruel" (LWW, Chapter 9, p. 152). Because Eustace's character is more thoroughly corrupted than Edmund's ever was, he requires a more radical treatment.

The treatment begins after he slips away to avoid doing his share of work and stumbles across a dragon's lair. After witnessing the death of the dragon, he enters the lair, discovers the dragon's treasure and falls asleep. What happens next is startling: "He had turned into a dragon while he was asleep. Sleeping on a dragon's hoard with greedy, dragonish thoughts in his heart, he had become a dragon himself" (VDT, Chapter 6, p. 466). Finally, in light of this experience, Eustace begins to see things as they really are:

> He realized that he was a monster cut off from the whole human race. An appalling loneliness came over him. He began to see that

the others had not really been fiends at all. He began to wonder if he himself had been such a nice person as he had always supposed. (VDT, Chapter 6, p. 466)

The final step in Edmund's transformation in *The Lion, the Witch, and the Wardrobe* is an encounter with Aslan (LWW, Chapter 13, p. 174). The same is true of Eustace's cure. Edmund, however, apparently received nothing more than a stern lecture from Aslan. Things are different with Eustace. When he encounters Aslan, Eustace, like Peter, Susan, and Lucy, is afraid. But Eustace's fear is greater; unlike them, he cannot approach Aslan or even glance at his face. He closes his eyes instead. In order to turn Eustace back into a human, Aslan tears off Eustace's dragon-scales with his claws. The process is, in a word, terrible: "The very first tear that he made was so deep that I thought it had gone right into my heart. And when he began pulling the skin off, it hurt worse than anything I've ever felt" (VDT, Chapter 7, pp. 474–75). After this painful process, Eustace "began to be a different boy. . . . The cure had begun" (VDT, Chapter 7, p. 476). Eustace was roused by Aslan's claws—the Narnian equivalent of God's megaphone.

Discovering Our Hidden Strengths:
Abraham and Shasta

Suffering may also serve a very different purpose besides exposing and correcting defects in our character. To see this, let's consider one of the most dramatic episodes in the Christian Bible, the binding of Isaac. This episode begins when God commands Abraham to take "your son, your only son Isaac, whom you love, and go to the land of Moriah, and offer him there as a burnt offering on one of the mountains that I shall show you" (Exodus 22:2). Without objecting or asking for an explanation for the troubling command, Abraham gets up bright and early the next morning and journeys to Moriah. He finds the mountain, prepares everything for the sacrifice, and raises the knife to kill his only son. At the last instant, God stops the proceedings with these words: "Do not lay your hand on the boy or do anything to him; for now I know that you fear God, since you have not withheld your son, your only son, from me" (Exodus 22:12).

This explanation for God's actions is puzzling; surely an all-knowing God wouldn't need to carry out such an experiment to discover the depth of Abraham's faith. Lewis, following St. Augustine (354–430 C.E.), suggests that "whatever God knew, Abraham at any rate did not know that his obedience could endure such a command until the event taught him."[5] In other words, God subjects Abraham to this ordeal so that *Abraham,* not God Himself, can discover the depth of Abraham's faith.

What this shows is that pain can be used not only to make clear to us our moral failings, but also to reveal and develop moral strengths we didn't know we had. Aslan uses this very technique in *The Horse and His Boy.* The episode I have in mind occurs as Shasta and Aravis, riding, respectively, Bree and Hwin, try to beat Rabadash's army to Anvard. A lion appears from nowhere and begins to chase them. Shasta and Bree are ahead and close to safety but the lion is right on the heels of Aravis and Hwin. Shasta, unable to get the terrified Bree to turn around, leaps off and runs back to face the lion himself. Weaponless, all he can do is shout at the lion to go home: "Then, to his utter astonishment, the lion, still on its hind legs, checked itself suddenly, turned head over heels, picked itself up, and rushed away" (HHB, Chapter 10, p. 272). Nobody, including Shasta himself, expected this sort of courage from Shasta. Bree observes that Shasta is "a child, a mere foal, who had never held a sword nor had any good nurture or example in his life" (HHB, Chapter 10, p. 275). Aravis admits, "I've been snubbing him and looking down on him ever since you met us and now he turns out to be the best of us all" (HHB, Chapter 10, p. 275).

The lion behind this episode is, of course, none other than Aslan himself. Just as God put Abraham to the test to teach Abraham about himself, Aslan puts Shasta to the test to teach Shasta about himself. The lessons our ordeals teach us are not always bad ones.

Just Deserts: Aravis

The Lord disciplines him whom he loves.
—HEBREWS 12:6

---

[5] Lewis, *Problem of Pain,* p. 101.

Lewis believed strongly in the traditional Retributivist Theory of punishment.[6] On this view, punishment is justified because, and only because, an offender deserves it, and only to the extent the offender deserves. Theories of punishment that ignore desert and focus instead on goals such as rehabilitation or deterrence inevitably fail to treat offenders with the respect and dignity to which moral agents are entitled. Indeed, "[i]f the justification of exemplary punishment is not to be based on desert but solely on its efficacy as a deterrent, it is not absolutely necessary that the man we punish should even have committed the crime."[7] Wrongdoing, Lewis believed, merits punishment, and justice demands that punishment be proportional to desert: "It is only as deserved or undeserved that a sentence can be just or unjust."[8]

This retributive function of pain is apparent in the episode just discussed, the scene in *The Horse and His Boy* in which Aravis and Shasta are attacked by a lion, and Aravis is raked by its claws. Earlier, Aravis had drugged her stepmother's slave, causing her to be whipped for oversleeping. Later, when Aslan reveals that he was the lion, he tells Aravis that "the scratches on your back, tear for tear, throb for throb, blood for blood, were equal to the stripes laid on the back of your step-mother's slave because of the drugged sleep you cast upon her. You needed to know what it felt like" (HHB, Chapter 14, p. 299). Here, Lewis suggests, the pain Aravis suffers is justified because it is the morally fitting response to her insensitivity and deception.[9]

Of course, even retributive punishment can serve important educational purposes that benefit us morally. Aslan says she "needed to know what it felt like." This knowledge helped her to see the true nature of her actions and to be sorry for them in a way that helped her become a better person.

---

[6] Lewis, "The Humanitarian Theory of Punishment," in *God in the Dock*, pp. 287–294.

[7] *Ibid.*, p. 291.

[8] *Ibid.*, p. 288.

[9] A similar retributivist vignette is found in *The Silver Chair* (Chapter 2, p. 558), when Aslan tells Jill that her task—rescuing Prince Rilian—will be harder because she endangered Eustace's life by showing off on the edge of a cliff.

Not a Tame Lion

All of this is relevant to a common misunderstanding about the nature of God's goodness that Lewis seeks to clear up in *The Problem of Pain*:

> By the goodness of God we mean nowadays almost exclusively His lovingness; and in this we may be right. And by Love, in this context, most of us mean kindness—the desire to see others than the self happy; not happy in this way or that, but just happy. What would really satisfy us would be a God who said of anything we happened to like doing, 'What does it matter so long as they are contented?' We want . . . not so much a Father in heaven as a grandfather in heaven—a senile benevolence who, as they say, 'liked to see young people enjoying themselves' and whose plan for the universe was simply that it might be truly said at the end of each day, 'a good time was had by all'.[10]

The grandfatherly deity Lewis describes is one who wishes only to make us feel as good as possible. If this were really the nature of divine goodness, then it's hard to see how the problem of pain could be solved. If God were good in this sense, surely the universe *wouldn't* contain so much suffering!

But in Lewis's eyes, this is not the real nature of divine goodness. God loves us all right; but because He loves us, He wants us to attain *real* happiness, not what we tend to think happiness is (namely, feeling good). We can attain real happiness only by becoming worthy of God's love, and we can only do that by becoming better people. An obvious question arises at this point: Why doesn't God just *make* us better—perfect even—to begin with? The answer is that God also wants us to have free will. He wants us to have the two great goods of free will and genuine happiness. The problem, from God's point of view, is that if He gives us the first thing (free will), we might use it to turn away from the second thing. Here, another question comes to mind: Isn't God all-powerful? And doesn't this give Him the power to guarantee that each of us will receive both free will and genuine happiness?

Like many philosophers, Lewis recognizes that being all-powerful doesn't mean the ability to do absolutely *anything*; at

---

[10] Lewis, *Problem of Pain*, p. 31.

best, it includes only the ability to do anything *that can be done at all*.[11] Some things are just plain impossible, and giving someone free will and also forcing her to become perfect is just plain impossible. Not even God can do it. Once He's given us free will, the best He can do is try to get us to improve ourselves *freely*. And one of the best ways He can do this—sometimes the only way He can do this—is to inflict pain on us. The moral transformations of Edmund and Eustace illustrate this point.

If this is right, then we can solve the problem of pain *and* the problem of how Aslan can be both good and terrible at the same time. The presence of pain in the universe seems incompatible with the existence of God only if we think of God's goodness as the senile kindliness Lewis describes. Once we understand the *true* nature of divine goodness, the incompatibility vanishes more quickly than Reepicheep can draw his sword! In fact, understanding divine goodness correctly enables us to see that it is precisely *because* God is good that He sometimes causes us to suffer. He hurts us to make us better, and He wants to make us better because He loves us. This, in a nutshell, is Lewis's solution to the problem of pain.[12]

What of the problem of understanding how Aslan could be good *and* terrible at the same time? Well, Aslan is the God of Narnia, and Aslan's goodness is just like God's goodness. This means that *because* Aslan is good, he's also dangerous, he might hurt you—he's *terrible*. Unless you are perfect (and no one is), you have something to fear from Aslan. Understanding the true nature of Aslan's goodness enables us to see that his kind of goodness *requires* that he also be terrible. We are reminded throughout the *Chronicles* that Aslan is not a *tame* lion. This is Lewis's way of hinting that Aslan's goodness is not the dotardly grandfatherly goodness that is concerned only with making you *feel* good. Instead, it's the real, terrible goodness that is concerned with making you *become* good.[13]

---

[11] *Ibid.*, p. 18.

[12] I haven't the space here to cover all aspects of Lewis's solution, and I've had to leave some important bits out. Some kinds of suffering—the sufferings of animals, infants, and the severely mentally handicapped, for example—can't plausibly be seen as opportunities for moral betterment. For Lewis's speculations on these kinds of suffering, see Chapter 22 in this volume.

[13] I would like to thank Greg Bassham, Jerry Walls, and Margaret Wielenberg for helpful suggestions on earlier drafts of this chapter.

19

Worthy of a Better God: Religious Diversity and Salvation in *The Chronicles of Narnia*

JAMES F. SENNETT

My title comes from my favorite character in *The Chronicles of Narnia,* Jewel the Unicorn, who appears in *The Last Battle.* Jewel is talking about Emeth, a brave and upright Calormene soldier, who accepts a challenge from Shift the Ape to go through the Stable Door, declaring that he would gladly die a thousand deaths for the chance to look once upon the face of his beloved god Tash. As Emeth approaches the Door, Jewel whispers to Tirian, the Last King of Narnia, "By the Lion's Mane, I almost love this young warrior, Calormene though he be. He is worthy of a better god than Tash" (LB, Chapter 10, p. 728).

The plot thickens several chapters later when the kings and queens of Narnia, enjoying their first moments in Aslan's country, come across a bewildered and confused Emeth, who tells them his remarkable story. Thinking he had entered Tash's domain, Emeth goes in search of his revered deity, only to encounter the great Lion, Aslan. Emeth describes the meeting as follows:

> "Then I fell at his feet and thought, Surely this is the hour of death, for the Lion (who is worthy of all honour) will know that I have served Tash all my days and not him. . . . But the Glorious One bent down his golden head and touched my forehead with his tongue and said, 'Son, thou art welcome.' But I said, 'Alas, Lord, I am no son of Thine but the servant of Tash.' He answered, 'Child, all the service thou has done to Tash, I account as service done to me.' . . . I overcame my fear and questioned the Glorious One and said, 'Lord, is it then true, as the Ape said, that thou and Tash are

one?' The Lion growled so that the earth shook . . . and said, 'It is false. Not because he and I are one, but because we are opposites—I take to me the services which thou hast done to him. For I and he are of such different kinds that no service which is vile can be done to me, and none which is not vile can be done to him.' . . . But I said . . . , 'Yet I have been seeking Tash all my days.' 'Beloved,' said the Glorious One, 'unless thy desire had been for me thou wouldst not have sought so long and so truly. For all find what they truly seek.'" (LB, Chapter 15, pp. 756–57)

Largely due to this passage, Lewis has often been accused of endorsing *universalism*—the view that all religions are basically the same, or that everyone will eventually be saved. Whether universalism is true is an important and much-debated issue in philosophy, as it raises fundamental questions about God, the nature of religious truth, divine justice, and life after death. In this chapter I will explore whether or not Lewis was a universalist, and see how he addresses questions of religious salvation in *The Chronicles of Narnia*.

"All Find What They Truly Seek"

There are many great religions in the world with many devout followers who live exemplary and upright lives. What does this imply in light of the fact that some of these religions, including orthodox Christianity, insist that they are the one true way to salvation or enlightenment?

To get a handle on these issues, let's begin with some working definitions of four views of religious salvation:

Universal Salvation is the doctrine that all people will be saved, regardless of their religious affiliation, or even if they have none.

Pluralism is the doctrine that all of the great religions are capable of saving people; there isn't any religion that is the "one true religion" or the "only way."

Inclusivism is the doctrine that there is only one true religion, but that it is possible for people to be saved by that religion without consciously or explicitly belonging to it.

Exclusivism is the doctrine that there is only one true religion, and that one must belong to that religion in order to be saved.

People have used the term "universalism" for each of the first three doctrines stated above. But these are definitely different positions. The first implies that all people will be saved, whereas neither the second nor the third does. And the third implies that there is only one true religion, which the second denies. So when we ask, "Was Lewis a universalist?" it's important to be clear which of these three views we have in mind.

It's clear that Lewis is not teaching universalism in the strongest sense—that of universal salvation—in the *Chronicles*. There are many, including the infamous Shift, who battle against Narnia at the Stable Door and do not pass into Aslan's country. There is also the strange and tragic story of the renegade dwarfs who are thrown into the Stable. They sit in the eternal sunshine and verdant wonderland of Aslan's country, but all they experience is the darkness of the Stable interior and the putrid odors that permeate a barn full of animals—a plight from which not even Aslan can deliver them. "'You see,' said Aslan, 'They will not let us help them. They have chosen cunning instead of belief'" (LB, Chapter 13, p. 748). And, in perhaps the saddest scene in the *Chronicles,* we learn that Queen Susan herself "is no longer a friend of Narnia" and will not be joining the grand processional further up and further in (LB, Chapter 12, p. 741).

So clearly Lewis isn't a universalist in the strongest sense. He doesn't believe that all people will be saved regardless of their religious convictions or lifestyles.

But was Lewis a pluralist? Is Emeth's worship of Tash just as legitimate as the Narnians' adoration of Aslan? We might be tempted to think so; after all, Emeth is welcomed into the Lion's Land. But don't forget Aslan's vehement denial that Tash and he are the same. "I and he are of such different kinds that no service which is vile can be done to me, and none which is not vile can be done to him" (LB, Chapter 15, p. 757). Aslan isn't saying that Emeth's service to Tash is just as worthy as service to Aslan. Rather, he's saying that what Emeth *thought* was service to Tash was *really* service to Aslan. In other words, Emeth was a servant of Aslan's, even though he didn't realize it.

So Lewis clearly isn't a religious pluralist. He doesn't believe that all religions are basically the same, or that all of them are equally viable means to salvation.

Aslan explains to Emeth that it is possible to serve the one true God even when one doesn't realize that that is what one is doing. You will find what you *truly* seek, even if you don't have a fully formed *understanding* of what you seek. Thus Lewis isn't a universalist or a pluralist—he's an *inclusivist*. Our definition of inclusivism includes two central claims: (1) that there is one true religion; and (2) that a person may be saved without explicitly practicing or even knowing about that religion. This view is not pluralism, for it claims that there is only one true religion. And it is not universal salvation, for it doesn't claim that everyone will be saved.

So we arrive at this answer to the question of whether or not Lewis is a universalist: he is, but only in the sense that he is an inclusivist who believed that the opportunity for salvation is universally available, even for those who in this life may not know the one true religion. While this is a far cry from the claim of universal salvation, it's still a position that many people find disturbing and unwelcome. The standard view of most conservative Christians is *exclusivism*—the claim that there is only one true religion, and that one can be saved only by accepting that religion in this life. In fact, the debate between exclusivism and inclusivism is a major issue among Christian philosophers and theologians today.

"There Is a Way into My Country from All Worlds"

Lewis expressed his inclusivism in many of his non-fiction writings. Here are just two of the most prominent passages (all emphases are mine).

> There are people in other religions who are being led by God's secret influence to concentrate on those parts of their religion which are in agreement with Christianity, and *who thus belong to Christ without knowing it.*[1]

---

[1] C.S. Lewis, *Mere Christianity* (San Francisco: HarperSanFrancisco, 2001), p. 209.

I think that every prayer which is sincerely made even to a false god or to a very imperfectly conceived true God, is accepted by the true God and that *Christ saves many who do not think they know Him.*[2]

With passages like these in mind, it's easy to spot expressions of inclusivism in the Narnia tales. The story of Emeth is the clearest illustration, but there are many others.

Perhaps the clearest evidence is simply the fact that the Narnian salvation story is not the Jesus story. There are intentional parallels, of course, in the story of Aslan's death on the Stone Table in *The Lion, the Witch, and the Wardrobe,* but they are by no means the same story. And even if they were, Aslan's death has redemptive power for Edmund only, not for anyone else. Redemptive hope in Narnia is shrouded in deep mystery, vague anticipation, and unclear prophecies. It looks and feels a lot more like the Jewish anticipations of a Messiah who would save them than the "blessed assurance" and confident expectation of the early church that the Messiah had already come.

Aslan is not Jesus; Narnia is not Christendom. And yet we have no trouble at all spotting the good news of God's welcoming love or the deep challenge of his call to holy living in the Narnia narratives. In the very process of creating these stories, Lewis demonstrates the ease with which God can communicate the basic elements of his gospel message in non-Christian contexts.

It won't do simply to dismiss these tales as allegory or parable. The issue is whether or not the gospel has the power to reach into contexts where it is not overtly acknowledged and nonetheless turn hearts and lives to God. If it does, then any such story will resemble the gospel story and be properly classified as parable or allegory. Besides, Lewis himself clearly signals that these stories are not mere allegories when, at the end of *The Last Battle,* Narnia and our world are blended together in the heavenly realm of Aslan's country. The Pevensie children, their parents, Lord Digory, King Frank and Queen Helen, and many others from our world join with the Narnians in a great parade of the redeemed. Lewis plainly doesn't intend for

---

[2] *Letters of C.S. Lewis,* revised and enlarged edition, edited by W.H. Lewis and Walter Hooper (New York: Harvest), p. 428.

us to think of the *Chronicles* as mere pictures of what God is really doing through the church, and only through the church. Jesus said, "Other sheep I have which are not of this fold" (John 10:16, AV). Lewis allows his imagination to explore some of the possible implications of that intriguing but enigmatic remark.

Lewis emphasizes the fact that the Narnia stories are not the gospel story in the mystical closing scene of *The Voyage of the "Dawn Treader."* In another scene reminiscent of the life of Jesus, Aslan appears to the travelers in the form of a lamb, frying fish for breakfast on the shore (VDT, Chapter 16, p. 540; compare John 21:1–14). The lamb tells Edmund and Lucy that they must find their way into Aslan's country from their own world.

> "What!" said Edmund. "Is there a way into Aslan's country from our world, too?"
> "There is a way into my country from all worlds," said the lamb.

The lamb then reveals himself as the Great Lion and informs them that they will never return to Narnia.

> "You are too old, children," said Aslan, "and you must begin to come close to your own world now."
> "It isn't Narnia, you know," sobbed Lucy. "It's you. We shan't meet you there. And how can we live, never meeting you?"
> "But you shall meet me, dear one," said Aslan.
> "Are—are you there, too, Sir?" said Edmund.
> "I am," said Aslan. "But there I have another name. You must learn to know me by that name. This was the very reason why you were brought to Narnia, that by knowing me here for a little, you may know me better there." (VDT, Chapter 16, p. 541)

Though the gospel story is not available in Narnia, the children nonetheless encounter God's truth in a way that draws them close to him, even though they do not yet know that "other name" by which he can truly be known.

Many other passages from the *Chronicles* provide evidence of Lewis's belief in the power of the gospel to touch those who have never heard of it. One of the most delightful is the wonderful story of the Dufflepuds, whose bizarre situation and magical caretaker seem as foreign to Narnia as the customs and religions of tribal cultures might seem to us. Yet when Jill asks how the magic she read from the Book of Spells worked, Aslan responds, "Do you think I wouldn't obey my own rules?" (VDT, Chapter 10, p. 498). And the magician Coriakin greets Aslan with the words, "Welcome, Sir, to the least of your houses" (VDT, Chapter 11, p. 499).

We need to look finally at a passage that some people claim proves that Lewis *wasn't* an inclusivist. When Jill Pole first enters Narnia in *The Silver Chair*, she does so via Aslan's country. Parched with thirst, she finds a stream, only to encounter a majestic lion blocking the way. She asks him to move, but he refuses. She asks if he will promise not to eat her. "I make no promises," he intones.

> "*Do* you eat girls?" she said.
> "I have swallowed up girls and boys, women and men, kings and emperors, cities and realms," said the Lion. It didn't say this as if it were boasting, nor as if it were sorry, nor as if it were angry. It just said it.
> "I daren't come and drink," said Jill.
> "Then you will die of thirst," said the Lion.
> "Oh dear!" said Jill, coming another step nearer. "I suppose I must go and look for another stream then."
> "There is no other stream," said the Lion. (SC, Chapter 2, pp. 557–58)

Aslan's bold proclamation that "There is no other stream" is not an affirmation of exclusivism. It is simply an acknowledgement of that great point on which inclusivists and exclusivists agree—that there is only one true religion, and ultimately one true God, that can provide salvation. What they disagree about is whether *overt acceptance* of that truth in this life is necessary for redemption.

With this distinction in mind, let's look again at the passage about the stream. Jill has no idea who Aslan is. Nor does he make any attempt to tell her who he is. He simply invites her to come and drink, and warns her that, if she doesn't, she will die. In the end Jill does drink, and her life is spared. But she still doesn't know who Aslan is. That information doesn't come until later. If there is a lesson here it is that it is *the water* that saves, not anything we know or believe about the water. But that is an inclusivist message, not an exclusivist one.

"I've Been Longing to Go to the North All My Life!"

Inclusivists and exclusivists agree completely about one thing. Both believe that all who are saved do eventually come to know and embrace the one true religion. This is the import of Aslan's climactic comment to Emeth, "All find what they truly seek." Where inclusivists part company with exclusivists is in their conviction that, while many people come to know and embrace the truth explicitly before death, there are some who do so only in the next life.

This idea of a pilgrimage journey to truth and salvation is dramatically illustrated in the story of Shasta in *The Horse and His Boy*. True, Shasta meets and comes to love Aslan when he reaches Archenland and Narnia, and lives out his days as a faithful believer in the true Narnian religion. Nonetheless, as we will see, his story nicely illustrates one of the primary motivations behind Lewis's inclusivism.

Shasta's preparation for his pilgrimage is evident from the beginning of his story. Hints are dropped that he is of "true Northern stock," as Bree puts it (HHB, Chapter 1, p. 210). The first thing we learn about him is that he "was not at all interested in anything that lay south of his home," but that "he was very interested in everything that lay to the North because no one ever went that way and he was never allowed to go there himself" (HHB, Chapter 1, p. 205). Shasta suspects from the start that there is more to life—and to himself—than is revealed in the world he has known. And he has an inkling of the direction he must go in pursuit of that something more.

It is no wonder, then, that he so readily responds to his evangelist, Bree, who brings the glad tidings of "Narnia and the North." Notice, however, that nothing has yet been said about Aslan, of Narnian devotion to him, or even of the evils of Tash and his followers. Bree's invitation to Shasta, like Christ's to Peter and Andrew (Matthew 4:19), is simple and straightforward: "Why don't you run away with me?" (HHB, Chapter 1, p. 209). His unhappy life with the fisherman, the threat of being sold to the Tarkaan, and the chance to fulfill his lifelong dream of seeing the North, all work together to make Shasta's decision an easy one.

The ensuing journey is one filled with adventure, danger, and seemingly endless opportunities for failure and defeat. Of special note are the many times he and his companions encounter lions along the way. However, the perils of the journey are seen in retrospect as providential course corrections steadily homing the travelers in on their goal.

This providential dimension to their journey has two crucial features. First, it is Aslan who is doing the guiding. When Aslan is escorting Shasta, unseen, through the foggy mountain pass from Archenland to Narnia, Shasta complains about all the lions he had encountered on his journey. "There was only one lion," Aslan replies. When Shasta asks how he knows that, Aslan answers:

> "I was the lion." And as Shasta gaped with open mouth and said nothing, the Voice continued. "I was the lion who forced you to join with Aravis. I was the cat who comforted you among the houses of the dead. I was the lion who drove the jackals from you while you slept. I was the lion who gave the Horses the new strength of fear for the last mile so that you should reach King Lune in time. And I was the lion you did not remember who pushed the boat in which you lay, a child near death, so that it came to shore where a man sat, wakeful at midnight, to receive you." (HHB, Chapter 11, p. 281)

Second, and more important for our purposes, Shasta had no idea that Aslan existed, let alone that he was working from the time of Shasta's birth to bring him to Narnia and to the truth. Shasta's pilgrimage was one of confused and ambiguous wanderings, indecipherable events, and little comprehension of the journey's development—except for the one constant guidepost, "Narnia and the North!"

Even when Shasta seeks answers from the unseen stranger on the mountain pass, pleading desperately, "Who *are* you?" Aslan answers only with the single word, "Myself" (HHB, Chapter 11, p. 281). For those who recall the passage (Exodus 3:13–15) in which God reveals to Moses that His name is "I AM," the theological implications of this answer are clear and profound. But for Shasta, the poor fisherman's son, the response is completely baffling.

"The Lion Will Know"

We know far more about Shasta than we do about Emeth. Nonetheless, in our brief encounters with this young Calormene, we see enough to know that he has indeed been on a similar spiritual journey. That Aslan has been guiding this journey is clear from the Lion's words to Emeth, quoted in the opening section of this chapter, and summarized with undeniable finality in his first four words: "Son, thou art welcome" (LB, Chapter 15, p. 757).

The similar paths of Emeth and Shasta are seen most clearly in their parallel reactions the first time they encounter Aslan. When the fog clears on the mountain pass, Shasta is finally able to see who has been walking beside him.

> Luckily Shasta had lived all his life too far south in Calormen to have heard the tales that were whispered in Tashbaan about a dreadful Narnian demon that appeared in the form of a lion. And of course he knew none of the true stories about Aslan, the great Lion, the son of the Emperor-beyond-the-Sea, the High King above all kings in Narnia. But after one glance at the Lion's face he slipped out of the saddle and fell at its feet. He couldn't say anything but then he didn't want to say anything, and he knew he needn't say anything. (HHB, Chapter 11, p. 282)

Emeth recounts his meeting Aslan thus:

> "Then I fell at his feet and thought, Surely this is the hour of death, for the Lion (who is worthy of all honour) will know that I have served Tash all my days and not him. Nevertheless, it is better to see the Lion and die than to be Tisroc of the world and live and not to have seen him." (LB, Chapter 15, p. 756)

There are three important similarities in these encounters, and one notable difference. The first similarity is that neither of them knows who Aslan really is. Emeth fears him as a demon, and Shasta—who had been spared the bogeyman stories with which Emeth was raised—has no idea who he is. Second, neither expects anything good from him. Shasta is too befuddled to expect anything at all, and Emeth expects only destruction. Third, and most important, they both recognize Aslan as worthy of worship and adoration. The immediate and unhesitating response of both is to fall at his feet, content to receive whatever doom he may pronounce.

This veneration is not due to awareness of Aslan's divinity. Neither knows who, or what, Aslan is. Rather, their reverence is stirred by a recognition, so deep within them that neither of them could have expressed it, that this Lion is the End to which their lives have been inexorably moving. They don't yet know the truth in all its fullness, but they are fully willing to accept that truth, whatever its consequences.

The one important difference is this: Shasta's encounter with Aslan takes place while he is alive, whereas Emeth's takes place after he has passed through the Stable Door into the Lion's Land. And this difference is of import precisely because it is not important at all. Aslan's ability to grant the grace that is the natural culmination of the journey is not limited by the confines of birth and death. A journey that is properly pursued will find fulfillment, whether in this life or the next. Emeth's redemption makes as much sense as Shasta's. In the context of the all important matter of searching after truth, the question of which side of the Stable Door Emeth stands on when he finds it strikes us as totally irrelevant—and it is. All that is relevant is what the Lion knows—that Emeth, like Shasta, was on the journey.

The parallels in the stories of Shasta and Emeth remind us again of the episode of Jill by the stream. Like them, she doesn't know who Aslan is. Yet, like them, she recognizes in him something to be believed, feared, and reverenced. She never questions his statement that "There is no other stream," even though it condemns her to the frightening dilemma of either approaching the Lion or dying of thirst. But step out she does, and it is this commitment to truth—even to a truth she could not begin to articulate—that signals her salvation and her fitness for the task Aslan gives her.

In keeping with Lewis's "mere Christianity," Shasta, Jill, and Emeth are all saved by their faith. And at the point where they make their faith commitments they have little idea of who or what they have faith in. But Aslan knows. And apparently, for Lewis, that is enough.

"Justice Shall Be Mixed with Mercy"

There remains only the question of why Lewis or any other Christian should be attracted to inclusivism. While a full-fledged defense of the view is well beyond the scope of this chapter,[3] I

---

[3] For detailed defenses of the doctrine, see John Sanders, *No Other Name: An Investigation into the Destiny of the Unevangelized* (Grand Rapids: Eerdmans,

will close our discussion with a few words on why this view is so appealing to a growing number of Christian clergy, scholars, and lay people.

One big reason is that inclusivism seems to be so obviously taught in scripture. The entire Hebrew Bible is the story of many, many people who were saved without believing in Jesus or becoming Christians—Abraham, Moses, David, and Elijah, to name just a few. Of course, these people lived before Jesus of Nazareth and before there was a Christian faith to respond to! But the key point is that they were saved despite the fact that they had no access to the gospel. They were separated from the gospel, notice, by a *chronological* gap, whereas today many are separated by a *geographical* or *cultural* gap. If God is willing to overcome the chronological gap, there is reason to believe he will overcome the geographical and cultural gap as well. For inclusivists, the salvation of the Old Testament saints demonstrates God's willingness to save those who respond to him to the best of their knowledge and ability, even when that does not enable them to acknowledge Jesus or become Christians in this life.

Second, inclusivism is supported by the essential Christian doctrine of God as a God of love, desiring the salvation of as many people as possible. It makes no sense to assert on the one hand that God "is not willing that any should perish, but that all should come to repentance" (2 Peter 3:9, AV), but to believe on the other hand that billions of people will be lost who never had even a chance in this life to become Christians. Furthermore, according to Christianity, salvation is by grace, not by works. Inclusivism allows God the freedom to work as he will to fulfill his desires for the salvation of people, rather than being restricted by the contingencies of time and place. Inclusivists are fond of saying that the deciding factor in salvation is not whether a person knows Jesus, but whether Jesus knows that person (see Matthew 7:23; 25:34–46).

Third, inclusivism seems to be demanded by the logic of morality and the orthodox view of God as morally perfect. It has

---

1992), pp. 224–267; Clark H. Pinnock, *A Wideness in God's Mercy: The Finality of Jesus Christ in a World of Religions* (Grand Rapids: Zondervan, 1992), pp. 149–180; and Terrance L. Tiessen, *Who Can Be Saved: Reassessing Salvation in Christ and World Religions* (Downers Grove: InterVarsity, 2004), especially Chapters 9 and 16.

long been recognized by ethicists that "ought" implies "can"—
that is, that if a person *should* do something, he *must be able* to
do that thing. We can't be faulted for not doing the impossible.
I can't be blamed for failing to run a mile in under three minutes; you can't be blamed for failing to heal all the cancer
patients in Milwaukee.

But given that becoming a Christian is necessary for salvation, it follows that if God condemns one who has never heard
the gospel, then he is punishing that person for failing to do
something she didn't have the ability to do. This would be
unjust. But God never treats anyone unjustly. So, some form of
inclusivism must be true.

Near the end of *The Horse and His Boy,* Aslan pleads with
the captured Calormene prince Rabadash to lay aside his pride
and accept the mercy of the good kings of Archenland and
Narnia. Rabadash's arrogance knows no bounds, however, and
Aslan has no choice but to short-circuit his blasphemous pro-
fanity by transforming him into a donkey. But then Aslan
assures Rabadash that "justice shall be mixed with mercy," and
that there is a remedy for his plight. "'You have appealed to
Tash,' said Aslan. 'And in the temple of Tash you shall be
healed'" (HHB, Chapter 15, pp. 307-8).

Some have seen this passage as evidence that Lewis was
indeed a universalist, or at the very least a pluralist. He seems
to be saying that Rabadash's pagan beliefs give him all he needs
from religion. However, a closer reading of the passage reveals
it to be a clear-cut inclusivist scenario. Aslan is clearly in control
of the entire situation, and any power Tash is able to wield is
strictly subject to the will and oversight of Aslan. Aslan specifies
the precise conditions under which Rabadash can be healed (he
must appear before all of Tashbaan as a donkey on the day of
the great Autumn Feast), and even places clear restrictions on
the extent of the healing (if he ever wanders more than ten
miles from Tashbaan, he will turn into a donkey again, this time
forever).

This is clearly inclusivist. There is no ultimate source of
divine favor except Aslan. However, Aslan's love for all creatures, Narnian and Calormene alike, often moves him to work
through whatever means necessary—even the temple of Tash
itself—to try to bring those creatures to him. Rabadash, like
Emeth, is worthy of a better god than the one he has served.

The love of God and his desire for "whosoever will" permeates the *Chronicles.* Justice is constantly mixed with, tempered by, even superseded by mercy. From the physically thirsty Jill Pole to the spiritually thirsty Emeth, from the intellectually challenged Dufflepuds to the emotionally restless Bree and his boy Shasta, Aslan is constantly doing everything he can to pave a way from God to his people, in this world and others.

20

The Atonement in Narnia

CHARLES TALIAFERRO and
RACHEL TRAUGHBER

In C.S. Lewis's *Chronicles of Narnia* there are friends and enemies, life and death, betrayals and reconciliations. Running through all seven books, but especially in *The Lion, the Witch, and the Wardrobe* and *The Magician's Nephew,* Lewis develops an account of reconciliation or atonement (literally: "at-one-ment") whereby someone who has done wrong may be reconciled and restored into fellowship with those he or she has wronged, including being restored in his or her relationship with the divine Aslan. At first glance, this portrait of reconciliation may seem shocking, but in the end, we suggest, it is illuminating and promising.

Lewis's treatment of the process of atonement bears a very close resemblance to what is known as the *Ransom Theory* (sometimes called the Christus Victor model) that was developed in early Christian theology. The theory (which we will describe in detail below) sees human history in terms of a dramatic case of enslavement, ransom, and liberation. We shall first explore the atonement in Narnia and then take note of its relation to the traditional Ransom Theory. The Ransom Theory has many critics, both Christian and non-Christian. While it was embraced by some important early Christian philosophers and theologians, most Christians today adopt other accounts of Christ's atonement. We believe that there is merit to the Ransom Theory, and so we will defend it both in light of its own virtues as well as in its particular role in Lewis's books. Our defense of both the Narnian *Chronicles* as well as the traditional Ransom Theory is needed, for at least one leading philosopher of religion today, John R. Lucas, expressly cites the *Chronicles* in connection with his objections to the Ransom Theory. We will begin with an exposition of Lewis's view of atonement in Narnia, followed by a discussion of Lucas's criticisms.

Can Evil Be Undone?

Throughout the *Chronicles*, the process of creation is treated as fundamentally good. In *The Magician's Nephew*, Aslan creates Narnia through song.[1] Beasts—those who can talk and those who can't—along with plants, minerals, and so on, all emerge from the Lion's voice in resplendent, creative, wild variety. This euphoric celebration of life highlights nature as vibrant, wondrous, and positive. Evil, on the other hand, is portrayed as fundamentally negative—a life-denying disfiguring of what is good. It is seen as a kind of distortion of the good, a parasite that feeds on what is healthy. This parasitic, predatory quality of evil can be seen in the character of the witch Jadis and, to a lesser extent, in Uncle Andrew.

Jadis pursues things she deems good (mainly power and domination), but these are all at enormous cost to others—she admits, for instance, to having vindictively destroyed an entire world. She has some understanding of Aslan as the source of creation, but she sees him as a force to be opposed and, if possible, killed. She promises Digory life, but ultimately this involves enslavement to her. By comparison, Uncle Andrew is almost comic, especially given his befuddled, blurry recollection of Jadis at the end of *The Magician's Nephew* (MN, Chapter 15, p. 106). Despite the humorous overtones of his personality, Uncle Andrew is willing to sacrifice the lives of children for his own desires, he threatens harm to a child's mother and, like Jadis, he wishes to kill Aslan (MN, Chapter 8, p. 63). All in all, Jadis and Uncle Andrew seem more like thieves than creators, and they both seek to oppress, control, or kill those who are good.

---

[1] Lewis's portrait of creation by singing is similar to that presented in J.R.R. Tolkien's *The Simarillion* (Boston: Houghton Mifflin, 1977), pp. 15–22.

This conflict of good and evil between Aslan, Jadis, and Uncle Andrew sets the stage for the adventures of Digory and Polly. In *The Magician's Nephew*, Lewis retells the Biblical story of the Fall as taking place in two worlds, Charn and Narnia, that the two children enter with the help of magic rings. It is in this account of wrongdoing and subsequent reconciliation that we get a glimpse of Lewis's view of atonement.

Digory and Polly are in a great hall in the dead world of Charn when Digory violently wrenches Polly's wrist and foolishly rings a bell that awakens evil in the form of the witch Jadis, who later enslaves Narnia as the White Witch. The way in which Digory eventually comes back to his senses and is reconciled with Polly and Aslan involves several steps. First, there is an admission of wrongdoing accompanied by sorrow and regret. In one scene, Aslan coaxes Digory into admitting his responsibility. Aslan asks:

> "How came she [Jadis] to be in your world, Son of Adam?"
> "By—by Magic."
> The Lion said nothing and Digory knew that he had not told enough.
> "It was my Uncle, Aslan," he said. "He sent us out of our own world by magic rings, at least I had to go because he sent Polly first, and then we met the Witch in a place called Charn and she just held on to us when—"
> "You *met* the Witch?" said Aslan in a low voice which had the threat of a growl in it.
> "She woke up," said Digory wretchedly. And then, turning very white, "I mean, I woke her. Because I wanted to know what would happen if I struck a bell. Polly didn't want to. It wasn't her fault. I— I fought her. I know I shouldn't have. I think I was a bit enchanted by the writing under the bell."
> "Do you?" asked Aslan; still speaking very low and deep.
> "No," said Digory. "I can see now I wasn't. I was only pretending." (MN, Chapter 11, p. 80)

In addition to admitting his guilt and expressing regret, Digory also needs to seek the forgiveness of those harmed.[2] Aslan asks

---

[2] Many reasons may be given for the importance of sorrow in reconciliation. Here are four: (1) As Roderick Chisholm has argued, it is a basic good to take pleasure in good and feel sorrowful about evil. (2) Insofar as a person is

Digory about his relationship with Polly, and then invites him to "undo" the harm he has created. Aslan asks Polly:

> "Have you forgiven the Boy for the violence he did you in the hall of images in the desolate palace of accursed Charn?"
> "Yes, Aslan, we've made it up," said Polly.
> "That is well," said Aslan. . . . "Are you [Digory] ready to undo the wrong that you have done to my sweet country of Narnia on the very day of its birth?"
> "Well, I don't see what I can do," said Digory. "You see, the Queen ran away and—"
> "I asked, are you ready," said the Lion. (MN, Chapters 11 and 12, pp. 82–83)

There is a suggestion here that in addition to admitting one's past wrongs, expressing sorrow, and seeking forgiveness, there must be repentance or moral reform as well as an "undoing" of the evil that one has committed. Can one make full restitution or, more radically still, somehow make it the case that the evil one has committed is done away with? This last task seems beyond our human powers. This is partly because, whatever restitution we make, we cannot change the past. Once you have done something evil, you cannot erase the fact that you did it. But Lewis suggests in *The Magician's Nephew* that while humans cannot undo evil, they can cooperate with Aslan (or God) in undoing the evil results that come from wrongdoing.

Aslan gives Digory the task of getting a magic apple from a tree in the garden of the West. Digory succeeds with the assistance of Polly and a winged horse (first known as Strawberry but later re-named Fledge). The apple is planted and it grows into the Tree of Protection. The tree may or may not be a symbol of the cross, but its power to protect Narnia seems part of an even greater protection that Aslan will provide at a great cost to himself. In a passage that hints at the sacrifice and resurrection of Aslan in *The Lion, the Witch, and the Wardrobe* (to be

---

responsible for some evil, guilt feelings (in proportion) are fitting, and presumably feeling guilty involves remorse and sorrow as opposed to mere regret. (3) Sorrow may be a sign of genuine reform or repentance. (4) Insofar as any pleasure was gained in the wrongdoing, sorrow in a sense secures (or is evidence) that there is no ongoing pleasure but a remorse that any wrongful pleasure was taken at all.

discussed below), Aslan tells all the Talking Beasts of Narnia: "Evil will come of that evil [Digory's wrong doing], but it is still a long way off, and I will see to it that the worst falls upon myself" (MN, Chapter 11, p. 80). We are not told just how Aslan will deliver Narnia from evil, though there is a suggestion that the only true way of protecting oneself from evil must be through action that is caring and not selfish. Aslan points out that the Tree has the power to protect Narnia, but if it is used for selfish reasons the results will be disastrous.

At the end of *The Magician's Nephew*, Digory is invited to take an apple from the Tree in order to cure his dying mother. In doing so, Aslan cautions Digory, "What I give you now will bring joy. It will not, in your world, give endless life, but it will heal. Go. Pluck her an apple from the Tree" (MN, Chapter 14, pp. 100–01).

We have here a hint that part of the way in which Aslan can "undo" evil involves healing and expansive life. Somehow, in a way that we don't yet see, the evil of Jadis, Andrew, and Digory is to be overcome by the re-assertion and transformation of the good creation by Aslan. To see how Aslan accomplishes this, let's turn to the treatment of evil and atonement in Lewis's *The Lion, the Witch, and the Wardrobe*.

Deep and Deeper Magic

Early Christian thinkers like Origen of Alexandria (around 185–254 A.D.) held that in sinning, human beings come under the bondage of Satan and the works of Satan: sin, evil, and death. To liberate those in bondage, Christ is offered as ransom. Christ switches places with the hostages; he is offered as an exchange or payment for the release of those held captive. By accepting this exchange, Satan is defeated, because Christ, as God incarnate, overcomes sin and death through his passion, crucifixion, and resurrection. This is the traditional Ransom Theory of Christ's atonement.

Before delving into the problems of this theory of atonement, let's see how the Narnian case of reconciliation runs parallel to the Ransom Theory.

In *The Lion, the Witch, and the Wardrobe*, evil is represented by Jadis, now known as the White Witch, who captivates Edmund with enchanted food and the promise of more food and power. As Edmund falls prey to the Witch's power, his personality deteriorates. He becomes mean, deceptive, and self-serving.

How is Edmund delivered from evil and reconciled with others, including Aslan? It becomes clear that Edmund cannot free himself. The Witch prepares Edmund to be sacrificed, but at the last minute he is rescued by the good Beasts of Narnia. Like Digory before him, Edmund undertakes the process of admitting past wrongs, expressing remorse, and repenting (LWW, Chapter 13, p. 174).

As in *The Magician's Nephew*, however, the problem of restitution arises: How can Edmund "undo" the evil he has done? This is complicated by the Witch's claim of ownership over Edmund. The Witch tells Aslan, "You at least know the Magic which the Emperor put into Narnia at the very beginning. You know that every traitor belongs to me as my lawful prey and that for every treachery I have a right to a kill" (LWW, Chapter 13, p. 175). Aslan then negotiates with the Witch and agrees to be sacrificed in Edmund's place. Aslan offers himself as a ransom for Edmund's release. When the moment comes for the Witch to kill Aslan, she gloats triumphantly:

> "And now, who has won? Fool, did you think that by all this you would save the human traitor? Now I will kill you instead of him as our pact was and so the Deep Magic will be appeased. But when you are dead what will prevent me from killing him as well? And who will take him out of my hand then? Understand that you have given me Narnia for ever, you have lost your own life and you have not saved his. In that knowledge, despair and die." (LWW, Chapter 14, p. 181)

As everyone knows who has read the book, Aslan dies and then returns to life. Later, he tells the children how he foiled the Witch's plan:

> "[T]hough the Witch knew the Deep Magic, there is a magic deeper still which she did not know. . . . [I]f she could have looked . . . into the stillness and the darkness before Time dawned, she would have read there a different incantation. She would have known that when a willing victim who had committed no treachery was killed in a traitor's stead, the [Stone] Table would crack and Death itself would start working backwards." (LWW, Chapter 15, p. 185)

A great battle ensues after the resurrection, in which Edmund plays a key role, and the Witch and her minions are finally over-thrown. In restoring Narnia to rights, Aslan returns to life all the good creatures the Witch had turned to stone.

Problems for the Ransom Theory

While the Ransom Theory was defended by Origen, Gregory of Nyssa, and other heavyweight early Christian thinkers, it was repudiated in the Middle Ages by Anselm, Abelard, and many influential theologians who followed. Christians looked else-where to understand how it is that Christ liberates people from sin, death, and Satan (if Satan in fact exists; none of the great Creeds of the Christian Church requires belief that he does). For example, it has been argued that Christ paid the penalty that was due to sin; that Christ's life is a perfect offering that satisfies what all creatures owe to God; and that through Christ's suffer-ing love we are divinely called to give up our self-centered desires and to seek a right relationship with God. A popular, current view that traces its roots back to Greek theology sees the atoning work of Christ in terms of people becoming transformed through their identification with Christ, coming to see the world through Christ's love.[3] The reasons why many Christians aban-doned the Ransom Theory are not hard to see.

Oxford philosopher John R. Lucas notes one major attraction of the Ransom Theory—the powerful way in which it captures the sense of liberation from the *captivity* of sin that many Christians have experienced. "Throughout its history," he notes, "Christianity has shown remarkable power to speak to, and save, those who have ended up at the bottom of the pile as a result of their own addictions and fecklessness. . . . If I am . . . in thrall to sin, and if I am freed by Jesus's death on the cross, it was the price he paid for my release."[4] Despite these attrac-tions, however, Lucas believes the Ransom Theory is objection-

---

[3] See, for example, John Hick's "Is the Doctrine of the Atonement a Mistake?" in *Reason and the Christian Religion*, edited by Alan Padgett (Oxford: Clarendon, 1994). For an extensive treatment of the atonement, see Richard Swinburne's *Responsibility and Atonement* (Oxford: Clarendon, 1989).

[4] J.R. Lucas, "Reflections on the Atonement," in *Reason and the Christian Religion*, pp. 266–67.

able, both in the world of Christian theology as well as in Narnia.

Lucas offers four major criticisms of the Ransom Theory: (1) It requires a literal belief in Satan. (2) It further requires that Satan has a right to torment and sacrifice those in his power. (3) It is religiously and morally repugnant to picture God working out a deal with Satan. And (4) God seems to deceive Satan, just as Aslan seems to deceive Jadis by appealing to Deeper Magic. In some classic theological texts, God is even described as tricking Satan by setting a trap for him. For an extreme statement of this outlook, consider medieval theologian Peter Lombard's line: "The cross was a mousetrap baited with the blood of Christ."[5] Isn't such deception an offensive strategy for God to use against evil?

We shall reply to each of these objections, thus defending what we see as valuable lessons from Lewis's *Chronicles* and from early Christian theology. This will involve modifying the Ransom Theory in places, but we believe that Lucas and others have thrown the baby out with the bathwater; the Ransom Theory, we shall argue, offers an illuminating, defensible portrait of atonement both in Narnia and in Christian theology.

Personifying Evil

Lucas's first objection is that the Ransom Theory requires belief in Satan. And this belief, he claims, is superstitious and ultimately inconsistent with the sovereignty of God.

C.S. Lewis first achieved fame with the publication of a book, *The Screwtape Letters* (1942), in which demons engage in written correspondence about wily ways to entrap people in vice. This masterpiece and other works of popular apologetics catapulted Lewis to the cover of *Time* magazine in 1947. While defending the rationality of belief in a supernatural evil force is necessary in Origen's version of the Ransom Theory, we believe that a form of the Ransom Theory still makes sense if "Satan" is treated as a metaphor for the binding power of evil. After all, as Lucas notes, it is a commonplace to think of evildoing on the

---

[5] Cited by H.D. McDonald in *The Atonement of the Death of Christ* (Grand Rapids: Baker, 1985), p. 144.

model of addiction in which persons have lost their freedom (being a slave to booze, sex, or eBay), and the New Testament repeatedly refers to evil in terms of bondage (Hebrews 2:15; Galatians 5:1; Romans 8:15) and the slavery of sin (John 8:34; Romans 6:17). Arguably, this bondage may involve a person being held captive by forces that he can't escape from without aid. Admittedly, it is a further step to picture such evil forces as a person (Satan), but we believe that Lewis has demonstrated, in *The Screwtape Letters* and elsewhere, the illuminating ways in which evil can be analyzed from a personal point of view. The personification of vices and virtues has generated a rich literature of allegory, including Bunyan's *Pilgrim's Progress*, Orwell's *Animal Farm*, and Lewis's own *The Pilgrim's Regress*. Even if there are no demons, Lewis has shown with great skill how the device of imaginary evil beings can bring to light how vices such as jealousy, anger, and pride can ensnare and dismantle a person's moral character. Compare Lewis's outlook with that of his friend, J.R.R. Tolkien. Tolkien employs a rich panoply of embodied supernatural beings (Morgoth, Sauron, Saruman) to explore and shed light on the nature of evil and the human lust for power. Invoking the supernatural (if only as metaphors) can bring to light important truths about the nature and power of evil.

In replying to the remaining three objections, we will adopt a nuanced picture of the Ransom Theory according to which evildoing has caught us in a trap that, for us, is inescapable. That trap is Digory's predicament: nothing he can do by himself can "undo" the evil he has unleashed. We humans simply lack the power to make full restitution for past harms. To offer a simplistic example, imagine two people (Pat and Kris) who quarrel and injure one another. They can ask forgiveness, express sorrow, repent, and maybe even laugh about things afterwards, but nothing can change the fact that harm was done. So, on our account, evildoing may place one in a bind beyond one's control, just as if one were enslaved by Jadis or Satan.

Satan's Lawful Prey?

Lucas's second objection is that the Ransom Theory requires that Satan (assuming he exists) has a moral right to enslave and torment those in his power, and that the recognition of such a right is inconsistent with Satan's totally corrupt character and God's goodness.

Because in our version of the theory, we are not imagining that Satan is a person who functions as an actual slave owner, our theory does not face Lucas's objection. But we will defend the following sense in which Lewis rightly portrays evil as meeting a fitting end in bondage. In one of his novels, *The Great Divorce*, Lewis describes Hell as something that people gradually *choose for themselves* by giving themselves over, bit-by-bit, to cruelty, selfishness, and other vices. His point is that once a person gives way to sin, they entrap themselves in a cycle of self-destruction. Consider the logical consequence of vanity. In mild forms, the vain person loves admiration and praise, but if the vanity becomes extreme, he finds he has no interest in others at all except as means to his own pleasure. After all, if he is so much more important, why should he care about others? In a haunting passage, Lewis writes that he believes that "the damned are, in one sense, successful rebels to the end; that the doors of hell are locked on the *inside*."[6]

The kind of impropriety that Lucas worries about in which the Devil is the rightful owner of sinners is bypassed in our account. What is preserved from the traditional Ransom Theory is the important insight that we can place ourselves in dire straits by our own wrongdoing. Indeed, the harm we bring on ourselves when we do this is the natural or logical consequence of wrongdoing. Obviously, some harms may be disproportionate, as when some relatively minor wrongdoing (like slightly exceeding the speed limit) results in some great harm (a bus full of children plunges over a cliff). And in this life, some wrongdoing may go completely unnoticed or appear to result in great benefits. But in much Christian theology, as in *The Magician's Nephew,* evil is mainly seen as a distortion of good things, a twisting, parasitic force. For example, when the vice of rage (not to be confused with a moral, passionate anger at injustice) goes to an extreme, it becomes a tyrannical, debilitating evil. When someone's violent rage brings on such evil (imagine that a person's violent, unprovoked rage causes him to burst a blood vessel), one may easily see the result as fitting ("He got what he

---

[6] C.S. Lewis, *The Problem of Pain* (New York: Macmillan, 1962), p. 127.

deserved"). As Lewis sees it, the fitting ill result of wrongdoing (the captivity or bondage of evil) is something that is ultimately brought on by the person doing the wrong. "It's not a question of God 'sending' us to Hell. In each of us there is something growing up which will of itself *be Hell* unless it is nipped in the bud."[7]

Before moving to the third objection, let's consider further the Witch's appeal to Deep Magic in *The Lion, the Witch, and the Wardrobe*. Aslan apparently recognizes the Witch's understanding of Deep Magic, for he tells the children after his resurrection that she did indeed know about it. The Witch does talk in terms of "lawful prey" and the "right to kill." In assessing this claim, notice first that there is no suggestion that the Witch has a *duty* to kill traitors. It must also be noted that Aslan himself clearly does not see any such duties; in fact, Aslan seems committed to liberating Edmund no matter what the cost.

Two further points need to be appreciated in reply to Lucas's objection to the Witch's role.

First, the fate of Edmund in *The Lion, The Witch, and the Wardrobe* vividly underscores the nature of allegiance and treachery. When you betray your siblings and place yourself under a vile, brutal power, that power may well bring about your own end. In a sense, by serving the Witch as Edmund did (placing his sisters, brother, and various Talking Beasts in peril), he winds up in her domain, which is a sphere of tyranny where she may "rightly" do as she pleases. After all, Edmund entered into the Witch's service; his misadventures with the Witch did not begin by her kidnapping him. By appealing to a "Deeper Magic," Aslan asserts that there is something deeper and more powerful than the tyranny we bring on ourselves.

Second, Lewis's story rightly highlights the way in which mercy and forgiveness can be in tension with justice. Forgiveness and mercy can involve doing something undeserved or even something that, from the standpoint of justice alone, should not occur. For example, imagine a criminal, rightly condemned to life in prison, who later repents her wrongdoing, makes all the restitution for past harm she can, and then does

---

[7] *God in the Dock*, edited by Walter Hooper (Grand Rapids: Eerdmans, 1970), p. 155.

heroic deeds, rescuing innocent persons from fires, inventing medicines that heal, and so forth. It may be that she deserves to remain in prison for what she did, yet out of mercy and forgiveness, a judge may let her go free. Arguably, this involves doing something that, from the standpoint of justice alone, one should not do. Perhaps something similar applies to Aslan's treatment of Edmund, where mercy ultimately triumphs over cruel "justice."

Let's Make a Deal?

Lucas's third objection to the Ransom Theory is that there is something religiously and morally repugnant in picturing God working out a deal with Satan. As Lucas asks rhetorically, why wouldn't God simply break the bonds of Satan by force? Two things can be said in reply.

First, we think that the metaphor of good and evil in negotiation is, in fact, illuminating. After all, evil is often disguised as something good. Jadis and Uncle Andrew want power, and power, so long as it is not exercised for evil, can be good. Often, the conflict between good and evil is disguised as a conflict between different types of goods, or as a clash over how something good should be pursued. The evil of Uncle Andrew was not that he wanted to explore other worlds, but the way he went about doing this (by endangering children and so forth). In Aslan's "negotiations" with the Witch, we don't see a conflict between better and worse options, but a truly terrible exchange in which Aslan gives his life in order to liberate a hostage. The "negotiation" here dramatically brings to light the way evil often leads to greater evil.[8] It also highlights how evil can call forth acts of courageous, sacrificial love.[9]

---

[8] For a recent work on the corrosive impact of evil and the human tendency to use negotiations and other devices to inflict harm, see *Humanity* by John Glover (New Haven: Yale University Press, 1999).

[9] The classic Biblical story of good and evil, negotiation and slavery and, finally, deliverance involves Joseph and his brothers (Genesis 37–50). An innocent man, Joseph, is sold into slavery by his brothers. The brothers report to their father that Joseph has died. As it turns out, while the brother's chief goal was to rid themselves of Joseph and to make money by selling him as a slave,

Second, Aslan does use force to overcome Jadis, just as Christ uses force to overcome Satan in the Ransom Theory. But here it is crucial to understand that the force involved must be such as to display the love of Aslan or God so that Edmund and others may truly put aside their bondage to evil and accept the liberation provided. Imagine a case where someone has been unjustly imprisoned. The bars of his prison are then broken and there is an easy opportunity for escape. What if the person refuses to escape and prefers instead to remain in his cell? Has he been truly liberated? Arguably not. In a sense, the willing prisoner has become his own jailer. In Narnia and the Ransom Theory there is a fitting, dramatic way in which Aslan and the God incarnate demonstrate their love by taking on the results of wrongdoing. If death is the ultimate outcome of relentless evil, then by suffering death they wind up bearing, and ultimately overthrowing or undoing, the work of evil. Aslan and the God incarnate achieve a profound, loving identification with Edmund and other wrongdoers by undergoing the fate that Edmund and others have brought upon themselves. And by overcoming that fate, they show Edmund and others the way out of evil.

Lucas charges that the Ransom Theory gives an account of the cost of atonement and its benefits but without explaining how the two connect. The connection may be seen in how God manifests abundant love by identifying with wrongdoers and then coaxing or cajoling them into a life of goodness, welcoming God's restoration after past harms. It is because persons matter in Narnia and the Ransom Theory that the liberation has to be seen as a profoundly moving exercise of divine love. God's merely overcoming evil by an omnipotent edict would likely lead us to think of God as more of a puppet master, a frightening impersonal *force*, as opposed to the picture we get in Narnia and the New Testament of a personal manifestation of divine love. The ultimate consummation of the atonement is achieved by our joining in God's (or Aslan's) superabundant power to bring new life out of horror and death.[10]

Joseph became a powerful steward in Egypt who rescues his father, brothers and their families from famine. In this narrative, a seemingly hopeless enslavement is turned upside down as it becomes one step in a process that ultimately achieves reconciliation for all.

[10] The Ransom Theory can take seriously the need to rescue a person from

Gotcha, Satan!

Lucas's final objection is that the Ransom Theory portrays God as deceiving Satan, and that it is improper to attribute any such unworthy action to God.

Let's consider Narnia first. In Lewis's story, did Aslan lie? Aslan didn't disclose the Deeper Magic during the negotiations. Of course, he may not have known of the Deeper Magic at the time, in which case there was no withholding. But assuming Aslan did know of the Deeper Magic, was it lying or somehow wrong not to disclose this? No. Except under highly unusual circumstances, wrongdoers are not entitled to full disclosure. Imagine someone has stolen your backpack and inside it there is a cell phone that regularly sends signals indicating its location. Have you deceived the person by not telling them that they should be careful to turn off the cell phone? In a hostage crisis, are you obligated to make full disclosure of all that might help the hostage takers? Surely not.

In responding to this last objection, it's helpful to note the dramatic features of the Ransom Theory. It is a tale in which evil is overcome by its own devices. In Origen's theology, Satan thought it would be great to take on the author of life itself. While we may not embrace this demonic supernaturalism, this portrait of evil fits many historical cases of evil. Think of the ways in which empires have been stretched by tyrants to the breaking point. In the modern era, Napoleon, Hitler, and Saddam Hussein (the list is not exhaustive) may all be seen as having lusted for power so intensely that they foolishly strove to dominate others far beyond their ability to control or destroy. This portrait of the self-destructive, ultimately foolish nature of evil is present throughout Hebrew and Christian scripture. "The fool has dug a hole and fallen into it" (Psalms 7:15). "Those who live by the sword, die by the sword" (Matthew 26:52). The

---

him or herself. Consider Shakespeare's *Macbeth*. In the play, the murderer Macbeth sinks further and further into a crisis of moral identity. At one time he is afraid *for* himself, fearing discovery, but later on he becomes afraid *of* himself. If he was to be rescued from his evil, he would have to be delivered from his past choices and character. This need for self-deliverance is one of the reasons why the Ransom Theory and the Narnian account of atonement must involve a dramatic process that truly liberates a person by the person himself truly renouncing his past evil and then coming to seek the good.

teaching here seems to be that evil has within it its own seeds of destruction.

Some of the imagery used, cited earlier, about how God lured Satan into making a deal is indeed crude. Thinking of the cross as a mousetrap, as Peter Lombard does, seems primitive and ugly. But in its defense one needs to appreciate the ugliness of the world in Lombard's Middle Ages. We believe there is a kind of humor to the image of a mousetrap. The image likens Satan and the powers of evil to a rodent! When you consider the brutal persecution of Christians in the first centuries, casting evil as a mouse takes guts and a sense of humor. Despite its comical aspect, however, the mousetrap image is not often used in the exposition of the Ransom Theory, for it only focuses on one aspect of the atonement—the defeat of evil—and does not address the broader issue of drawing people away from evil and toward God through the resurrection.

Worth a Deeper Look

We have not fully defended the truth of the Ransom Theory. Much more would need to be said to do that! In his other writings, Lewis doesn't explicitly endorse the Ransom Theory, but he does insist that it is pivotal to Christianity to affirm that Christ provides people with the way of salvation and atonement, even if there are very different accounts of just how this is accomplished. We have argued that the Ransom Theory, so routinely dismissed historically and by modern critics, has much to commend it as a coherent, illuminating account of atonement, both in Christian theology and in *The Chronicles of Narnia*.

21

The Green Witch and the Great Debate: Freeing Narnia from the Spell of the Lewis-Anscombe Legend

VICTOR REPPERT

Oceans of ink have been spilled about C.S. Lewis over the past sixty or so years, and quite frankly a good deal of it is sheer nonsense. A prime example of this is the claim that *The Chronicles of Narnia* represents a retreat from his previous career as a Christian apologist. According to this widely accepted account, Lewis abruptly abandoned Christian apologetics after suffering a humiliating defeat in a 1948 debate with Oxford philosopher Elizabeth Anscombe. At the time of the debate, Anscombe was in her late twenties and relatively unknown. Indeed, her critique of Lewis was her first purely philosophical publication.[1] She went on to become one of the most distinguished philosophers of the twentieth century, and was appointed to the chair at Cambridge previously held by Ludwig Wittgenstein, under whom she had studied and whose works she had translated.

The legendary debate with Anscombe took place at a meeting of the Oxford Socratic Club[2] on February 2nd, 1948. In his book *Miracles*, published the year before, Lewis argued that naturalism—the claim that only physical reality exists—is irrational and self-defeating. Anscombe sharply criticized the argument, claiming that it was confused and based on the ambiguous use of key terms. According to the "Anscombe legend," Lewis not

---

[1] See G.E.M. Anscombe, "A Reply to Mr C.S. Lewis's Argument that 'Naturalism' is Self-Refuting," reprinted in *Metaphysics and the Philosophy of Mind*, Volume 2 of *The Collected Philosophical Papers of G.E.M. Anscombe* (Minneapolis: University of Minnesota Press, 1981), pp. 224–231.

only admitted that Anscombe got the better of the exchange, but recognized that his argument was wrong. Further, as a result of the exchange, Lewis gave up on Christian apologetics. According to Humphrey Carpenter, one of the purveyors of the Anscombe legend, "Though [Lewis] continued to believe in the importance of Reason in relation to his Christian faith, he had perhaps realized the truth of Charles Williams's maxim, 'No one can possibly do more than decide what to believe.'"[3]

The biographer A.N. Wilson brings *The Chronicles of Narnia* into the legend by suggesting that Lewis abandoned the "adult" approach of coming to faith through rational argument, in favor of a non-rational, fideist (purely faith-based) approach through children's stories. In the *Chronicles*, he suggests, the emphasis is on trusting faith and firm conviction, not on rational evidence. There, the great virtue is the willingness to believe, even in the teeth of a mountain of counter-evidence, if called upon to do so. Religious truth is acquired through the imagination of the child, and not through intellectual analysis, as Lewis had previously supposed.

According to Wilson, this radical shift by Lewis was mainly due to his debate with Anscombe. Before this encounter, he had been something of an intellectual bully who had become a hero to many because of his debating prowess and his cleverness in defending the Christian faith. But Anscombe reduced him to a child by "cutting the bullying hero down to size."[4] This, Wilson argues, "was the greatest single factor which drove [Lewis] into the form of literature for which he is today most popular: children's stories."[5] Reduced to a child himself, Lewis reverted to writing stories that would reflect what he had become.

Furthermore, Wilson adds a particularly colorful twist to his theory when he suggests that the Green Witch of *The Silver Chair*, who attempts to persuade the children that Narnia does

---

[2] An undergraduate debating society whose purpose was to discuss issues surrounding Christian faith. Lewis was the first president of the club, a position he held at the time of the debate.

[3] Humphrey Carpenter, *The Inklings: C.S. Lewis, J.R.R. Tolkien, Charles Williams, and Their Friends* (Boston: Houghton Mifflin, 1979), p. 217.

[4] A.N. Wilson, *C.S. Lewis: A Biography* (New York: Norton, 1990), p. 214.

[5] *Ibid.*, p. 211.

not exist, was inspired by Anscombe.[6] In short, Narnia was Lewis's own escape hatch when reality, as forced upon him by the sober philosophical dialogue of the Anscombe exchange, proved too difficult for him to handle.

Now it should be pointed out that Wilson appears to be a writer hostile to Lewis's own Christian beliefs.[7] But sometimes we also find Christians making a good deal of the Anscombe legend.[8] These Christians, I suspect, are much more attracted to Lewis the myth-maker than they are to Lewis the Christian apologist who appeals to reason. Consequently, they are happy to contend that Lewis came to realize, after the encounter with Anscombe, that rational apologetics was not as effective as Lewis had claimed in his earlier writings. But is Lewis the author of Narnia really a radically different person from Lewis the Christian apologist?

Separating Fact from Fiction

If we look at the public record of what happened in the Lewis-Anscombe debate, we find the following. Lewis had argued in *Miracles* that any argument for naturalism is "self-refuting," that is, saws off the very plank on which it stands. For naturalism implies that all causes are irrational physical causes. But if that is so, then the thought "naturalism is true" is itself the result of irrational physical causes. But we have no reason to trust any belief that results entirely from irrational physical causes. Thus any argument for naturalism undercuts itself, because if naturalism is true, there could never be any reason to believe that it is true.

Anscombe objected that Lewis confuses irrational causes with non-rational causes, and fails to distinguish "reasons" from "causes." An argument is valid, she pointed out, when the conclu-

---

[6] *Ibid.*, p. 226.

[7] It's worth noting that John Beversluis, one of Lewis's most severe philosophical critics, judges that Wilson's views are badly misguided. See his "Surprised by Freud: A Critical Appraisal of A.N. Wilson's Biography of C.S. Lewis," *Christianity and Literature* 41:2 (1992), pp. 191–92.

[8] See for instance the article by Cary Stockett, "The Inconsolable Secret, Part II: Lewis's Apologetics of the Heart," http://www.christianity.com/partner/Article_Display_Page/0,,PTID307566/CHID562734/CIID1418382,00.html

sion follows logically from the premises. Why a person was led to assert the argument is irrelevant to its logical validity or strength. Even crazy or drunk people sometimes assert good arguments.

In 1960, Lewis substantially revised his original argument against naturalism in a new edition of *Miracles*. There, he acknowledged the importance of the reason-cause distinction but argued that for rational thought to be possible, reasons and causes must ultimately coincide. In other words, for a belief to be justified, it is not enough for the belief to be supported by good reasons. Those reasons must cause the person to hold the belief. And according to naturalism, only non-rational causes, not reasons, can cause beliefs. Thus, the very distinctions on which Anscombe insisted actually reinforce Lewis's argument that naturalism undercuts itself.

It's clear that Lewis was initially dispirited by the Anscombe debate. His pupil Derek Brewer remembers Lewis speaking dejectedly of the "fog of war, the retreat of infantry thrown back under heavy attack."[9] Another friend, Hugo Dyson, claims that in the immediate aftermath of the debate Lewis was in a state of near-despair, feeling he had "lost everything and come to the foot of the Cross."[10] It may be that Lewis was more disappointed in his own performance in the debate than he was convinced that Anscombe had shown his argument to be wrong. In fact, in the very issue of the *Socratic Digest* in which Anscombe's essay appeared,[11] Lewis offers essentially the same counterattack that he published many years later in the new edition of *Miracles*, showing that his own doubts about his argument were short-lived, if they existed at all.

A Change of Course?

So did Lewis move away from rational apologetics after this incident or repudiate his earlier views? While it is clear that there is a shift in his writing away from books like *The Problem of Pain*, *Mere Christianity*, and *Miracles*, it is doubtful that the debate

---

[9] Derek Brewer, "The Tutor: A Portrait," in James T. Como, ed., *C.S. Lewis at the Breakfast Table and Other Reminiscences* (New York: Harcourt, Brace, 1992), p. 59.

[10] Quoted in Wilson, *C.S. Lewis*, p. 213.

[11] No. 4 (1948), pp. 7–15.

with Anscombe had anything to do with it, or that there was any essential change in his views.

First, Lewis was not a philosopher or a Christian apologist by profession. Some people devote their lives to the work of Christian apologetics; William Lane Craig and J.P. Moreland are well-known examples. If one of them were to stop writing apologetics, we might need an explanation. Lewis may be recognized in retrospect as the most influential apologist of the last century but that was not his primary vocation. Although he had studied philosophy as an undergraduate, his professional career was as a Professor of medieval and Renaissance literature. He wrote Christian apologetics partly to fill what he thought to be a void in Christian writing in his time, and partly in response to requests by others.[12] There is no evidence that he had any major apologetical works planned after *Miracles* that went unwritten due to the Anscombe exchange.

But this by no means shows that Lewis had lost interest in apologetics or confidence in its value. Although he wrote no overtly apologetical *books* after *Miracles*, he wrote several substantive apologetical *essays* in the years after the famous debate. In "Is Theism Important" (1952), Lewis affirms the importance of theistic arguments, and says, "Nearly everyone I know who has embraced Christianity in adult life has been influenced by what seemed to him to be at least probable arguments for Theism."[13] In "On Obstinacy of Belief" (1955), Lewis defends Christianity against the charge that while scientists apportion their beliefs to the evidence, religious people do not, and are therefore irrational.[14] In "Rejoinder to Dr. Pittenger" (1958), Lewis defends his Christian apologetics against criticisms from a prominent theologian, hardly what you would expect him to do if he thought his career as an apologist had been misguided.[15] The essay "Modern Theology and Biblical Criticism" (1959) is a stinging assault on

---

[12] Lewis wrote *Miracles* partly in response to a complaint from Dorothy Sayers that there were no good up-to-date books on the subject. See *C.S. Lewis: A Companion and Guide*, edited by Walter Hooper (San Francisco: HarperSanFrancisco, 1996), pp. 343–44.

[13] Lewis, *God in the Dock*, p. 173.

[14] C.S. Lewis, *The World's Last Night and Other Essays* (New York: Harcourt Brace, 1952), pp. 13–30.

[15] Lewis, *God in the Dock*, pp. 177–183.

modern Biblical scholarship of a skeptical variety, the sort of scholarship that is currently represented by members of the Jesus Seminar.[16] If that essay is not a piece of Christian apologetics, then I simply do not know what the term means.

Second, a defender of the Anscombe legend must confront the fact that Lewis revised and expanded the controversial third chapter of *Miracles*. If the argument against naturalism had been proven wrong, why in the world would Lewis devote more space in his book to the disgraced argument? All one needs to do is to compare the length of the original and the revised chapter and one cannot fail to realize that Lewis considered the revision to be an important project, fully worthy of the serious effort he gave it. One simply does not revise a book and extensively expand an argument one thinks has been proved wrong.

Third, it is a mistake to suppose that if an author writes something that has an emotional appeal to it, rationality has been abandoned. This is to commit what I like to call the Star Trek fallacy. In the first generation of *Star Trek*, logic is represented by Mr. Spock, who is supposed to be purely rational and therefore free of emotion. Dr. McCoy, on the other hand, represents the emotional side of human nature, who opposes Spock's emphasis on logic. But surely, one wouldn't reason at all without some passions at work, perhaps a passion to reason well or to discover the truth. Indeed, as Lewis argues at length in *The Abolition of Man*, emotional responses can be rational or irrational, and to downplay the emotions as "mere" feelings is to undercut the life of reason, not to uphold it.[17]

In fact, the Narnia books can themselves be seen as works of broadly Christian apologetics. Lewis's close friend, J.R.R. Tolkien, was finishing *The Lord of the Rings* at the same time Lewis was beginning *The Chronicles of Narnia*. One of his central aims in writing *The Lord of the Rings*, Tolkien wrote, was "the elucidation of truth, and the encouragement of good morals in this real world, by the ancient device of exemplifying them in unfamiliar embodiments."[18] Lewis's Narnia books are

---

[16] C.S. Lewis, *Christian Reflections* (Grand Rapids: Eerdmans, 1967), pp. 152–166.

[17] C.S. Lewis, *The Abolition of Man* (New York: Macmillan, 1947), pp. 13–35.

[18] *The Letters of J.R.R. Tolkien*, edited by Christopher Tolkien (Boston: Houghton Mifflin, 1981), p. 194.

inspired by a similar view of moral fiction. In the *Chronicles,* through his use of both Christian allegory and imaginatively compelling portrayals of good and evil, Lewis seeks to engage both the emotions and the reason in recognizing the beauty of Christian values and ultimately the truth of the Christian world view.

The Professor's Trilemma

In *Mere Christianity* Lewis offers his most famous argument for Christian belief, an argument that has come to be known as Lewis's Trilemma. The argument centers on how we should regard Jesus's claims to be God. According to Lewis, the fact that Jesus claimed to be God drastically reduces our options on how to view him. In particular, the idea that Jesus was a great moral teacher who was not God seems to be ruled out by the massive error involved in falsely claiming to be God. Lewis writes:

> You must make your choice. Either this man was, and is, the Son of God: or else a madman or something worse. You can shut Him up for a fool, you can spit at Him and call Him a demon; or you can fall at his feet and call Him Lord and God. But let us not come with any patronising nonsense about His being a great moral teacher. He has not left that open to us. He did not intend to.[19]

I will not here discuss whether or not this argument is a good one. It has, of course, been criticized by some and defended by others. My point now is simply that when the Pevensie children are trying to assess the credibility of Lucy's claim to have visited another world through the wardrobe, Professor Digory Kirke, the owner of the house, offers a closely similar argument:

> "Logic!" said the professor half to himself. "Why don't they teach logic in these schools? There are only three possibilities. Either your sister is telling lies, or she is mad, or she is telling the truth. You know she doesn't tell lies and it is obvious that she is not mad. For the moment then and unless any further evidence turns up, we must assume that she is telling the truth. (LWW, Chapter 5, p. 131)

---

[19] C.S. Lewis, *Mere Christianity* (San Francisco: HarperSanFrancisco, 2001), p. 52.

Now this strikes me as a very odd passage for someone who, according to the Anscombe legend, has abandoned rational apologetics in favor of the imagination. Not only is Professor Kirke (who, we eventually find out, has been to Narnia himself) presenting an argument with exactly the same structure as the Trilemma, we find him emphasizing the importance of logic and wondering why they don't teach it in the schools. The Professor could have used any number of ways of persuading the children to believe Lucy, but what he offers is a logical argument.

Is Anscombe the Green Witch?

Wilson's attempt to identify the Green Witch from *The Silver Chair* with Anscombe is surely one of his most fanciful speculations. Lewis himself made some comments about reviewers in his own lifetime who speculated on how his books came to be written:

> My impression is that in the whole of my experience not one of the guesses has on any one point been right; that the method shows a record of 100 per cent failure. You would expect that by mere chance they would hit as often as they miss. But it is my impression that they do no such thing. I can't remember a single hit. But as I have not kept a careful record my mere impression may be mistaken. What I think I can say with certainty is that they are usually wrong.[20]

On the basis of this experiential claim concerning Lewis's own contemporary reviewers, I would have to place the probability that the Green Witch has anything to do with the Anscombe incident as pretty close to zero. The fact is, there are not only obvious but massive differences between the Witch and Anscombe that make identifying the two absurd. Besides the fact that she was not an evil, shape-shifting, non-human witch, Anscombe was a Roman Catholic Christian who believed as firmly in Supernaturalism as did Lewis. What she denied was that Lewis had a good argument for Supernaturalism in *Miracles*. The Witch, by contrast, is trying to get Eustace, Jill, Puddleglum and Rilian to accept Underworld as the only world. Second,

---

[20] Lewis, *Christian Reflections*, p. 160.

while Anscombe strove to make people aware of certain distinctions that she thought undermined Lewis's case, the Green
Witch strums on an instrument in order to place a spell on her
captives in order to dull their thinking and make them accept
the idea that Overworld doesn't exist. Finally, the Marsh-wiggle's
reply to the Witch is, after all, an argument for believing in
Narnia, not an appeal to blind faith, as can be seen in the chapters by Lovell and Menuge in this volume. Anyone who knows
anything about the career of Gertrude Elizabeth Margaret
Anscombe cannot take seriously the possibility that the Witch
speaks for her.

Prudence and Faith in *The Chronicles*

Perhaps we can best exhibit the relationship between *The
Chronicles of Narnia* and Lewis's apologetics by looking at
Lewis's discussion of the virtues of prudence and faith in *Mere
Christianity*. Lewis, following an old Christian tradition, identi-
fies the Four Cardinal Virtues as Prudence (sometimes called
Wisdom), Temperance, Courage, and Justice, to which he adds
the Three Holy Virtues of Faith, Hope, and Love. He defines
Prudence as "practical common sense, taking the trouble to
think out what you are doing and what is likely to come of it,"
and reminds us that Christ taught us to be not only "as harmless
as doves" but also "as wise as serpents." He continues:

> He wants a child's heart but a grown-up's head. . . . The fact that
> you are giving money to a charity does not mean that you need not
> try to find out whether that charity is a fraud or not. . . . It is, of
> course, quite true that God will not love you any less, or have less
> use for you, if you happen to have been born with a second-rate
> brain. He has room for people with little sense, but He wants every
> one to use what sense they have. . . . God is no fonder of intel-
> lectual slackers than of any other slackers. If you are thinking of
> becoming a Christian, I warn you, you are embarking on some-
> thing which is going to take the whole of you, brains and all.[21]

Like many passages in Lewis, this one has tremendous contemporary relevance. Many people in the Christian community (and

---

[21] Lewis, *Mere Christianity*, pp. 77–78.

outside of it) have been slack in their intellectual responsibilities, and the results have been disastrous. The mass suicide in Jonestown, Guyana, and the suicide of the Heaven's Gate cult in California are grim reminders of what happens when religious people give up on thinking critically and simply follow what a leader says. Or to take less dramatic examples, but ones closer to home, think about how millions of Christians get caught up in spiritual fads like the recent "prayer of Jabez" phenomenon or the sensational eschatology of the *Left Behind* series. How many people have given money they can hardly afford to television evangelists, only to find out that the money went for air-conditioned dog houses and visits to sleazy motel rooms? The Christian community suffers greatly whenever it is intellectually lazy and careless.

Think carefully about Lewis's claim that "God wants a child's heart but a grown-up's mind." The great virtue of children, Lewis thinks, is not that they believe blindly, in the teeth of whatever evidence there might be against their cherished beliefs. In fact, Lewis says, "Most children show plenty of 'prudence' about doing the things they are really interested in, and think them out quite sensibly."[22] And just as Lewis refuses to insult the intelligence of children in *Mere Christianity*, he refuses to do so in *The Chronicles of Narnia*. So not only does he emphasize the virtue of prudence, he tells us that whatever Christians might mean by saying that we ought to be childlike, it has nothing to do with believing contrary to the available evidence.

In his discussion of the virtue of faith in *Mere Christianity* Lewis explains what faith is, distinguishing it from the fideistic notion that faith is believing contrary to the evidence. He writes, "I am not asking anyone to accept Christianity if his best reasoning tells him that the weight of the evidence is against it. That is not the point at which Faith comes in." He continues:

> Now Faith, in the sense in which I am here using the word, is the art of holding on to things your reason has once accepted, in spite of your changing moods. . . . That is why Faith is such a necessary virtue: unless you teach your moods "where they get off," you can never be either a sound Christian or even a sound atheist, but just a creature dithering to and fro, with its beliefs really dependent on

---

22 *Ibid.*, p. 77.

the weather and the state of its digestion. Consequently one must train the habit of Faith.[23]

Given the analysis of faith in this passage, it's easy to see that the virtue of faith and the virtue of prudence are perfectly compatible. It is the task of apologetics to show that as prudent human beings, we can nevertheless exercise Christian faith. We are not expected to exercise prudence in, say, the purchase of a used car, but exercise faith when it comes to selecting one's religious beliefs. Rather, prudence and faith fit together like a hand in a glove. Prudence is the virtue of thinking things through; faith is the virtue of acting on what one knows to be true, even in the face of emotional impulses to think otherwise.

An opponent of Christian apologetics, on the other hand, thinks that the faith of the Christian is exercised when the believer accepts beliefs that, if he were exercising the kind of prudence required in other contexts, he would not accept. The life of prudence and the life of faith are at odds for the anti-apologist.

But after the exchange with Anscombe, did Lewis conclude that faith was indeed a matter of steadfastly accepting Christianity, even though the weight of the evidence is against it? The evidence strongly suggests otherwise. Consider this passage in *The Lion, the Witch, and the Wardrobe*, where Edmund betrays his siblings and justifies his actions by saying that he couldn't be sure that Aslan was good and the White Witch was bad.

> "Because," [Edmund] said to himself, "all these people who say nasty things about her are her enemies and probably half of it isn't true. She was jolly nice to me, anyway, much nicer than they are. I expect she is the rightful Queen really. Anyway, she'll be better than that awful Aslan!" At least, that was the excuse he made up in his own mind for what he was doing. It wasn't a very good excuse, for deep down inside him he really knew that the White Witch was bad and cruel. (LWW, Chapter 9, pp. 151–52)

Lewis's point here, obviously, is that Edmund's mistake lies in "believing" what he really knows not to be true. His action in this case displays neither true faith nor prudence.

---

[23] *Ibid.*, pp. 140–41.

For a second example, consider the dwarf Trumpkin in *Prince Caspian.* Though he is skeptical about the stories of Old Narnia and Aslan, he is nevertheless a virtuous character, while Nikabrik, who accepts the existence of the "supernatural," is wicked, because he attempts to call up the White Witch to expel the Telmarines. There are, of course, less virtuous skeptics in Narnia; Ginger the Cat and Rishda Tarkaan in *The Last Battle* are examples. But their lack of virtue is not due to failure to believe contrary to the evidence; rather, their failure has to do with attempting to exploit the beliefs of the Narnians for their own benefit.

Also in *Prince Caspian,* Lucy's faith fails, because she has seen Aslan and knows he is there, but nevertheless fails to follow him. At no point in the *Chronicles* is any character criticized for lack of "faith" in the fideistic sense of failing to believe something that runs counter to the evidence.

It is in *The Last Battle* that we find the strongest illustration of Lewis's belief in the consistency of prudence and faith. The story begins when Shift the Ape finds a lion-skin, and persuades Puzzle the donkey to put it on and pretend to be Aslan. Like a modern-day religious charlatan, Shift persuades Puzzle that he is really doing what Aslan wants by pretending to be Aslan, and persuades Puzzle that he really knows best and that, after all, Puzzle isn't very clever. When Puzzle realizes that he has been duped by the Ape, he says,

"I see now," said Puzzle, "that I really have been a very bad donkey. I ought never to have listened to Shift. I never thought things like this would begin to happen."

"If you'd spent less time saying you weren't clever and more time trying to be as clever as you could—" began Eustace but Jill interrupted him.

"Oh leave poor old Puzzle alone," she said. "It was all a mistake; wasn't it, Puzzle dear?" And she kissed him on the nose. (LB, Chapter 8, p. 713)

Now, although Jill is right in saying that it was inappropriate for Eustace to lecture the now-repentant Puzzle about listening to Shift, Eustace is also right in saying that Puzzle should have used the brains he had to exercise prudence and stop listening to the Ape. Merely following a leader and doing what one is told can be really dangerous if what one is told is a lie. An irrational faith, a willingness to exempt claims from rational scrutiny, is not a virtue; it is precisely what gets many of the characters in Narnia into trouble. Animals like Puzzle are as harmless as doves, but if they fail to be as wise as serpents, they end up being bamboozled by the likes of Shift in Narnia, just as many people are taken in by television evangelists in our world.

The view of faith and reason in the *Chronicles* is exactly the same as that in *Mere Christianity*. The life of prudence, of forming one's beliefs intelligently and carefully, taking the evidence into serious consideration, and the life of faith, are perfectly compatible with one another. The two virtues are not opposed to one another. Rather, they are two sides of the same coin. Lewis believed that before he encountered Anscombe, and he believed it afterwards when he wrote *The Chronicles of Narnia*. To suggest otherwise is to fly in the face of a mountain of contrary evidence. You have to have a lot of "faith" to believe the stories Wilson and others tell about C.S. Lewis. You have to believe them even though your best reasoning tells you the weight of the evidence is against them.

22

Some Dogs Go to Heaven: Lewis on Animal Salvation

GREGORY BASSHAM

> The Lord is mindful of his own, and will save both man and beast.
> —GEORGE MACDONALD

One of the things readers love best about C.S. Lewis's *Chronicles of Narnia* is all the captivating Talking Animals. Everyone has his or her favorite: Reepicheep, the hyper-gallant and courteous mouse; Strawberry, the faithful cab horse who gets his wings; Mr. and Mrs. Beaver, the very soul of good-hearted hospitality; Jewel, the faithful and noble unicorn. And of course the big kahuna himself, Aslan the lion, King of Beasts and son of the great Emperor-beyond-the-Sea, who, even though he isn't a *tame* lion, loves to romp with children and let them bury their faces in his mane and plant kisses on his nose. Lewis's good friend, J.R.R. Tolkien, was right: one of the "primordial human desires" satisfied by works of fantasy is the desire to "hold communion with other living things."[1] In *Narnia* Lewis succeeds in fulfilling this deep-seated desire as few other authors have.

We are fond of these animals, and so are delighted to find them, and other Talking Beasts, present in the Narnian heaven (Aslan's country) after Aslan brings Narnian history to a close. In a remarkable passage at the end of *The Last Battle*, Lewis describes a kind of Last Judgment for all the living and dead

---

[1] J.R.R. Tolkien, "On Fairy-stories," in *The Tolkien Reader* (New York: Ballantine, 1966), p. 13.

rational creatures of Narnia, including Talking Animals. Roused from their woodland homes and final resting places by Dragons and Giant Lizards, millions of creatures come rushing toward Aslan, who stands in front of the Door to the Narnian heaven. Among the creatures are all manner of rational Narnian creatures—"Talking Beasts, Dwarfs, Satyrs, Fauns, Giants, Calormenes, men from Archenland, Monopods, and strange unearthly things from the remote islands or the unknown Western lands" (LB, Chapter 14, p. 751). Some Talking Animals—those who look upon Aslan's face with fear and hatred—are transformed into ordinary non-talking animals, and then swerve to Aslan's left and disappear into a "huge black shadow," never to be seen by the children again. Other Talking Animals, those who look on Aslan's face with love, swerve to his right and join the throng of creatures that move "further in and further up" into Aslan's kingdom.

Conspicuously absent from this diverse array of creatures are any ordinary non-Talking animals. All the "Dumb" Narnian horses, bears, rabbits, beavers, and so forth are apparently destroyed by the Dragons and Giant Lizards, or else perish in the floods and eternal icy cold that mark the final end of Narnia. When Narnia is no more, we are told that all "of the old Narnia that mattered, all the dear creatures, have been drawn into the real Narnia through the Door" (LB, Chapter 15, p. 759). From this it would seem to follow that, in Lewis's view, only the Talking Animals "mattered." This is puzzling, because in several other works Lewis argues that non-human animals do "matter" and that at least some animals may go to heaven.[2] Why did Lewis exclude non-rational animals from his Narnian heaven, and what should believers in an all-powerful, loving God think about the possibility of animal immortality?

All Narnian Creatures Great and Small

Lewis himself clearly loved animals. To his friends, he was always "Jack," a nickname he chose himself in childhood after

---

[2] C.S. Lewis, *The Problem of Pain* (San Francisco: HarperSanFrancisco, 2001 [1940], Chapter 9; C.S. Lewis, "The Pains of Animals: A Problem in Theology," reprinted in *God in the Dock: Essays on Theology and Ethics*, edited by Walter Hooper (Grand Rapids: Eerdmans, 1970), pp. 161–171.

the death of his beloved dog, Jacksie. As a boy, he wrote endless stories about "Animal-Land," a world he invented, populated by talking, "dressed animals." As an adult, he strongly condemned cruelty to animals,[3] shared his house in Oxford with a large community of cats and dogs, and once remarked that a "man with a dog closes a gap in the universe."[4]

In the *Chronicles*, mistreatment of animals is always a sign of moral wickedness or blindness. The books condemn Uncle Andrew for conducting cruel experiments on animals (MN, Chapter 10, p. 76), the Calormenes for abusing horses and other animals (LB, Chapter 2, p. 680 and Chapter 12, p. 738; HHB, Chapter 1, p. 209 and Chapter 9, p. 268), Jadis for flogging Strawberry the horse without mercy (MN, Chapter 7, p. 55), and the Telmarines for silencing the beasts and trees (PC, Chapter 4, p. 338). When Aslan first creates Narnia, he commands the Talking Animals to cherish the Dumb Animals and treat them gently (MN, Chapter 10, p. 71), and admonishes King Frank to treat the Talking Animals "kindly and fairly," and not to allow any of his "free subjects," human or animal, "to hold another under or use it hardly" (MN, Chapter 11, p. 82).

This isn't to say that Narnia is a place in which all animals are treated as equals. On the contrary, it is a hierarchical world in which animals are placed under the rule of humans (MN, Chapter 11, p. 81) and Dumb Beasts are "given to" the Talking Beasts, along with the woods, fruits, rivers, and stars (MN, Chapter 10, p. 71). Ordinary horses are ridden and used as draft animals, but "no one in Narnia or Archenland ever dreamed of mounting a Talking Horse" (HHB, Chapter 14, p. 303). Humans and Talking Beasts are permitted to hunt Dumb Beasts (LWW, Chapter 17, p. 195; LB, Chapter 1, p. 671) and use them as food (SC, Chapter 16, p. 656; VDT, Chapter 2, p. 435), and even Aslan serves up a feast that includes pigeons and animal tongues (LB, Chapter 13, p. 747). The only vegetarians in the *Chronicles* are silly, "up-to-date" people like Eustace's parents who wear a "special kind of underclothes," take bogus health supplements like "Plumpton's Vitaminized Nerve Food," and believe in all

---

[3] C.S. Lewis, "Vivisection," reprinted in *God in the Dock*, pp. 224–28.
[4] C.S. Lewis, *The Four Loves* (New York: Harcourt, Brace, 1960), p. 79.

sorts of kooky, straight-laced ideas, like not leaving clothing lying on beds, and avoiding smoking and drinking (VDT, Chapter 1, pp. 425, 430).

We see an example of this sharp distinction between Talking and non-Talking animals when Puddleglum, Jill, and Eustace discover in the castle of the Giants that they have not been eating ordinary deer-meat:

> Suddenly Puddleglum turned to them, and his face had gone so pale that you could see the paleness under the natural muddiness of his complexion. He said:
> "Don't eat another bite."
> "What's wrong?" asked the other two in a whisper.
> "Didn't you hear what those giants were saying?. . . 'They say that when [the stag] was caught he said, "Don't kill me, I'm tough. You won't like me."'"
> For a moment Jill did not realize the full meaning of this. But she did when Scrubb's eyes opened wide with horror and he said, "So we've been eating a *Talking* stag." . . .
> "We've brought the anger of Aslan on us," [Puddleglum] said. . . . "If it was allowed, it would be the best thing we could do, to take these knives and drive them into our own hearts." (SC, Chapter 9, p. 608)

The idea that there is a gulf—a difference in kind rather than degree—between rational and non-rational creatures has long been part of the Christian moral tradition. Many Christian thinkers have agreed with Thomas Aquinas, the greatest philosopher of the Middle Ages, that rational creatures (angels and humans) are created in the "image" of God, but non-rational creatures (plants and animals) are not.[5] In Lewis's view, "the superiority of man over beast is a real objective fact, guaranteed by Revelation."[6] But this superiority, Lewis argues, doesn't mean that humans have a right to treat animals cruelly, or that animals cannot go to heaven. To see why, let's turn to Lewis's famous discussion of animal immortality in his book *The Problem of Pain.*

---

[5] Thomas Aquinas, *Summa Theologica*, I-I, Q. 93, art. 2.
[6] Lewis, *God in the Dock*, p. 226. Lewis quotes Jesus's remark that "You are of more value than many sparrows" (Matthew 10:31).

Is Lassie in Heaven?

Why might a theist—someone who believes in an all-powerful and loving God—be at least open to the possibility of an afterlife for animals? Lewis cites two reasons.

First, many humans love and cherish their pets. They bond with them, befriend them, and are befriended by them in return. In some cases, Lewis speculates, this bond may be so close that God will not permit even death to break it. Just as in some mysterious way a husband and a wife become "one body" through the sacrament of marriage, perhaps beloved pets will enjoy a kind of "derivative immortality"[7] in and through the raised bodies of their owners.

In his book, *The Great Divorce*, Lewis presents a fictionalized version of this idea. In a dream, the narrator boards a bus and embarks on a journey through heaven and hell. In heaven he encounters a woman of unearthly beauty, Sarah Smith, who is accompanied by a large troupe of singing and dancing spirits. Behind the spirits come a quite different band of followers:

> "And how . . . but hullo! What are all these animals? A cat—two cats—dozens of cats. And all these dogs . . . why, I can't count them. And the birds. And the horses."
>
> "They are her beasts."
>
> "Did she keep a sort of zoo? I mean, this is a bit too much."
>
> "Every beast and bird that came near her had its place in her love. In her they became themselves. And now the abundance of life she has in Christ from the Father flows over into them."[8]

Of course, as Lewis himself points out,[9] any such mediated or derivative immortality will affect only a tiny percentage of all the animals that have ever lived on earth, not to mention any animals that may dwell on other planets. Presumably, neither wild animals nor ill-treated domestic animals would be included—though Lewis does speculate that at least some wild animals might attend on risen humans and be part of their heavenly

---

[7] Lewis, *The Problem of Pain* (New York; HarperCollins, 2001 [1940], p. 145.

[8] Lewis, *The Great Divorce* (New York: HarperCollins, 2001 [1946], pp. 119–120.

[9] Lewis, *The Problem of Pain*, p. 144.

"train".[10] The key point for Lewis, though, is that pet owners do have good reason to hope that they will someday be reunited with their departed nonhuman friends.

The Healing of Harms

A second reason why theists should be open to the idea of animal immortality, Lewis suggests, is that it may help to solve the vexing theological problem of pain. As Erik Wielenberg explains in Chapter 18 above, the problem of pain is the challenge of trying to understand why (or whether) an all-powerful, all-knowing, perfectly loving God would permit all the suffering and evil that exists in the world. When it comes to *human* suffering, Lewis claims, we can see at least the glimmerings of a satisfactory answer in terms of three interrelated concepts. First, God has created humans with the gift of *free will*, and sometimes we misuse that gift in ways that cause suffering and pain. Second, some human suffering can rightly be seen as *just punishment* for our moral failings and transgressions. Finally, a world with real hardships and challenges seems to be a precondition for the exercise of many virtues (for example, courage or compassion) and more generally for *moral and spiritual growth*.[11]

When it comes to *animal* pain, however, none of these stock solutions seems to be available. As Lewis remarks, "So far as we know beasts are incapable either of sin or virtue: therefore they can neither deserve pain nor be improved by it."[12] The possibility of animal immortality might help in two ways. First, if, as millions of Hindus and Buddhists believe, all living things go through multiple reincarnations, at least some animal pain might be explained as *deserved or self-chosen* suffering resulting from choices made in a previous life. The idea might go something like this. Suppose Smith is a particularly swinish person—selfish, gluttonous, and greedy. On the Hindu-Buddhist view, after he dies he might be reborn as a pig and suffer a variety of piggish tribulations as a fitting punishment for his bad character. Or

---

[10] *Ibid.*, p. 146. Lewis also whimsically suggests that God might find a useful role for *mosquitoes* in hell. *Ibid.*, p. 141.

[11] Lewis, *Mere Christianity* (New York: HarperSanFrancisco, 2001 [1952], pp. 47–49.

[12] Lewis, *The Problem of Pain*, p. 132.

imagine that Jones, while hanging out in some celestial rest stop waiting for his next incarnation,[13] accepts an extra-credit assignment from God to live as a deer that gets devoured by a wolf. Jones's choice would seem to be meritorious because it contributes to the balance of nature and the good of evolutionary progress. Moreover, since his act is freely chosen, violates no one's rights, and will be amply rewarded by God, the suffering would seem to be justified.

For Lewis, solutions like this simply won't wash. Christians, he says, "know nothing of previous existences."[14] The Biblical view, rather, is that "it is appointed for men to die once, and after that comes judgment" (Hebrews 9:27), to be followed by either eternal happiness or eternal punishment (Matthew 25:46).

There is another way, however, in which the idea of animal immortality might help in solving the problem of pain. God might be justified in permitting animal pain if He *compensates* animals for their undeserved sufferings in some sort of afterlife. Consider a sickly fawn that barely survives a brutal winter and then is eaten alive by a pack of wolves in the early spring. How could God—or any being—be justified in bringing into existence a creature that He knows will live a short, miserable life, ending in a horrible, painful death? Things may appear very different, however, if the fawn's death serves a good purpose (for example, biological diversity) and is more than amply compensated in an afterlife. If the fawn's short, suffering-filled life is but "Chapter One" of a "Great Story" that "goes on forever: in which every chapter is better than the one before" (LB, Chapter 16, p. 767), even the fawn, if it could speak, would presumably proclaim in the end: "The judgments of the Lord are true and righteous altogether" (Psalms 19:9).[15]

At first blush, therefore, the compensation argument seems like a promising solution to the problem of animal pain. Lewis, however, sees serious problems with the argument. First, he claims, the idea of almighty God paying "damages" to His crea-

---

[13] Compare Plato, *Meno* 81a–b.

[14] Lewis, *The Four Loves*, p. 153

[15] John Wesley, the eighteenth-century founder of Methodism, offers a similar argument in his remarkable sermon "The General Deliverance" (Sermon 60), available online at www.ccel.org/w/wesley/sermons/sermons-html/serm-060.html.

tures is an unworthy assertion of divine goodness. Second, very few animals are capable of experiencing pain, so there is no need for God to compensate them for any undeserved suffering. Finally, the very concept of an afterlife makes no sense for most animals because they have no "soul" or "self" that is capable of surviving death. Let's consider these arguments in turn.

God in the Dock

First, Lewis argues, the idea of God compensating animals for their sufferings is inconsistent with God's wisdom and goodness:

> A future happiness connected with the beast's present life simply as a compensation for suffering—so many millenniums in the happy pastures paid down as "damages" for so many years of pulling carts—seems a clumsy assertion of Divine goodness. We, because we are fallible, often hurt a child or an animal unintentionally, and then the best we can do is to "make up for it" by some caress or tid-bit. But it is hardly pious to imagine omniscience acting in that way—as though God trod on the animals' tails in the dark and then did the best He could about it! In such a botched adjustment I cannot recognize the master touch; whatever the answer is, it must be something better than that.[16]

Clearly, a perfect, all-knowing God can't do anything in a botched or inadvertent way. This, however, isn't what the compensation argument claims. What the argument claims is that God *knowingly* created a world in which immense animal suffering would occur,[17] but that this is justified because (1) such suffering is necessary for the achievement of a great and overriding good[18] and (2) the animals' suffering will be more than

---

[16] Lewis, *The Problem of Pain*, p. 145.

[17] Whether God's "original" (pre-Fall) plan envisioned animal suffering is debated by Christian theologians. For a classic argument that God originally intended animals to be both pain-free and immortal, see Wesley, "The General Deliverance." For a contrary view, see Aquinas, *Summa Theologica*, I-I, Q. 96, art. 1.

[18] Exactly what that "great and overriding good" is, of course, open to debate. My own answer would be: A self-evolved world of great beauty and biological diversity that serves as a fitting environment for moral and spiritual development.

fully compensated in a life to come. There is nothing clumsy, botched, or unworthy about such an arrangement.

No Pain, No Claim

Second, Lewis rejects the compensation argument because he thinks very few animals can actually feel pain. Many animals, he admits, are "sentient," that is, capable of sensing and feeling. But in order to experience pain animals must be "conscious," that is, have a mind or soul that is capable of experiencing their sensations and feelings as a connected series of sensations and feelings. An animal's "nervous system delivers all the letters A, P, N, I, but since they cannot read they never build it up into the word PAIN."[19] Lewis admits that apes, elephants, and the higher domestic animals probably have at least some rudimentary consciousness, and thus can experience some degree of pain. "But a great deal of what appears to be animal suffering," he suggests, "need not be suffering in any real sense. It may be we who have invented the 'sufferers' by the 'pathetic fallacy' of reading into the beasts a self for which there is no evidence."[20]

In claiming that most animals are "sentient" but not "conscious," Lewis is following the lead of the famous French philosopher René Descartes (1596–1650).[21] According to Descartes, animals are just automata—complex machines that can neither think nor feel pain. Scientists in Descartes's day who accepted this view of animals, we are told,

> administered beatings to dogs with perfect indifference and made fun of those who pitied the creatures as if they felt pain. They said the animals were clocks; that the cries they emitted when struck were only the noise of a little spring that they had been touched, but that the whole body was without feeling. They nailed the poor animals up on boards by their four paws to vivisect to see the circulation of the blood which was a great subject of controversy.[22]

---

[19] Lewis, *Problem of Pain*, p. 142 (italics omitted).

[20] *Ibid.*, p. 137.

[21] René Descartes, *Discourse on Method*, Part V; "Letter to Henry More," *Philosophical Letters*, translated and edited by Anthony Kenny (Oxford: Oxford University Press, 1970), p. 66.

[22] Quoted in Tom Regan, *The Case for Animal Rights* (Berkeley: University of California Press, 1983), p. 5.

To claim, however, that animals cannot feel pain flouts both common sense and science. When humans are in pain, their pulse races, they breathe rapidly, natural pain-killers (endorphins) are released, and they often cry out, groan, whimper, or struggle violently to escape. Many animals respond in exactly the same way. Moreover, higher animals "have all the physical structures which seem to be involved in the production of sensations of pain, and, as far as the physiological evidence goes, these structures seem to work in the same way in other mammals as in man."[23] In fact, primates that have been taught sign language can communicate directly that they are in pain, just as humans can.[24] Thus, Lewis's claim that few if any animals can feel pain is no longer credible in the light of contemporary science.

Does God Care a Fig for a Newt?

Finally, Lewis argues that very few animals have a "soul" or "self" that is capable of surviving death. By "soul" or "self," Lewis means "a permanent bed along which . . . different portions of the stream of sensation roll, and which recognizes itself as the same beneath them all."[25] In other words, to have "soul" or "self" in Lewis's sense requires (1) a consciousness that is capable of experiencing a series of sensations *as a series*, and (2) an awareness of one's consciousness, or oneself, as persisting through time. Lewis thinks that dogs and other higher domestic animals, through long contact with their masters, may develop a soul or self, but that very few wild animals are likely to do so.[26] Thus, it would make no sense to speak of an afterlife for, say, a newt:

---

[23] G.C. Grindley, quoted in John Hick, *Evil and the God of Love*, second edition (San Francisco: Harper and Row, 1978), p. 311.

[24] Donald G. McNeil, Jr., "Did the Cat Really Say, 'I Want to Be Alone'? Sorry, It Said Meow," *New York Times* (September 7th, 2004), p. F3. Koko the gorilla has developed a vocabulary of one thousand signs and can form simple sentences.

[25] Lewis, *Problem of Pain*, p. 135. Lewis uses the terms "self," "soul," "ego," "personality," and "consciousness" interchangeably. This is a mistake. Nearly everyone would agree that humans (and perhaps some animals) have "personalities"; whether they have "souls" or "selves" in the metaphysical sense is more debatable.

[26] *Ibid.*, p. 146.

If the life of a newt is merely a succession of sensations, what should we mean by saying that God may recall to life the newt that died today? It would not recognize itself as the same newt; the pleasant sensations of any other newt that lived after its death would be just as much, or just as little, a recompense for its earthly sufferings (if any) as those of its resurrected—I was going to say "self", but the whole point is that the newt probably has no self. . . . There is, therefore, I take it, no question of immortality for creatures that are merely sentient.[27]

This argument is unconvincing for several reasons.

First, even if a newt isn't "conscious" in Lewis's sense, this doesn't prove that it has no soul. Lewis would admit that humans that are sleeping or in a persistent vegetative state have souls, even though they are not presently conscious. Perhaps newts, like humans in a persistent vegetative state, have souls, but souls that are not able to achieve conscious awareness due to the physical limitations of their brains. Once the newt dies, however, its soul will be released from the limitations imposed by its tiny newt brain, and will once again become conscious. This, in fact, is precisely what hundreds of millions of Hindus and Buddhists believe.[28]

Second, even if a newt has no soul, this doesn't mean that the newt cannot continue to exist in an afterlife. Christians believe that humans will someday be *resurrected*; that their bodies will be restored to life, freed from all diseases and infirmities, and will continue to exist for all eternity. Perhaps newts, too, will be resurrected as part of a "new heaven and new earth" (Revelation 21:1), a time when, as St. Paul declares, all creation "will be set free from its bondage to decay and obtain the glorious liberty of the children of God" (Romans 8:21).

Third, even if newts have no soul, God could presumably restore them to life and *give* them souls, much as Aslan transformed Strawberry the cab horse into a Talking, winged horse (MN, Chapter 9, p. 69).

Finally, even if a newt has no awareness of self, and so couldn't "recognize itself as the same newt" in any sort of after-

---

[27] *Ibid*, pp. 141–42.

[28] For a succinct defense of the view that animals have souls, see Richard Swinburne, *The Evolution of the Soul* (Oxford: Clarendon, 1986), pp. 180–83.

life, this wouldn't mean that immortality for such a creature would have no meaning or value. It would have value for the newt because it would presumably be a life full of newtish pleasures (lazing on rocks, sipping mosquito-flavored tropical drinks, or whatever). It might also have value for *other* creatures in the afterlife who value diverse forms of life, as indeed God presumably does too. And as we have seen, an afterlife in which animals are compensated for their undeserved sufferings might help to explain why a loving God might permit such sufferings. Even animals that have no "selves" and are unaware that they are being compensated would still benefit,[29] just as a human being who was suffering from advanced Alzheimer's would benefit from being fed, cared for, and loved.

In short, Lewis's arguments against animal immortality are unpersuasive. Many animals clearly do suffer, and there could conceivably be some sort of life after death for animals. Indeed, any fully satisfactory solution to the theological problem of pain may require positing such an afterlife.

Further Up and Further In

Lewis is to be commended for his courage in raising the unfashionable issue of animal immortality and for recognizing that at least a few animals may be saved. My only complaint is that he didn't open the Door to animal salvation much wider than he did.

Of course, it isn't hard to see why Lewis chose not to include any non-Talking animals in his Narnian heaven. Lewis freely admitted that his unconventional views of animal immortality were highly "speculative."[30] Moreover, in the pre-animal rights days of the 1950s, when the Narnia books were written, placing animals in heaven would have raised issues for many readers and would have added a needlessly controversial element to the books.

---

[29] Assuming they would *want* to exist in heaven. In Lewis's defense, it might be said that only those animals who are drawn in by our love, and desire our companionship, would also desire to be with the Son, which is essentially what heaven is. For a response along these lines, see Stephen H. Webb, *Good Eating: The Christian Practice of Everyday Life* (Grand Rapids: Brazos, 2001), Chapter 7.

[30] Lewis, *God in the Dock*, p. 166.

Were Lewis writing the Narnia books today, animal-lover that he was, I like to think he would have written a different ending to *The Last Battle*, one in which Aslan welcomes both Talking and non-Talking Animals into his heavenly realm, and says to all and sundry: "The term is over: the holidays have begun. The dream is ended: this is the morning" (LB, Chapter 16, p. 767).[31]

---

[31] Thanks to Steve Webb, Jerry Walls, Bill Irwin, and Dave Baggett for many helpful suggestions, and to Yuki "Snow" Hirose, whose unpublished paper, "Back to Narnian Freedom and Dignity: C.S. Lewis's Theology of Animals," stimulated me to think afresh about these issues.

The Adventurers

GAYNE ANACKER is Dean of the College of Arts and Sciences and Professor of Philosophy at California Baptist University, Riverside, California. He also currently serves as Vice President of the C.S. Lewis Foundation, Redlands, California. In an earlier life, he was founding President of Community Christian College, also based in Redlands, California. His intellectual interests include ethics, Great Books, intellectual history, and philosophy of religion. He is still waiting for his invitation to join the crew of the *Dawn Treader*.

GREGORY BASSHAM is Chief Duffer of the Philosophy Department at King's College, Pennsylvania. A frequent contributor to the Popular Culture and Philosophy series, he is the co-editor of *The Lord of the Rings and Philosophy* (2003) and co-author of *Critical Thinking: A Student's Introduction* (second edition, 2005). He had to get to know some devilishly queer people to get where he is today.

DEVIN BROWN is Professor of English at Asbury College, where among other things he teaches a class on Lewis and Tolkien. He is the author of *Inside Narnia: A Guide to Exploring* The Lion, the Witch and the Wardrobe (2005) and a novel for young people titled *Not Exactly Normal* (2005). He is looking for a wardrobe that opens on a land where it's always Christmas and never winter.

TIMOTHY CLEVELAND is an Associate Professor and Tisroc of the Philosophy Department at New Mexico State University. He is the author of *Trying Without Willing: An Essay in the Philosophy of Mind* (1997) as well as articles on the philosophy of action, philosophy of logic, and metaphysics. He is still looking for a magician to remove his uglifying spell.

JANICE DAURIO is Professor of Philosophy at Moorpark College. Her philosophical interests include ethics and the philosophy of religion, and her literary interests run from C.S. Lewis and J.R.R. Tolkien to Jane Austen and Anthony Trollope. She has published articles in *History of Philosophy Quarterly*, *Philosophers Annual*, and *Downside Review*. Her sister and three brothers were startled to learn that if the White Witch had served her cappuccino, as she served Turkish Delight to Edmund, she too might have betrayed her siblings to the Witch.

BILL DAVIS is Professor of Philosophy and Chair of the Philosophy Department at Covenant College. He is the author of "Choosing to Die: The Gift of Mortality in Middle-earth" in *The Lord of the Rings and Philosophy*, as well as chapters on moral philosophy in *Introduction to Ethics* (2000) and on philosophical theology in *Reason for the Hope Within* (1999) and *Beyond the Bounds* (2003). He is still having his dragon skin torn off.

KARIN FRY is an Assistant Professor of Philosophy at University of Wisconsin, Stevens Point. Her research interests include continental philosophy, aesthetics, social and political philosophy, and feminism. Though technically a daughter of Eve, she prefers to think of herself as a daughter of Lilith.

LAURA GARCIA teaches Philosophy at Boston College, specializing in philosophy of religion and metaphysics. She also writes on sex, marriage, and personalist feminism, taking the radical view that the three are compatible and mutually reinforcing. Her favorite C.S. Lewis books are *The Chronicles of Narnia* and *The Great Divorce* (which isn't about divorce).

WENDY C. HAMBLET is a Canadian philosopher who teaches Philosophy at Adelphi University, where her research focuses upon the problems of peaceful engagement within and among human communities, especially communities that have suffered histories of radical victimization. She is the author of *The Sacred Monstrous: A Reflection on Violence in Human Communities* (2004) and *Savage Constructions: A Theory of Rebounding Violence in Africa* (2005), as well as a number of articles in professional journals. Hers is a high and lonely destiny but somebody's gotta fulfill it.

KEVIN KINGHORN follows daily in the footsteps of C.S. Lewis. But this is not because Kevin is a literary genius. He simply lives in Oxford and happens to pass many of Lewis's old haunts on the way to work everyday at Oxford University, where Kevin took his doctorate and now teaches. Kevin frequently gives "C.S. Lewis tours" to family and close friends visiting Oxford—at what he describes as very reasonable rates. Kevin also contributed a chapter to *Superheroes and Philosophy*. He holds office hours without appointments only between nine and ten p.m. the second Saturday each month.

STEVE LOVELL completed his doctoral thesis, *Philosophical Themes from C.S. Lewis*, at the University of Sheffield, England. Having tried his hand as a mathematics teacher he still wonders, with Professor Kirke, "What do they teach them at these schools?"

GARETH B. MATTHEWS is Professor of Philosophy at the University of Massachusetts in Amherst. He is the author of a number of books and articles on ancient and medieval philosophy, including *Socratic Perplexity and the Nature of Philosophy* (1999) and *Augustine* (2005). He has written extensively on philosophy and children, including *The Philosophy of Childhood* (1994) and he writes a regular column on children's stories for the journal, *Thinking*. For a hobby he collects and refinishes antique furniture. He has a special interest in old wardrobes.

ANGUS MENUGE is Professor of Philosophy at Concordia University Wisconsin, and Associate Director of the Cranach Institute (www.cranach.org). Dr. Menuge has edited three books, including *C.S. Lewis: Lightbearer in the Shadowlands* (1997), and is the author of *Agents Under Fire: Materialism and the Rationality of Science* (2004). As a reminder of his former career as a lumberjack, he wears a special kind of underclothes.

TIMOTHY MOSTELLER is an Assistant Professor of Philosophy at Biola University. He is the author of *Relativism in Contemporary American Philosophy* (2006), and is publishing philosophical articles in philosophy of religion and ethics. His students regularly interrupt his classes with chants of, "Keep it up, Doc! Keep it up! You're talking like a book."

ADAM PETERSON is Instructor of Philosophy at Asbury College. He earned the M.A. in 2005 from St. Louis University, which involved working closely with Eleonore Stump. His main philosophical interests are ethics, metaphysics, and philosophy of religion. As a child Adam read the *Chronicles of Narnia* with his father, and then he put aside fairy tales for a time. But he is now—just as Lewis predicted Lucy Barfield would do when she grew older—picking it up, dusting it off, and reading it afresh. Aslan appears even bigger to him today than he did years ago.

MICHAEL L. PETERSON is Professor of Philosophy and Chair of that department at Asbury College. He is author of *Evil and the Christian God* and *With All Your Mind*, and co-author of *Reason and Religious Belief*. He is editor of *The Problem of Evil: Selected Readings* and *Philosophy of Religion: Selected Readings* and co-editor of *Contemporary Debates in Philosophy of Religion*. Mike is General Editor of the Blackwell series "Exploring Philosophy of Religion" and Managing Editor of *Faith and Philosophy: Journal of the Society of Christian Philosophers*. He has fond memories of reading the *Chronicles* with his son Adam many Narnian years ago, but now writing about it with Adam makes it seem as if no time at all has passed.

VICTOR REPPERT teaches philosophy and religion at Glendale Community College in Glendale, Arizona, and is the author of *C.S. Lewis's Dangerous Idea: In Defense of the Argument from Reason* (2003). He frequently takes baths in asses' milk.

BRUCE REICHENBACH is Professor of Philosophy at Augsburg College. He has written over fifty articles and book chapters on diverse topics in philosophy of religion, ethics, theology, and religion. His most recent books are *Introduction to Critical Thinking* (2001), *On Behalf of God: A Christian Ethic for Biology* (1995), and *Reason and Religious Belief* (third edition, 2003), co-authored with Michael Peterson, William Hasker, and David Basinger. "What is education? I should suppose that education was the curriculum one had to run through in order to catch up with oneself, and he who will not pass through this curriculum is helped very little by the fact that he was born in a most enlightened age" (Kierkegaard).

THOMAS D. SENOR is Associate Professor of Philosophy and Chair of the Philosophy Department at the University of Arkansas. He has published papers on the philosophy of religion, theory of knowledge, philosophy of mind, and political philosophy; he has also served on the Program Committee of the Central Division of the American Philosophical Association and the Executive Committee of the Society of Christian Philosophers. Senor reports that in addition to clothes, his closets contain skeletons but are bereft of pathways to magical kingdoms.

JAMES F. SENNETT is Professor of Philosophy and Interdisciplinary Studies at Lincoln Christian College and Seminary in Lincoln, Illinois. He has written two books and edited two others, and has published over two dozen articles in professional and academic journals and books. His latest book is *This Much I Know: A Postmodern Apologetic* (2005). He never meant to be a magician.

CHARLES TALIAFERRO, Professor of Philosophy at St. Olaf College, has authored or edited seven books, most recently *Evidence and Faith: Philosophy and Religion since the Seventeenth Century* (2005). He has written on C.S. Lewis in the *Scottish Journal of Theology* and in a short work on prayer, *Praying with C.S. Lewis* (1999). Like the Professor in *The Lion, the Witch, and the Wardrobe,* he is a devoted enthusiast for Plato.

RACHEL TRAUGHBER has studied philosophy and music at the Institute for the International Education of Students (Vienna) and at St. Olaf College. Raised in the Azores, when she is not performing or practicing music, she wishes she were exploring an archipelago of islands in the *Dawn Treader.*

JERRY L. WALLS is Professor of Philosophy of Religion at Asbury Seminary in Wilmore, Kentucky, where he has taught since 1987. He had the good fortune to get to know Greg Bassham while they were graduate students together at Notre Dame. Among his books are *Heaven: The Logic of Eternal Joy* (2002) and (with Scott Burson) *C.S. Lewis and Francis Schaeffer* (1998). He would like to have lived in the happy peaceful centuries in Narnia when the only things that could be remembered were things like dances and tournaments. He assumes Notre Dame, Kentucky, and Texas Tech (or whoever was coached by the Narnian equivalent of Bobby Knight) won the Lion's share of those tournaments.

STEPHEN H. WEBB is Professor of Religion and Philosophy at Wabash College. He is the author of eight books, including *American Providence* (2004) and *The Divine Voice* (2004). He likes writing about sound in part because he is losing his hearing. His favorite C.S. Lewis book is *Perelandra,* which he loves to teach. When not writing, he is able to maintain a peaceful state of mind though surrounded by his wife, three children, and two barking dachshunds, simply by muting his hearing aids. He is currently working on a book about Bob Dylan, who sings like a lion, although perhaps not The Lion.

ERIK WIELENBERG is Assistant Professor of Philosophy at DePauw University. He is the author of *Value and Virtue in a Godless Universe* (2005) as well as various articles in ethics and the philosophy of religion. He is currently working on a book on the views of C.S. Lewis, David Hume, and Bertrand Russell. Erik wants to warn readers that many succumb to the sickly sweet lure of philosophy, and few return to the sun-lit lands.

The Marsh-wiggle's Index